Soul Liberty

Soul Liberty

The Evolution of Black Religious Politics in Postemancipation Virginia

Nicole Myers Turner

The University of North Carolina Press CHAPEL HILL

Set in Merope Basic by Westchester Publishing Services
Manufactured in the United States of America

The University of North Carolina Press has been a member of the Green Press Initiative since 2003.

Library of Congress Cataloging-in-Publication Data
Names: Turner, Nicole Myers, author.
Title: Soul liberty : the evolution of black religious politics in postemancipation Virginia / Nicole Myers Turner.
Description: Chapel Hill : University of North Carolina Press, [2020] | Includes bibliographical references and index.
Identifiers: LCCN 2019032126 | ISBN 9781469655222 (cloth : alk. paper) | ISBN 9781469655239 (paperback : alk. paper) | ISBN 9781469655246 (ebook)
Subjects: LCSH: African American churches—Virginia—History—19th century. | African American churches—Political activity—Virginia. | African American Christians—Virginia—History—19th century. | African American Christians—Political activity—Virginia. | Slaves—Emancipation—Virginia. | Virginia—Politics and government—1865–1950.
Classification: LCC BR563.N4 T854 2020 | DDC 261.7089/960730755—dc23
LC record available at https://lccn.loc.gov/2019032126

Cover illustrations: J. H. Waddell, Matthew Fontaine Maury, and Carter Godwin Woodson, *Map of Virginia*, 1871 (Library of Congress Geography and Map Division, G3880 1871 .W3); and William Ludwell Sheppard, "The First African Church, Richmond, Virginia," *Harper's Weekly*, June 27, 1874, 545 (Library of Congress Prints and Photographs Division, LC-USZ62-117891).

The Fulcrum version of this book, which includes enhanced content, can be located using this link: https://doi.org/10.5149/9781469655253_Turner.

To Eisa

Contents

Figures, Graphs, Maps, and Tables

FIGURES

GRAPHS

MAPS

TABLES

Note from the Author about the Digital Humanities and This Book

THE THREE VERSIONS OF *SOUL LIBERTY*

This book expands the digital humanities by appearing in three versions published by the University of North Carolina Press: first, the *print book*; second, a *verbatim open-access (OA) e-book*; and third, an *enhanced OA e-book* on a companion website hosted by Fulcrum, an innovative publishing platform launched by Michigan Publishing at the University of Michigan Library. The Fulcrum version of the book can be located using this link: https://doi.org/10.5149/9781469655253_Turner.

The print book and verbatim OA e-book contain three charts, three illustrations, and four maps. The Fulcrum enhanced OA e-book contains the complete text found in the print and the verbatim e-book—and more. It contains vignettes featuring interactive maps that allow the reader to better follow the argument about how black religious politics evolved by clicking within the text to see different configurations of layers on the related maps. A link in the resources will connect to the digital project website where the interested reader can re-create the maps or explore further.

MY TURN TO THE DIGITAL HUMANITIES

I turned to technologies of mapping as a method to interpret the archive of black religion and politics in postemancipation Virginia because I initially viewed the archives I used as lists of geographically based information. The lists of people and churches I found in the records of the Baptist, Zion Union Apostolic, and Episcopal churches and the manuscript collection of political magnate William Mahone contained a wealth of geographic and social information. As I read through nearly thirty years of annual state convention minutes and diocesan council journals, and scattered records of the Zion Union denomination and four regional associations in Southside, with the longest extant runs of minutes over the same period, I found lists of individuals who participated in the meetings and their hometowns; of all the churches that were associated in the conventions and their post office boxes; and of delegates who were sent from their local associations to meetings in other regions of the state. Similarly, Mahone's voluminous archive of correspondence revealed robust geographic information about political networks and strategy. In addition to the hundreds of letters he received from throughout the state in the months leading up to the 1879, 1883, and 1889 elections, he gathered names of churches and pastors from correspondents in 1883 and again in 1889. He organized this information into lists by county. That Mahone specifically canvassed black churches as part of his political machine drew my attention and was something I wanted to better understand. But an explanation was not easily culled from the canvass reports. These lists by themselves did not yield much beyond what was already known about Mahone's engagement with black churches.

My understanding was transformed when I decided to map the information I was gathering in order to visualize the political landscape. I chose to map the churches, conventions, and election returns as separate layers of a single map. I thought that being able to view each layer separately and then in different configurations might help me to better understand the relationship between these elements. But I could not process the changing outlines of the boundaries of the conventions, the locations of hundreds of churches, and the results of six elections efficiently by hand. With the help of Laurie Allen, a university librarian, I learned to use ArcGIS well enough to create maps of the convention boundaries, the membership reports, and the electoral returns as a way to explore the potential relationship between churches and political outcomes.

This approach turned out to be pivotal to my understanding of the relationship between black church networks and the political action in which black Virginians engaged. In fact, I might have missed the most significant insight gained from the laborious process of transcribing the churches' and participants' information had I only used my archival research notes. I probably would not have understood how church networks established through the associations suffused the political culture of black Virginians and provided the foundation for the political turn that reinforced the idea among white politicians and black religious folks that black churches were an important network to engage. Thus, mapping shifted my focus to the robust ways that black religious folks conceived, nurtured, and used these networks, a perspective that has been too easily elided, even in narratives that acknowledge the existence of these black church networks as part of Mahone's political organizing strategy. The sense of connection and political efficacy black Virginians cultivated evolved because of the associations' regular meetings. I implicitly knew that churches were important sites, but I did not know exactly how they became so. Reading the maps alongside the archival evidence made that relationship clearer.

With all the information I gathered to explain how black religious politics evolved and especially how black churches as sites of political organizing came to be, the two-dimensional maps reproduced in this printed version simply cannot fully express the intellectual architecture of both the research design and the method. This print version cannot make underlying data freely available and easily manipulatable, nor can it expand beyond the many and well-established limitations of two-dimensional maps that attempt to contain, explain, erase, and elide ambiguity and complexity. Neither could the two-dimensional maps in this book speak to the political abuses that the mapping of black communities has effected. These concerns properly belong in a study of black religious politics, especially one that fully deploys maps as a method of analysis.

Another venue was required to address these concerns and then to share the findings of the study more broadly: a black digital humanities project, to be exact. Such a project would not simply use digital tools to explore African American religious history but go beyond that to center black people's lives and ideas, and engage in an act of recovery and representation characteristic of work that resides at the nexus of black history and digital humanities, as Kim Gallon argues in "Making a Case for the Black Digital Humanities" (in *Debates in the Digital Humanities 2016*, edited by Matthew K. Gold and Lauren F. Klein, University of Minnesota Press, 2016). With the assistance of Erin White, Shariq Torres and Todd Easter of Virginia Commonwealth University Libraries and Jeff Everhart and Tom Woodward of the Virginia Commonwealth University AltLab, I began working on the website, Mapping Black Religion (www.mappingblackreligion.com).

The digital project in the form of a website with interactive user interfaces and deep maps would afford the opportunity to make not just the argument of the book but also the underlying data more widely available. And the interactive version of the maps created using black religious folks' self-documentation would deploy a spatial methodology for exploring religious history.

Discussions with my UNC Press editor, Elaine Maisner, and others at both the Press and Fulcrum about publishing the book on Fulcrum's open-access (OA) platform as an enhanced e-book brought the chance to explore a new frontier in academic publishing—a frontier that could bring together the print book with the website by featuring my e-book with significant enhancements hosted by Fulcrum.

This new formulation—the enhancement—incorporates some of the interactivity of the website into the book and makes it much more than a book: it makes an enhanced e-book that expands the argument and allows you to see, as I have, how layering data can raise new questions and answer them, and how making spatial geography central to the narrative of history using digital methods can expand the explanatory power of archival research.

The enhanced e-book serves as a provocation to more questions and more research as you click to view different layers of maps that undergird the book's argument and connect to the website to explore further. The enhanced e-book invites conversation by moving this author's voice from the center to the side and to the center again as you read and consider my argument and conclusions and then my evidence and analysis. Realizing the enhanced reading experience that the digital humanities affords was the goal. Thus, the enhanced e-book is two arguments in one—one about black religion and politics, and the other about how we can use digital tools to enhance and expand study and interpretation in the humanities.

N.M.T.
July 2019

Acknowledgments

Someone asked me, "What makes it possible for you to do your best work?" Over the long gestation of this project, I learned that good company, time, and financial support are the keys. I am grateful that my cup has run over in these areas. It is my great honor to acknowledge the many sources here.

First, I want to give thanks to God who makes all things possible.

Research that involves traveling to archives and generous amounts of time to think, write, and workshop cannot be sustained without financial support. I am grateful for the generous funding I received from the Mellon Fellowship of the Virginia Historical Society and the John Hope Franklin Fellowship of Duke University's Rare Book, Manuscript, and Special Collections Library for support of the early stages of my research, and for Virginia Commonwealth University faculty start up funds for research support and conference attendance. I am indebted to Bill Blair and the Richards Civil War Era Center for the postdoctoral fellowship that allowed me time to reconsider the project and deepen my approach. A teaching release from VCU's Humanities Research Center (HRC) afforded me much needed time to finalize revisions of this manuscript while being in conversation with excellent colleagues. I acknowledge the encouragement and support that Richard Godbeer and Brooke Newman have shown to me and my cohort of fellows.

Good company comes in many forms. My deep gratitude goes to my church family at St. Paul's Community Baptist Church in Brooklyn, New York, and my pastor, the Reverend Dr. Johnny Ray Youngblood, in whose company and under whose leadership my interest in this subject matter was provoked and encouraged. Excellent teachers have fostered my development as a researcher and thinker. I am grateful to Mary Frances Berry, Anthea Butler, Steve Hahn, Stephanie McCurry, and Barbara Savage, who shepherded me through doctoral studies. Tracey Hucks, who alerted me to the possibility of studying religion in graduate school, and Michael W. Harris, who helped me find my methodological home, deserve special thanks.

Workshopping chapters at conferences allowed me to consider provocative questions and sharpen my thinking. I am pleased to acknowledge the opportunities given to me at the CLAW Symposium, organized by Adam Domby and Simon Fraser at the College of Charleston and at the invitation of Adam Bond at the Samuel Dewitt Proctor School of Theology at Virginia Union University. Generous audiences at the annual meetings of the Association for the Study of African American Life and History, the American Historical Association, the American Society of Church Historians, and a very memorable African American Digital Humanities conference at the University of Maryland, College Park, offered insightful comments on various aspects of the project.

Archivists and librarians make this work possible in so many ways. I am especially indebted to folks who have helped me orient myself to the various and voluminous archives. At the Library of Virginia, Brent Tarter was as welcoming and resourceful as other researchers had promised he would be. Lucius Edwards and Jessica Johnson were hospitable and accommodating during each of my visits to the Johnston Memorial Library at Virginia State University. I especially enjoyed Mr. Edwards's tour of Petersburg and Pocahontas Island. Leslie Rowland oriented me to the Freedmen and Southern Society Project's records. Deborah Price (St. Paul's College Archive) and Julia Randle, Christopher Pote, and Joseph Thompson (African American Episcopal Historical Collection, Bishop Payne Library, Virginia Theological Seminary) helped me find my way in their collections, pointing out records of interest to me.

Research staff in libraries and archives made the work possible, but folks close to home made the journey more enjoyable. My fellow graduate students in the History Department at the University of Pennsylvania, the Fontaine Society, and the Africana Studies Summer Institute helped me to have a balanced and supported experience. My thanks go to Yea Afolabi-Pillischer, Joanna Cohen, Abigail Cooper, Jack Dwiggins, Kim T. Gallon, Clem Harris, Richara Heyward, Angela McMillan Howell, Ricardo Howell, Matt Karp, Will Kuby, Alicia Lee, the late Chike Lloyd, Sarah Manekin, Erik Mathisen, Maisha Phillips, Maryan Soliman, Mecca Jamilah Sullivan, Khadijah Costley White, and Brandon Teray Woods. The Africana Studies Summer Institute and the Center for Teaching and Learning (CTL) provided generative, stimulative, and supportive environments in which I could think and serve. Special thanks to Bruce Lenthall and Cathy Turner of the CTL for their leadership and guidance.

In the world of scholars, there are many brilliant and generous interlocutors. I have enjoyed many conversations that have shaped my project and my intellectual journey in important ways. For sharing their thoughts and good conversation, I thank Gabeba Baderoon, Brandon Bayne, Bill Blair, Adam Bond, Kimberly N. Brown, Melanie Buffington, Cara Burnidge, Emily Clark,

Ana Edwards, Antonio Espinoza, Andrew Friedman, Brett Grainger, Rachel Gross, Michael R. Hall, Mathew Cooper Harriss, Errol A. Henderson, Cheryl Hicks, Justine Howe, Elizabeth Jemison, Kathryn Lofton, AnneMarie Mingo, Bernard Moitt, Brooke Newman, Crystal Sanders, Leigh Schmidt, Katherine Shively, Asali Solomon, Brandi Summers, Dan Vaca, Heather Williams, and Nan Woodruff. For sharing research references and for reading chapter drafts—contributions that have enriched the work—I thank Sarah Jane Brubaker, Chris Cynn, Hilary Green, Melis Hafez, Errol A. Henderson, Shermaine Jones, Kathryn Lofton, Karen Rader, and Heather Williams. Special thanks to John Kneebone, who read the entire manuscript during the busiest time of the academic year. I am also grateful to my cohort of HRC fellows with whom this project and its extension have been incubated. Winnie Chan, Ryan Smith, and Faedah Totah have workshopped chapters and shared readings that have refined my ideas. I appreciate the insightful comments and suggestions offered by Elsa Barkley Brown, Alison Gise-Johnson, Thavolia Glymph, Faith B. Harris, Tera Hunter, Laurie Maffly-Kipp, and Giuliana Perrone. I am grateful for the guidance of my editor, Elaine Maisner. Readers Mary Beth Mathews and Kidada Williams pushed my analysis and inspired me with their rigorous and thoughtful feedback. Any shortcomings are mine.

Writing can be the loneliest part of this work. However, I was never completely alone thanks to my writing partners: Robert Goldberg, Kim P. Fields, and Rachel Gross. I have been fortunate to have the assistance of researchers: Laura Ague and Antoinette Brown. And when I needed to step away from the computer and enrich other aspects of my being, my girls have been the best companions: Trelane Clark, Lanita Culinane, Ellen C. Scott, Ingrid Walker-Descartes, and Candice Watkins. Caregivers Kenyatta Allison, Genevieve Cervantes, and Cristal Marte helped me balance work and family. And my family support network—April Byrd, Lauren Entrekin, Ryan Keaton, Simone Knight, Melissa Margolis, David and Stacey Smith, and Deb Yorkman—showed up in countless ways to make this journey a little easier.

My posse—my family—rolls deep. They hold me up and they hold me down in every way. With love and gratitude I acknowledge them: the late Emily Warner, elder historian Thelma Reese, Thelma Hannah, Hellen Turner and the late Daniel Turner, Sr., and Traci and Wil Wilkerson. My siblings are the best friends I did not choose; Dwayne Childs, Tosca Myers, and Clayton Myers are gifts who keep me laughing and focused on faith. Gwendolyn Warner has been my stalwart prayer warrior, covering me every step of the way. My parents, Dolores Myers and Harmon Myers, with constant faith and love, gave me a great foundation. I am ever grateful for their sacrifices and guidance.

I could not do this work without a partner who shares the work of having a family and making a life. Dan Turner did not type a single word of this work, but he is in every one of them. His love and support have made this work possible in immeasurable ways. Eisa Turner brings so much light, love, and laughter into each day. He has shared "mommy time" with this book—not quite the sibling he would like—for his entire life. For his good cheer and patience nonetheless, it is to him that I dedicate this work.

Abbreviations in the Text

ABHMS	American Baptist Home Mission Society
AME	African Methodist Episcopal
AMEZ	African Methodist Episcopal Zion
BBA	Bethany Baptist Association
BCBA	Bluestone Colored Baptist Association
BRFAL	Bureau of Refugees, Freedmen and Abandoned Lands
BTS	Branch Theological School
CABMC	Consolidated American Baptist Missionary Convention
CSBA	(Colored) Shiloh Baptist Association
CME	Christian Methodist Episcopal
DMS	Diocesan Missionary Society
FSSP	Freedmen and Southern Society Project
GFB	George Freeman Bragg Papers
JACPEVA	Journal of the Annual Council of the Protestant Episcopal Church in Virginia
MP	Mahone Papers
MSRC	Moorland Spingarn Research Center
NNBA	Northern Neck Baptist Association
NUBA	Norfolk Union Baptist Association
PETS	Protestant Episcopal Theological Seminary
RBMSCL	Rare Book, Manuscript and Special Collections Library
RZUA	Reformed Zion Union Apostolic

VBSC	Virginia Baptist State Convention
VHS	Virginia Historical Society
VSU	Virginia State University
ZUA	Zion Union Apostolic

Soul Liberty

Introduction

In May 1872, Rev. Henry Williams Jr., pastor of the Gilfield Baptist Church, was elected to the Petersburg Common Council. He took his seat alongside two fellow church members and several other citizens of Petersburg, Virginia, including a member of the all-black congregation at St. Stephen's Episcopal Church. In his capacity as city council member, Williams presented a proposal to restrict from appointment to the police force any man judged to be a drunkard and a proposal to extend a city street. Through these contributions, Williams showed himself to be equal parts moral guardian and administrator, roles he also fulfilled as pastor at one of Petersburg's leading black churches.[1]

Williams's election to the Petersburg Common Council came seven years into his leadership of Gilfield and two years after black men in Virginia received the right to vote. Among the first cohort of Petersburg's elected officials in 1870 were lay members of Williams's congregation. These pioneer church members and politicians established a foundation for black church members' contributions to policy and governance of the city. They also set a precedent for black political engagement that would come to be a highly scrutinized and politically powerful platform for black people during the postemancipation period.

Williams served only one term and then returned his focus to leading his church and supporting the spread of the Baptist state and regional conventions throughout the state. Williams's brief foray into politics highlights an important if understudied facet of the postemancipation period—the intersection between religion and politics and how the relationship between the two realms developed. Though scholars have long debated the role of the church in black political struggles and chastised it for its sometimes limited participation, this study aims to explore the relationship between black religious institutions and black political participation in Virginia during the postemancipation period—one of the signal moments of political and cultural transformation in the African American experience—in order to understand how the relationship evolved rather than to judge it.[2] Moreover, this study draws important cues from the early twentieth-century studies of black churches, which were descendants of the postemancipation churches I study.[3] Hence, I explore questions of leadership, organization, membership, and politics, but I ground my analysis in the particularities of the postemancipation era. My central findings expose how the intersection of religion and politics in the African American experience of the late nineteenth century shaped black political participation. In so doing, this study offers a nuanced perspective on the process that shaped the dialogic moments of engagement and withdrawal that characterized the relationship between black religion and politics after emancipation.[4] This study describes how black Christians in postemancipation Virginia pursued soul liberty—a combination of religious freedom, righteousness, equity, and justice—through their churches, conventions, and seminary education. Their efforts were shaped by the shifting political context from emancipation to citizenship. The expressions were not uniform or easily pegged to one political orientation or another because the political terrain was so complex. Though the goals were clear, the ways they could be manifest were very much shaped by the context. Black religious politics of the postemancipation period was dynamic, responsive, and a bit hard to pin down.

TWO CENTRAL CONTENTIONS direct this study. First, I argue that the relationships between black religious institutions and political institutions changed from slavery to emancipation because black people went from being property to being citizens. As formerly enslaved people became citizens, they continued to negotiate the means to obtain the resources that would make real the freedom for which they had prayed and fought. The particular tasks of defining black capacity for obtaining political office, securing education, and negotiating biracial coalitions called on churches and other institutions to perform in different ways. The false binary of viewing churches as either engaged or disengaged with worldly circumstances oversimplifies the more nuanced reality of their members' simultaneous spiritual exultation over emancipation and material concern for the social, political, and economic aspects of freedom. Consequently, I explore how the context shaped the shifting orientations of churches in relationship to political participation.[5] The black churches of Reconstruction were not caught between being an opiate or an inspiration; they were caught in the position of mediating black life on totally new terms. When coupled with the aims and practices of democratic politics and party development, the function and structure of churches and conventions not only made churches vulnerable to political exploitation but also caused a merger of values, such that women were marginalized while ministerial leadership was lionized.[6] These developments also shaped racial identification in a way that influenced interracial politics, which were so central to the period.

My second point derives from the first. I aim to disrupt the leadership paradigm that focuses attention on the male ministerial elite by drawing attention to the processes that demarcated ministerial positions as male. Some scholars explain the apparent overlap between ministerial and political leadership in terms of educational attainment, divine appointment, and the authority that being a minister provided.[7] I argue that though limited, theological education provided the context for the development of black Protestants' interracial political strategies and the development of gendered roles and ideas among theological students.

Further, I expand the view of the relationship between leaders and politics beyond the pulpit to the pews. To examine only the leaders who were ministers limits consideration of other church members who held political office. For example, not only did Rev. Henry Williams and Rev. Guy Powell—a minister and politician from Brunswick County—hold elected and appointed offices, but so did church officers and members, an even deeper indication of the level of overlap between church people and political leadership and participation.[8] Moreover, churches as collective bodies provided the votes necessary to bring elected officials to power. Furthermore, looking only at ministers as political leaders excludes women's political participation completely. Scholars only reinforce the structural processes that excluded women when they approach the interpretation of religion and politics this way. That approach omits the places within churches and religious spaces where women may have exercised control, including in church meetings, where they could vote and exercise leadership by conducting prayer meetings. By approaching the narrative of the political preacher with some skepticism, I capture the development of that role. Looking at the laity destabilizes the notion that men were made for the ministry (in black churches, anyway).

A LOCAL STUDY OF Petersburg and the surrounding counties structures and anchors my approach, allowing me to represent the dynamic evolution of black religion and politics. Examination of census returns, local election returns, newspapers, and church and convention minutes allows the interwoven threads of community, social, and political life to come into full view. Documenting interactions between church members, between members and leaders, and between churches and government officials at this level is essential to articulating a clear sense of the evolution of political movements, for as Steven Hahn posits, the best way to understand a political movement is "by analyzing how its participants directly experienced social changes."[9] Focusing on the development of church conventions, like the statewide Virginia Baptist State Convention; a handful of regional associations spread across the Tidewater and Southside regions, like the (Colored) Shiloh Baptist Association and the Bluestone Colored Baptist Association; and the Zion Union Apostolic Church gives a sense of the local roots of black church organization. This approach, coupled with a prosopography of the church community and an examination of census data, Freedmen's Bureau records, traveler accounts, and city government records, provides insight into the lived experience of the community. The voluminous William Mahone Papers, which include his correspondence with political agents throughout Virginia, provide a window into the evolution of coalition politics within the state.

Before I delve into an overview of Virginia politics, let me offer a brief discussion of my conceptualization of politics. While significant advances have been made in expanding the definition of politics for African Americans, who have spent the majority of their existence in the United States excluded from the formal arena of electoral politics, a concerted focus on this very aspect during the postemancipation period is very much in order.[10] With the passage of the Thirteenth, Fourteenth, and Fifteenth Amendments, and related revisions of state constitutions, formerly enslaved people became citizens and black men part of the electorate. This does not suggest that the tools of evasion, misdirection, and doublespeak characteristic of the infrapolitics employed by those excluded from the formal arena were no longer necessary. The dynamics of power, domination, and resistance that characterized the relationships between slave owners and the enslaved remained in place for a long time. Freedpeople had to work for their former owners for wages or crop shares and had to depend on white benevolence to develop their first generation of educated people. These relationships required negotiation.[11] The stark contrast between the enslaved past and the emancipated present was most powerfully articulated in legal and political terms.[12] Social and cultural transformations were fuzzier. While earlier generations of scholars have depicted black people as political dupes at worst and as politically naive at best, my study credits these new citizens with working to protect their own interests.[13] I follow them as their gaze shifted to realizing the soul freedom they had dreamed, prayed, and fought for. For some, freeing the spirit required voting and holding office, which allowed them to participate in the distribution of resources and defining the terms of that freedom.

In addition to focusing on black participation in electoral politics, I examine the terms of the biracial political coalition evident within the Readjuster movement of the late 1870s and early 1880s. This biracial coalition effectively fulfilled what was Virginia's era of Reconstruction and is an important example of how Reconstruction attempted to remake American society—the very idea of American democracy—without slavery.[14] Major General William Mahone—political titan, railroad magnate, and a former Confederate—spearheaded the movement of western white farmers, urban lawyers, and freedpeople.[15] At its apex, the movement united black and white Republicans against Conservatives, later called Democrats, known for their support of paying the state's debt (which included debts accrued while West Virginia was still part of the state and while black people were enslaved) at full face value and at the expense of public education. They were called Funders based on their position regarding the debt. By the time the Readjusters—so named because of their belief that the debt should be "adjusted"—built a majority coalition in Virginia's General Assembly in 1879 and elected William E. Cameron as governor in 1881, schools had been shut down for lack of funding. With control of the state and general assembly, however, Readjusters effected Virginia's de facto Reconstruction, welcoming black people into almost all levels of political participation (as voters, delegates, and state legislators, but not as elected federal officials) and supported legislation that reduced the debt burden, secured state-funded education, funded a college for black people, banned the whipping post, and established an insane asylum for black people so that the mentally ill would no longer be stigmatized and treated poorly by being placed in jail.[16] Black people's political aims were achieved through the coalition and with its political support at the legislative level.[17]

One of the ways I interpret the intersection of religion and politics is through the ways that William Mahone and his organizers viewed black churches. Early in the movement, they seemed to be unaware of black churches and their roles in the community because there were few references to them in the correspondence. In 1883, however, Mahone actively sought information about black churches and their leaders after someone recommended he do so. Underlying the view of black voters as individuals and constituents, however, was the view of black people as members of organized churches. I replace emphasis on Mahone's attempt to marshal information about black churches in preparation for the 1883 state election and his 1889 gubernatorial bid with a focus on the church convention networks that were already extant.[18] Mahone's rudimentary contact lists paled in comparison to what black church conventions already knew about their constituents. In the distance between the two was the voting power of black churches. Comparing Mahone's lists to the voter polls, election returns, and church conventions' statistical information reveals just how much political power black churches potentially wielded and suggests a nascent awakening in Mahone to what twenty-first-century politicians now believe to be true: the way to reach black voters en masse is through their churches.[19] Readjusters needed blocs of votes, not individuals, to retain political office. Black churches became important parts of the Readjusters' political strategy.

IF I DEFINE political participation in a traditional way, the way I locate politics is not traditional. One way that the expanded definition of politics aids the interpretive frame of this study is in the expansion of places where one may find political activity. One cannot overlook the political gaze of Baptist conventions held coterminously with Republican Party conventions and later the state constitutional convention. Church convention participants were concerned with demonstrating their fitness for political participation through these conventions, making these religious spaces explicitly political projects.[20] These conventions and churches were also implicated in the long history of black religion as being resistant to oppression and articulating hope for democratic freedom. They were implicitly political in this way as well as through reflecting the internal dynamics of class and gender politics and by acting as sites of discourse.[21]

When looking at religion in Petersburg, the great diversity of black institutionalized religion comes into view, dispelling the tendency to focus on the two great black denominations—the Baptist and the African Methodist Episcopal churches. Though the Baptists were no doubt the preeminent denomination in Petersburg and the Southside region, the small but mighty congregation of St. Stephen's Episcopal Church contributed to the life and leadership of the community. In fact, in Petersburg, the Episcopal Church dominated the education scene, forming common schools and even a seminary for black ministers, while the Baptists dominated in nearby Richmond. Even more intriguing is the fact that the black Episcopalians were descendants of enslaved people, which challenges the tendency to associate the Episcopal Church with high church culture. The Baptist churches of Petersburg included a mix of free black and formerly enslaved people, producing their own mixture of high church and low church culture. For example, Rev. William H. Sherwood described how First Baptist Church of Petersburg held two different services—an early service for the professional members and a later service for the domestic workers.[22] The Zion Union Apostolic (ZUA) Church, an independent black denomination founded in Southside, adds further diversity to the black religious landscape. The ZUA and Colored Methodist Episcopal (later, Christian Methodist Episcopal, CME) churches were the only two independent black denominations founded in the South, and the ZUA Church was founded solely by black people.[23]

The diversity of denominations highlights the theme of interracial cooperation and interracial politics at the root of Readjuster movement coalitions and Reconstruction-era politics. This study reveals that politics was shaped by the racial positioning of the denominations and of black people within the denominations. I gain insight into interracial politics through the perspectives of independent black denominations like the ZUA Church, cooperative black denominations like the black Baptists, and integrated black people in the Episcopal Church. I explore how these churches framed their postemancipation projects and how their efforts changed over time.

In this study of religion and politics, which challenges leadership paradigms and draws on a past with liberating potential, the place of women in black religion is a theme that also emerges. One of the central conundrums of religion and Christianity generally and black religion in particular is the overwhelming dominance of women as churchgoers and men as ministers and leaders.[24] More important than the question of why this hierarchy existed is the question of how women could be agents in such a paradigm.[25] Some have argued that women wielded the power of the purse as the central financiers of black churches (as members and fund raisers), power over church leadership through selecting ministers and voting on their tenure, and even power over certain female-oriented and female-led spaces, like the Woman's Convention in the Baptist and Pentecostal traditions.[26] I am, however, less concerned with women's contributions than I am with tracing how women's roles became circumscribed to the pew and the Woman's Convention. There were no women's conventions under slavery (though there were separate women's spaces).[27] It would be easy to ignore the absence of women from leadership in postemancipation church conventions, but the acknowledgments of their donations and the listing of their names among the paying, supporting members of the conventions beg attention to the ways that women were present and their place circumscribed in these gatherings. Moreover, when the church developments are read alongside the changes in the local political sphere, the limiting effects of the overlap of church and state for black women in some churches become clearer. It is certainly helpful to acknowledge the ways that women participated in formal politics from the periphery, as Elsa Barkley Brown so deftly demonstrates, but it is also important to unveil and examine the forces that pushed and circumscribed them to the narrowest of peripheries.[28]

THIS PROJECT DEPLOYS geographic information system (GIS) mapping as a means to understand and interpret the social and political worlds of Virginia's black religious folk. It undertakes this endeavor in a nonpositivist manner by recognizing how mapping has been used to impose boundaries on black people and how the mapping of a racial landscape has tended to produce segregation, ghettoization, and gentrification or limited black resources and opportunity.[29] This study upends these dominating practices by viewing the community map from the vantage point of black Virginians. Producing maps has simply given visual form to the great amounts of spatial data that black people gathered about themselves and that they used to form their religious and political communities. In this process, this study works to codify and to recognize the "invisible landscapes" that postemancipation black Virginians "carr[ied] in their heads."[30] Further, in addition to interrogating mapping practices of domination, this project deploys maps that destabilize the Cartesian map emphasis on political landscapes and boundaries by mapping patterns of movement and networks.[31] The maps produced as part of this study also invite a particular kind of engagement with the past, a visual engagement that can awaken a historical consciousness that remains dormant when just the lists of locations and names are considered in their tabular form.[32] Instead, mapping and viewing maps is an act of historical consciousness, not unlike the process of viewing photographs of historic places. As Alan Trachtenberg explains in his introduction to William E. Williams's photography collection, the work "demonstrate[s] how the historical can be achieved as a moment of consciousness. The mental effort is to make sense of each image and in making sense, to make history, a conscious effort to alter consciousness. It's the pictures that bring us here and hold us, but as an ensemble of pictures, words, and physical objects, the array itself assumes the heightened dimension of the historical."[33] The maps included in this study are not photographs of historical locations but representations of historical spaces and historical communities and thus, like Williams's photographs, opportunities for and reflections of historical interpretation.

The historical interpretation that shapes these maps takes seriously black feminist studies and postcolonial scholars' critiques of positivist uses of GIS maps and technologies. Like feminist scholars who introduced the feminist subject—the researcher who recognizes herself—and the feminist object—the inclusion of women's experiences and spaces on maps—this study renders aspects of black life and black spaces on the maps that would otherwise have had little concern with them.[34] And the purpose is not for domination, not for cooptation, but for greater visibility and understanding of the black subject. This project then also contributes to understanding how communities are made through mental maps and what mapping practices beyond physical map making—whether cartographic and by hand or digital via GIS—were inherent in the lives of black and white southern people of the nineteenth century.

AT THE 1871 Consolidated American Baptist Missionary Convention—the first attempt to create a national Baptist convention—attendees placed themselves within the historical lineage of Baptists in America by likening their postemancipation struggle to Roger Williams's pursuit of "soul liberty" in colonial Rhode Island. Paramount in the attendees' consideration was how they could freely live their religious lives. As the narrative that follows suggests, this pursuit of soul liberty took black Christians through the thickets of government agencies, through negotiations within churches and church convention leadership, and ultimately into the realm of electoral politics, where the pursuit and realization of soul liberty was fully amplified.

Soul liberty is the balancing task that postemancipation African Americans engaged in and pursued. They sought freedom to worship—soul freedom down to the very core of their being, where nothing could hinder them. They pursued it through gaining control of their own worship spaces and by securing leadership posts in their churches, at conventions, and later in the electoral political realm. In so doing, they came to define liberty in practices that involved negotiating within the community in such a way that the dialectics of freedom and unfreedom became more pronounced. As black men gained more political freedom to participate, the limitations of the broader political context for black women became more apparent. Additionally, liberty entailed negotiating the boundaries within the community of interconnected people. Thus, liberty was an expansive concept with many directions and expressions, and contrary to the conventional understanding of liberty as unbounded, it came with both constraints and the freedom of interpretation.

The full extent and significance of the intersection between black religion and politics cannot be understood without exploring at the local level the contours and dynamics of the interactions between white and black people, congregations and ministers, and churches and electoral politics. This local study of black churches at the crossroads of emancipation demonstrates the challenges and triumphs that black religious institutions experienced and how they brokered resources and effected change at the very moment and place in which their members found their feet. As a consequence, Virginia is no synecdoche.[35] Its story does not stand in for the story of every black church community. Through this brief exploration, however, the black church can begin to have a history through which the nuances of the pursuit and meaning of soul liberty can be better understood.

CHAPTER ONE

Making a New Religious Freedom

In the fall of 1865, Reverend Jeremiah R. V. Thomas, pastor of the Immanuel African Methodist Episcopal Church in Portsmouth, Virginia, wrote to General Oliver O. Howard, commissioner of the Freedmen's Bureau, for help resolving a property issue. In 1863, the black members of Immanuel had left the Methodist Episcopal Church, South, and joined the African Methodist Episcopal Church. Though the members changed their denominational affiliation, their church building continued to be owned by white trustees in the Methodist Episcopal Church, South. This arrangement was in accordance with the laws of the South, which prohibited enslaved people from owning property and prevented black people from holding offices in the church.[1] This was the policy even though the black church members had paid two-thirds of the $7,500 cost of building the church. Reverend George Baines, the white former pastor and trustee, wanted to claim the church, so Reverend Thomas needed quick assistance. "Believing that you will do us justice," Thomas wrote, "we write for advice."[2]

The matter was referred down the chain of command to Charles E. Johnson, assistant superintendent at Norfolk, who had a ground-level view of the circumstances. Johnson uncovered additional details that added complexity and depth to the situation. White trustees had in fact purchased the church, but the property was intended to be "for the <u>exclusive use</u> of the <u>Colored people</u>." While the black members raised most of the money, the white people of the Dinwiddie Methodist Episcopal Church made up the difference. The church came under the control of the black members when the Union Army occupied the city and required Reverend Baines to turn over the keys. At that point, the church members elected their own trustees and decided to join the African Methodist Episcopal (AME) Church.[3] This situation was likely further complicated because in 1863, the War Department gave all the titles for property of the Methodist Episcopal Church, South, to the Methodist Episcopal Church, North.[4]

Legal documents did not coincide with reality, however. The official deed describes the property as being for "the use of members of the Methodist Episcopal Church, South." There was no mention of the actual use by the African American members. In reality, enslaved people did most of the work of establishing a church, with some assistance from white people, but were not recognized as legal actors. Thus, the enslaved people relied on the support of white trustees and church leaders for recognition. This arrangement put black church members like those of Immanuel in a tenuous position once emancipated. Some of the white trustees wanted to exploit the legal loophole and keep the church, while other trustees were willing to give the church over to the freedpeople. To add insult to injury, Reverend Baines insisted on preaching at the church, though many members remained offended by his earlier pronouncement that "it was no more sin to sell a 'nigger' baby from its Mother than it was to sell a calf from a cow." Thus, Immanuel's black trustees wrote General Howard in the hope that the U.S. government could give them some relief where the Methodist Episcopal Church, South, and the state legislature would not.[5]

Encapsulated in this case are the tangled threads of antebellum southern religion, race relations, and politics that were being pulled apart by the transformations that emancipation brought. The complicated dynamics of slavery that allowed enslaved people to purchase land were exposed. The authority that white people had and that held such arrangements in place was being challenged by freedpeople seeking autonomy. Obtaining land on which to live and work was an important step toward the freedom, independence, and self-determination freedpeople sought after emancipation.[6] Likewise, securing church property was a significant step in this direction, as the Immanuel case demonstrates. Freedpeople also rejected the hypocritical white preacher who dared to continue preaching in the era of freedom with the same lips and in the same spirit that denigrated their humanity and affirmed the system of slavery. The transition to freedom, which included the religious freedom to worship where, when, and with whomever they chose, included being aided by the federally established Bureau of Refugees, Freedmen and Abandoned Lands, which not only mediated labor disputes, rationed food, and monitored abandoned land but also mediated disputes over church property. The Freedmen's Bureau was for all intents and purposes "the government" to the freedpeople.[7] Through the negotiations that freedpeople engaged in with the Freedmen's Bureau, this case also upturns the view of black people as novices in the landownership process. As major contributors to and stewards of church property while enslaved, black people were already de facto landowners. In the postemancipation period, however, they ran the risk of losing their property due to legal loopholes.

In the first year of emancipation, freedpeople dealt with white Christians in interracial settings or separated themselves from white leadership into their own independent churches and denominations. This new independence brought its own challenges of defining community and establishing leadership. While Immanuel's members made their break from white leadership after the Civil War's end, some black churches had longer legacies of independence, which placed them on a firmer footing for maintaining and developing their independence from white people after emancipation. Not all black Christians chose to separate from white churches, though. This chapter shows that the struggle to secure soul liberty could also take place within predominantly white churches, such as those in the Episcopal Church. Where the explicit attempts to maintain control over black worshippers manifested in disputes over land for the Immanuel AME Church, black Episcopalians struggled for recognition within the Virginia diocese. In addition to navigating within the church, emancipation brought black worship under different legislative control than had been established after Nat Turner's rebellion. Under slavery, legislation attempted to curtail black worship by prohibiting enslaved people from gathering without a white person in attendance. After emancipation, Freedmen's Bureau agents charged with shepherding the process of Reconstruction on the ground took an active role in mediating disputes about freedpeople's worship and land. Black religious folks found themselves negotiating with government agents and missionaries to undo the culture of surveillance initiated after Turner's rebellion. This chapter presents the first stage of the formation of black religious politics. Black religious institutions navigated the racial dynamics of freedom, race, place, and power through disputing property ownership, establishing independent churches and denominations, and interacting with the Freedmen's Bureau and white Christian missionaries to secure autonomous worship.[8]

Black Religion's Antebellum Roots

The power dynamics the Immanuel AME Church sought to reorient had deep roots in the antebellum formulations of enslaved and free black religious life. As the shared purchasing responsibility reflected, enslaved and free black people demonstrated autonomy in the antebellum period. Enslaved people in religious space, especially, lived out the tensions between autonomy and control. In the hush harbors where enslaved people worshipped clandestinely and independently, they developed a separate identity for themselves.[9] In the interracial churches and in their interactions with patrollers who tried to control black religious ideas, expression, and freedom, enslaved and free black people perceived the contradictions between their independent worship and the attempts to curtail it. As a result, they developed their own critiques of the Christianity of enslavers. Thus, the antebellum religious landscape embodied the contradictions that informed the contests over race, place, and power that became more explicit and more pronounced after emancipation.

During the antebellum period, the religious terrain of slavery in the South had a great variety of expressions and institutions. On the one hand, there were the independent religious worship sites of the "hush harbor" tradition; on the other hand, there were formal Christian institutional worship spaces, both black and white. All these locations had their own politics and political significances for black and white people, enslaved and free. In the hush harbor, enslaved people mapped "rival geographies" and articulated a politics of freedom through movement to illicit spaces at unapproved times.[10] Moreover, enslaved people practiced a politics of spiritual resistance that transcended the physical boundaries of church buildings and spiritual gatherings through the ways in which they formed community identities with one another, which superseded possible identification with their masters, and through the ways they defined God.[11]

In the white-led institutional churches, the slaveholders and white preachers attempted to use the church sermon to discipline and control the minds and bodies of enslaved men and women within hearing range. In these spaces, both enslaved and slaveholders tried to "[use] religion socio-politically to control one another."[12] In addition to the white-led institutional churches, there were also independent black churches in the South during the pre-emancipation period.[13] In these churches, the politics of place developed slightly differently, as the members were both free and enslaved and still had to endure some aspects of the surveillance that participation in worship with white people entailed.[14] The coexistence of these three institutional spaces meant that there was not one single arbiter of the existential questions that religious institutions addressed, nor a single arbiter of the interpersonal dynamics that people gathering together in these spaces created. Antebellum black religious politics was shaped by black people's proximity to white practitioners and by the ways space was organized, which varied across geographies and time.

The hush harbor independent and clandestine worship spaces were characterized by enslaved people's resistance to white domination through the act of "stealing away"—secretly removing oneself from the plantation.[15] In these secret meetings, the members gathered with their own leaders to commune with the spirits. Here they developed their own ideas about and relationship with God. Eugene Genovese describes how enslaved people were able to create space within Christianity for themselves. He claims that they actually had a good measure of freedom in their religious spaces. Had they not had such space, Genovese argues, "folk belief might have remained an antithesis, and the slaves might have had to make the hard choice between Christianity and an anti-Christianity." Instead, separate worship spaces in the churches allowed the enslaved to develop independent Christianity. Planters did not want to enforce the laws that forbade enslaved people to gather because they believed that religion made the enslaved more docile.[16] Despite planters' beliefs, any space enslaved people had to create spiritual community was powerful political space. The power of these gatherings was further emphasized by the patrollers' constant attempts to disrupt meetings where the enslaved sought to worship their own God in the ways that they saw fit. Patrollers often targeted the times and places where enslaved people would be meeting in an attempt to enforce the boundaries of slavery,[17] but in so doing, they also gave ammunition for the development of a democratic propensity toward religious freedom.

Not all enslaved people had to "steal away" to worship. Some slaveholders actually built praise houses on their plantations so that enslaved people would not leave in order to go to worship services. One can only imagine how the proximity of the plantation praise house to the slaveholder stifled or shaped these religious services, however. Accounts of enslaved preachers who preached one message in the presence of white people and another in the slave quarters, out of earshot of white people, indicates the creative resistance enslaved people enacted in these instances of smothering surveillance.[18] Mrs. Julia Frazier captured the challenges of white and black people worshipping together in the story of an enslaved person named John who would always holler in church. The slaveholder challenged him, saying that if John could keep quiet during services, he would get John a new pair of boots. John stayed quiet as long as he could before exclaiming, "Glory to God! Boots or no boots, glory to God!"[19] A slaveholder's efforts to define an enslaved person's worship experience could not be fully realized.

There were also enslaved and free black people who stood outside religious organization—formal or informal. According to Mollie Booker, a free black woman, free black people were not allowed to go to church.[20] Indeed, some enslaved people were not permitted to go to church or any kind of worship service. In many cases, this prohibition stemmed from slaveholders' fear that a gathering of enslaved people could lead to an insurrection.[21] In other cases, they simply belonged to slaveholders who did not adhere to any religious faith and thus did not intend to secure any kind of catechism for the enslaved. Others went to white churches but were not allowed to participate in the service except for the singing or were subjected to a portion of the service geared just toward the enslaved.[22]

All these differences in black religious life created space for critiques. Independent black churches represented black struggles toward religious freedom and simultaneous critiques of racism within white Christianity.[23] Independent black churches existed throughout the North and South from the late eighteenth century into the antebellum period. Freed and free black people who had grown weary of white racism in religious institutions formed the first independent black denominations. Among these was the African Methodist Episcopal Church, which Richard Allen founded in 1816. This denomination and other independent churches were often motivated by critiques of the racist politics of the parent or related churches and denominations, but they also reflected denominational affinities.[24] In fact, Richard Allen affirmed his commitment to Wesleyan Methodism and claimed this commitment as being among his motivations for starting the AME denomination.[25] Meanwhile, one of his fellow protesters from St. George's Episcopal Church, Absalom Jones, chose to remain within the Episcopal Church. These independent congregations, like the hush harbors, posed continuous challenges to southern white Christianity and to the power dynamics of slavery.

As these independent churches and denominations challenged the racism among white Christians, they also explicitly challenged the theology of white southern Christian churches. Fugitives and freedpeople were critical of Christian slaveholders because they doubted the slaveholders' Christian beliefs. To them, "Christian slave owner" was an oxymoron. Refugees and self-emancipating slaves, whose narratives provide insight into what enslaved people thought during the antebellum period, offered strenuous critiques of white Christian southerners. Many proclaimed that they would have more strongly preferred a gambler, thief, or non-Christian as a slaveholder than a Christian one.[26] Common wisdom was that Christians were the harshest slaveholders, giving little food and clothing and whipping enslaved people most wantonly. A heathen, as the self-emancipated slaves put it, would more readily feed and clothe the enslaved and perhaps, most importantly, leave them alone on Sunday. As one woman noted, it was the Christian slaveholders who demanded the most work from enslaved people on Sundays: "The Christians will oppress you more. For instance, the biggest dinner must be got on Sunday. Now, everybody that has got common sense knows that

Sunday is a day of rest." There was a fundamental contradiction in Sunday being the day when the largest family meal was served and when the standards for preparing and presenting the meal were most strenuously enforced, leaving the opportunity for an enslaved house servant to receive a severe beating for any misstep.[27] An enslaved person could not properly be Christian in such a setting, where her labors were most in demand on Sunday. Sabbaths were whites-only days. These practices were symbols of white Christian hypocrisy. These dynamics also informed the context of independent black churches.

Some interracial churches found the racial dynamics of worshipping together to be too much to endure and therefore separated into black and white churches. In some instances, the split was the result of a protest; in others, it was amicable. In 1815, an interracial Methodist Church in Charleston, South Carolina, experienced some of the fissures that racial tensions created. There, the white members tried so hard to stifle black power within the congregation that the black members separated from the church and sought ordination for their leaders through the AME Church, leaving the Methodist Episcopal Church, South, altogether.[28] In other cases, the impetus for separation of black and white church members was less acrimonious, but the results were the same. In Petersburg in 1800, black and white members of the Davenport Church separated: the white members established their church on Market Street, the main thoroughfare in the city, and the black members established their church—the Sandy Beach Church (later known as Gilfield Baptist Church)—in the Pocahontas area of Petersburg, near the Appomattox River.[29]

Though the split was amicable, the question of property ownership loomed in the background of Sandy Beach's founding. Two historians of the Gilfield Baptist Church differ over whether or not black church members owned the Sandy Beach property because they were reported to have paid $250 of ground rent in 1815. Historian Luther Porter Jackson, on the authority of a contemporary lawyer, argues that one could "hold title to the land and yet continue to pay a fee called ground rent."[30] By contrast, Gilfield Baptist Church clerk Richard Kennard claimed that the church did not own the land at Sandy Beach in Pocahontas. Jackson concluded that whether or not they owned the land, the church certainly owned its building. With such confusing practices, it is no wonder that black church people faced challenges over property ownership. The church had many free black members who were also landowners and thus presumably familiar with landowning practices and laws. Many of them owned property near the second site of what would become

Gilfield Baptist Church. Even still, the presence or involvement of white trustees, who wanted to stop them from building a new building, indicated that there was still some oversight by white people, even if they were ultimately unable to impose their will on the congregation. Jackson writes, "The Church had one great trouble to combat in building the brick house. The trustees who believed with those who were opposed to the new building, would not give their consent until one half of the money was raised, but those who favored the building showed the pessimistic trustees that the Church was her own soverign [*sic*]; then the trouble ended and the building went on to completion."[31]

The tradition of autonomous churches in the Baptist polity created space for independent black Baptist churches to be formed even if they had white trustees and white overseers. Separate black Baptist churches in the South dated back to the 1750s with the African Bluestone Baptist Church in Mecklenburg County, Virginia, and the Silver Bluff Baptist Church in South Carolina.[32] The exact cause of the split within the Davenport Church is not known, but some clues to the cause and significance may be found in the details of the numbers of church members, the legal terms of land ownership, and the leadership that emerged after the split. In 1820, membership of the church on Market Street—formed by whites who had left Davenport to establish a separate church—numbered just 28 compared to the membership of Gilfield (née Sandy Beach), which numbered 422.[33] The separation of the black and white churches in 1800 followed decades of interracial worship that emerged out of the revivals that spread evangelical fervor over the southern rural religious landscape. In 1800, this interracial worship space, where black and white people preached to and ministered to one another, came to an end, and the era of the independent black church of Gilfield commenced. These cases notwithstanding, the independent black churches were continuously under some form of surveillance because of white fears of insurrection, and many independent antebellum black congregations had white preachers as de jure leaders.

Gilfield Baptist Church's history, an example of antebellum independent black church formation, is rooted in the interracial past of southern Christianity.[34] Despite the split in the church's membership, Gilfield remained under white leadership for most of its antebellum existence, reflecting the leadership patterns of many black churches in the antebellum South.[35] From its inception, almost all of Gilfield's pastors were white, save Sampson White, who served from 1837 to 1838.[36] It is notable that White's very short tenure occurred six years *after* Turner's rebellion led southern state and local governments, including Petersburg's, to prohibit all-black gatherings and require a white man to be present.[37] Even though Gilfield had white pastors, there was no shortage of black leadership. In fact, during the early years of the church's existence, the preachers came from the congregation.[38] There were many men who were recognized as capable preachers, but according to Jackson, where the church initially managed to share the leadership roles among the many preachers, this became unwieldy and the church members decided to seek one regular pastor whom they called in 1815. William Pittman, a white man, was their first pastor.[39] From 1815 to the end of slavery in 1865, Gilfield elected three of its six pastors, which suggests that they took an active role in determining who their leaders—black and white—were. By the time of Reverend William N. Robinson's pastorate in 1857, the leadership of the church was shared. This negotiation did not go on long because Robinson was Gilfield's last white pastor. After the war ended, he peaceably resigned because he recognized the desire of the church's members to be self-governing. In the fall of 1865, the church called the Reverend Henry Williams Jr., who was born free in Spotsylvania County but raised in Ohio, to the helm of the church.[40]

In November 1865, Williams was passing through Petersburg on a missionary trip, like so many religious people did in the immediate aftermath of the Civil War. At the time of his trip, Gilfield was waiting on the minister they had called to replace Reverend Robinson, but he had not yet reported to his post.[41] Gilfield invited Williams to preach, and upon hearing him, the congregation offered him the pastorate; he accepted. Williams brought his wife, Madaline Carter Williams, back to the state of his birth, and he assumed the pastorate of Gilfield.

The congregation that Williams was called to pastor was one of Petersburg's leading ones. Like its nearest comparable church, First Baptist Church—also known as the Harrison St. Baptist Church—it was large in size and had a mixed congregation of black people who had been free before the war and those who had become free. Although Gilfield had a number of free black members due to Revolutionary-era manumissions, there were also a number of enslaved members who had shared in the leadership and governance of the church.[42] Before the Civil War, most of Petersburg's black people were enslaved (66 percent in 1860).[43] The enslaved population grew during the Civil War, and a subset of these enslaved people formed Petersburg's other major church, St. Stephen's Episcopal Church. But Gilfield differed from St. Stephen's and Harrison St. because it almost immediately secured stable black leadership. Williams remained pastor of Gilfield for the next thirty-five years, whereas Harrison St. had a succession of pastors and instability for nearly a decade, and St. Stephen's first rector, a black man, left after three years, disgusted over the racism within the Episcopal Church, and was replaced by Giles B. Cooke, a white rector.

Some churches carried a lineage of negotiating freedom within the parameters set by white trustees and quickly sought independent black leadership after emancipation, while others continued the negotiations. These churches also had the good fortune not to have had land disputes of the sort that Immanuel AME Church of Portsmouth did.

The antebellum black religious experience involved significant contests about the meaning and practice of the Christian faith. Where slaveholders tried to control or limit the content, expression, and practice of Christianity, enslaved and free black people inserted their own traditions and developed trenchant critiques. In this context, there existed two Christianities.[44] One was a black Christianity of resistance to racism and exploitation and a critique of hypocrisy that fed a commitment to democracy and freedom. The other was a white Christianity of domination and control, a "handmaiden of slavery."[45] The dominant social and economic relations of slavery held these two approaches in dynamic relationship. Once the institution was removed, the terms of the relationship began to shift, as the Immanuel case and the formation of other independent churches after emancipation demonstrate.

Independent Black Church Development After Emancipation

Many freedpeople migrated from the country to the cities or vice versa to get away from slaveholders or to test the limits of their new freedoms.[46] In many cases the migration was not just physical but also spiritual, with freedpeople tending to leave the churches of their enslavers to affiliate with churches of their own choosing.[47] For some of Virginia's freedpeople, this was the Baptist or AME Church, which reemerged in the South after having been all but banned in Virginia and South Carolina after the Turner and Vesey rebellions.[48] For others, the new religious freedom meant a completely new denomination, as was the case with the formation of the Zion Union Apostolic Church. In these surroundings, freedpeople began to build new communities that reinforced their community allegiance and sense of belonging among fellow freedpeople. Freedom brought the chance to negotiate openly for resources and responsibility rooted in the precept of black autonomy. These negotiations took place within independent black churches and in predominantly white churches in which black people remained. Some black people expected an immediate shift, as reflected in the developments at

St. Stephen's Episcopal Church, the first black Episcopal Church in Virginia. At the same time, gender dynamics of black church leadership emerged. These dynamics, which fostered Victorian manhood for black men and erased black women's participation, can be seen in the creation of churches by black women and the pursuit of patriarchal authority by some black men.

While most studies of black religious institutions in the postbellum period focus on the increasing numbers of independent black Baptist and Methodist Churches, very little attention has been given to black people who remained within the predominantly white denominations.[49] And yet these narratives are just as illuminating about the religious, racial, and political landscape of the postemancipation period. These freedpeople approached the postemancipation interracial religious community with a desire for autonomy and a sense of expectation akin to what those freedpeople who separated into independent black churches felt. The St. Stephen's Episcopal Church of Petersburg—formed by the Braggs, a family of freedpeople, with assistance from a white priest—exemplifies this experience. The church emerged in the postemancipation period out of collaboration between a black woman and a white Episcopalian priest.

The Bragg family migrated to Petersburg from Warrenton, North Carolina, immediately after the Civil War ended. By 1860, free black people made up a good portion of Petersburg's population, numbering about 3,000, and together with enslaved people (about 5,924) nearly equaled the number of white people in the city (9,324).[50] Thus, there were a large number of black people who were present in Petersburg during the war and who had witnessed the Battle of the Crater, a massive slaughter of black Union soldiers by a battalion of Confederate soldiers under General William Mahone's charge.[51] The Bragg family, however, was part of a migration of black people from North Carolina and Southside to the city.[52]

According to a history written by Carrie Bragg Campbell, sister of George Freeman Bragg Jr., the family had been affiliated with the Episcopal Church in North Carolina and when they moved to Petersburg, they affiliated with the city's Grace Episcopal Church.[53] The Bragg family matriarch, Caroline W. Bragg, was credited with working along with Grace's rector, Reverend Churchill J. Gibson, to establish a separate mission church for black people based in the Stringfellow Chapel, which had been "used by the Soldiers during the war."[54] That church, St. Stephen's Episcopal Church, grew into one of Petersburg's noted black churches, and one of the bulwarks of black Episcopalians in the state. It developed a school and secured educational opportunities for the city's black children and later black ministers. Out of this church and school came an unlikely partnership between freedpeople and former Confederates that paralleled, if not informed, later interracial political alliances, like the Readjuster movement.

Gumption was not enough to get St. Stephen's recognized as a parish by the Annual Council of the Virginia Diocese, however. Under the leadership of black rector Reverend Joseph S. Atwell, whom Bishop Francis McNeece Whittle had sent to Petersburg in the fall of 1868 and who was ordained to the priesthood by Bishop John Johns on May 7, 1869, St. Stephen's applied for admission as a parish but was denied. Atwell was so frustrated with the diocese's decision and unaccustomed to this level of racism that—having come from the Kentucky diocese, where he had led black churches into connection on other occasions—he left for St. Stephen's Church in Georgia, which was recognized by the Georgia diocese. Virginia's diocese, however, preferred to keep its black parishes under the leadership of the white parishes, and it was not easily budged from its position.[55]

Narratives of black church formation often highlight the role played by men and obscure the presence and participation of black women. One salient example is the narrative of the exodus of black members from St. George's Episcopal Church in Philadelphia, which gave birth to what would become the AME Church. In accordance with Richard Allen's account, his and Absalom Jones's presence is often noted, but the presence of numerous women is often overlooked.[56] This omission is curious given the seeming parity of representation of black men and women in black churches after emancipation. Sister Bragg's salient role in helping to organize the St. Stephen's Episcopal Church places black women squarely in the place of black religious church origins, which is also evident in the names of individuals who were among the first to gather in worship in these houses. These records usually suggest groupings of husbands and wives, parents and children, and siblings and single individuals who were both male and female.[57]

Perhaps the occlusion of black women from church origin stories reflects the political dynamics of the postemancipation period, in which black men worked to cultivate political coalitions with what historian Glenda Gilmore described as "the Best Men."[58] It is more likely that for black churches, the male-dominated origin stories were a narrative conceit that addressed some of the contemporary concerns of black men creating a meaningful freedom and of later historians grappling with interpreting the significance of black churches in black community life.[59]

The early history of the Zion Union Apostolic (ZUA) Church (later, the Reformed Zion Union Apostolic Church), compiled by church historian

Rev. James Oliver Allen and published by the church's general education board, is one example. Allen's manuscript was heavily edited before being published. This account of the church's history provides clues about the development of the church's leadership and amplifies major thematic concerns about black ministerial leadership.

The ZUA Church began from a congregation of freedpeople who separated from the Baptist and Episcopal Churches in Brunswick and Mecklenburg counties. They were soon joined by a black missionary from Philadelphia, James Howell. According to Howell, going south was also a fulfillment of his calling: "I came like Abraham," he reportedly said. "I left Philadelphia not knowing anything except God told me to go. God has something for me to do here."[60] A freeborn black man, Howell came to Southside toward the end of the Civil War because he had heard that some AME missionaries had gone to Virginia to establish mission fields.[61] Howell—who, according to church historian Rev. James Oliver Allen, had been unable to rise above the position of elder in the AME Church due to his limited education—also saw an opportunity to remake himself and to reform the errant AME Church in his move to the South. Howell wanted to become a minister and bring the AME Church back around to the fundamental principles of Methodism.[62]

While Howell's narrative paralleled that of black people in other denominations who sought to gain control over their own destinies from white folks, he also sought independence from overbearing black ecclesiastical structures that denied him access to institutional recognition and power. This theme of retaining autonomy continued to resonate through the formation of the ZUA Church and black religious associations during Reconstruction. Howell must have been extremely frustrated by his failure to advance in the denomination. According to Allen, "[the church] was the one place where [Howell] felt complete and free."[63] Allen depicted the problems that Howell faced in terms that have come to be the standard interpretation of the significance of the church in black life. It was the one place where a black man could feel like a man. Outside he had to scrape and shuffle and defer to white men and women. But inside the church, Allen asserted, "he could feel equal to every other man. He could speak up and speak out. He could oppose and defend. He could elevate himself from pew member to choir member or official."[64] With such an expectation of progress and validation, Howell was frustrated by his inability to rise beyond the position of elder simply because he had only obtained a grade school education.[65]

Howell came to Virginia in 1864 and went to Petersburg, where he found the city suffering from desolation and destruction.[66] After trying to find work and start a church in Norfolk, Hampton, and Newport News with little success, Howell decided to board a train and get off where the spirit led him. In Five Forks (now Skipwith), in Mecklenburg County—five miles west of Petersburg—he got off the train to stretch his legs and started a conversation with a bystander. This person noted that there was a significant population of black people, mostly Episcopalians but also some Baptists, who had separated from the white churches and were meeting at the courthouse. This group of separatists did not have regular pastoral leadership. Howell decided to stay in Five Forks and soon united with the separatists worshipping at the Boydton courthouse.[67]

Howell established himself as a leader among these religious dissidents. Traveling between Boydton, Virginia, and Warrenton, North Carolina, he befriended several men who would become leaders in the ZUA Church. Among them were Nicholas Coleman, George Washington Taylor, Samuel Barner, and Wilson Taylor (Mecklenburg); John McDowell Bishop, Charles and Alfred Brown, Miles Green, Phillip Farrer, and Payton Edwards (Brunswick); and Alfred, Macklin, and Washington P. Russell, and Hercules "Harkless" Coleman (Palmer-Springs, Warrenton, North Carolina).[68] Some of the dissidents formed a Baptist church at Boydton, and others formed the St. Paul Zion Church. Howell worked to help form other churches, and on April 1, 1869, Howell and several other leaders gathered to organize the churches into a formal denomination. Together they created the structure for what they called the Zion Union Apostolic Church. They arrived at this position after three days of praying and searching. Out of this convention, they nominated Rev. James R. Howell and Rev. Sandford M. Dodge to compile their plans and present them to their members at the follow-up meeting in October 1869.[69]

Howell represented the great opportunities black people encountered on the new terrain of the South. A man who had been denied the opportunity to advance in religious leadership in a northern free denomination came to the South and was able to become the founding leader and later bishop of the second all-black religious denomination in the South. Notably, Howell's efforts allowed him to secure a position that affirmed his masculine identity and placed the pursuit and attainment of leadership roles for black men within the formation of Victorian manhood. Like members of the masonic lodges after emancipation, some black ministers were able to use the trappings of the ministry and the rituals of the church to claim their manhood in comparison to white men, by obtaining positions of equivalent stature and, in relationship to black women, by establishing patriarchal relationships between the pastor and the congregation, especially the women.[70] This Victorian manhood included an emphasis on domesticity that redeemed both black manhood and black womanhood.[71] Howell's pursuit of the pulpit had as its backdrop the limitations on black manhood and citizenship rights that living in the antebellum United States entailed. Like the AME ministers and the men who opposed black women preachers, those seeking the pulpit were concerned with their own masculinity.[72] Howell can be likened to these ministers because he fit the mold of the rugged itinerant minister forging a path to ministry through the wilderness.[73] Though the landscape for articulating black manhood through ministry became defined by the issue of women preaching, the initial steps were forged through securing the pulpit.

The Freedmen's Bureau and Black Religious Practice

While freedpeople negotiated within and with extant denominations to redefine their religious lives, external governmental and religious agencies were also significant interlocutors for freed religious institutions. The Freedmen's Bureau, created by an act of the U.S. Congress in 1865, was the first governmental agency following the military to take an active role in defining freedom for the freedpeople. Tasked with assisting the freedpeople and administering abandoned lands, the Freedmen's Bureau also brokered the assistance of northern missionaries to fulfill the many demands the transition surfaced. Together the bureau and the missionaries redefined the terms of the contest over the meaning and practice of Christianity. In addition to negotiating conflicts over land, the Freedmen's Bureau also negotiated conflicts between religious freedom and labor. Northern missionaries and Freedmen's Bureau agents went even further in their efforts to shape the lives of freedpeople in the areas of education, family life, and gender roles. Through their work, these agents shaped the context in which freedpeople made a new religious freedom.

The Freedmen's Bureau was the first iteration of "the government" with which freedpeople engaged.[74] In the case of black churches, they found the bureau's agents both champions and challengers. Though the bureau's agents had little authority in the confiscation of property, they did have the unfortunate responsibility of informing the freedpeople who had worked abandoned land during the war that those lands were to be returned to their Confederate owners.[75] Beyond how the agents behaved, however, an image of hopeful and independent people searching for ways to make freedom meaningful is reflected in the correspondence of Freedmen's Bureau agents.

A resilient church community responded to the arson burning of First African Baptist Church in Petersburg in May 1866. Apparently the same perpetrators, whom Freedmen's Bureau agents referred to as "rebels," also attempted to burn down the Gilfield and St. Stephen's churches, but the fires were quickly extinguished before much damage could be done.[76] The loss of independently owned black property was a tragedy, but Petersburg rallied to the support of First African Baptist Church. The city offered a $5,000 reward for the capture of the guilty persons, while citizens and church members raised enough money to rebuild the church. Freedmen's Bureau agent Stuart Barnes was surprised at the faithful response of Petersburg's freed black community; he thought they would be angry at the violent affront. Instead, they were hopeful. The hearty, supportive response of the city's inhabitants did much to encourage such sentiments.[77]

Burning black churches and schools in the postemancipation period was an all too common expression of white angst and anger about the transitions going on in southern society. The churches were particular targets because of their institutional independence. The schools drew attention because of the liberating potential of education that had been withheld from enslaved people. That these two institutions often shared the same physical space made the target all the more attractive.[78] Moreover, the independence they represented made these large edifices clear declarations of the change in social relations. In the cases of arson and attempted arson, the black churches discovered the Freedmen's Bureau's and city government agents' support of their survival. The Freedmen's Bureau seemed to understand the landscape of conflict as shaped by the former Confederates or "rebels" lashing out against the freed black religious spaces. And the city government took the position of standing against violent acts of intimidation by offering an incentive to bring the individuals to justice. In the first few months of emancipation, freedpeople found political allies among government officials.

In the instance of the First African Baptist Church arson, the Freedmen's Bureau needed only to watch the city respond quickly to the violence committed against its black inhabitants. In other instances, freedpeople requested that the bureau aid them in establishing their own churches. In Richmond, church members requested that the wood from the Chimborazo Hospital be given to them to use to build a church.[79] If, as was noted in the case of the Immanuel AME Church, the bureau could do little to override the dictates of state law—one of the clear directives given to agents and especially magistrates—the bureau could sell or otherwise dispense with land acquired as a result of the war. However, just how the bureau was supposed to handle distribution of the land remained unclear. The bureau was supposed to administer abandoned lands that had belonged to former Confederates and had been confiscated. But just as there was no legal mechanism to secure slave property in churches to the community, there was no legal apparatus to provide for the redistribution of land. Sherman's Field Order No. 15, which set aside 400,000 acres along the coast of Georgia and South Carolina and promised freedpeople 40 acres and a mule, did not hold legal weight.[80]

Besides the lack of legal muscle, there was a lack of political will among the nation's top leadership to secure land for the freedpeople. President Andrew Johnson quickly undercut the bureau's ability to administer abandoned lands when he issued his Amnesty Proclamation on May 29, 1865, which offered most former Confederates a pardon and the restoration of their land upon taking an oath. To reinforce the results of Johnson's Amnesty Proclamation, in October 1865 Stuart Barnes and other agents throughout the state held meetings with the freedpeople in which they told them in no uncertain terms that they would not be receiving land and that they would have to work for their former owners.[81] Johnson's proclamation put the bureau in the unfortunate position of restoring lands to former rebels rather than using it to aid the freedpeople in getting their footing. Consider, for example, the investigation into the ownership of Huguenot Springs in Powhatan County, whose owner had died, putting the property under the control of executors. Though the property had been occupied by the United States during the war, General Patrick advised the owner that the government did not intend to keep it, so the executors took possession of the land with the intent to sell it without any formal order from the U.S. government. Freedmen's Bureau agents thus spent a couple of weeks untangling the details in order to allow former Confederates to sell the land.[82] In these circumstances, then, southern land under the bureau's control dropped from 75,653 acres in 1865 to 50,000 in 1866 and under 10,000 in 1868.[83] As many as twenty thousand black people were evicted from land in southeast Virginia following Johnson's proclamation.[84]

Not much of the land restored to former Confederates was in Southside, however. There was a maximum of nine properties in the second subdistrict, which included Petersburg, City Point, Dinwiddie, Prince George, Chesterfield, Halifax, and Powhatan counties.[85] While Petersburg was the last theater of the Civil War before the fall of Richmond, it was never occupied by the Union, and so there was not a lot of land under federal control. Of the small amount of land under bureau control after the war, all that was left by March 1867 in the second subdistrict was one piece of Confederate government property and one parcel of private property.[86] Although hope for land redistribution may have been small to start, federal policies ensured that it would be impossible.

The bureau's role as arbiter of conflicts between freedpeople and their white employers drew it into discussions about black religious practices. Independent black worship presented an immediate conflict with lingering practices of inequality in church leadership, and it became an even more pronounced conflict when it affected labor. This was the subtext to complaints about worship services led by Mother Howard, a black female missionary from Philadelphia. Agent J. W. Sharp, assistant superintendent in Surry County, received reports "from citizens of the neighborhood" that Mother Howard held worship services on Sunday night that lasted until Monday morning and made the freedpeople late to work. At a white employer's request, Sharp spoke to Mother Howard and her companion, "a colored man from Philadelphia named Dawson," about her comportment. Sharp reported that he visited the meeting and found 150 men and women there. The attendees behaved in a "becoming and orderly manner," he wrote, "unless great excitement and much loud shouting and shrieking could be otherwise construed by those who are not advocates of a demonstrative form of worship."[87] Clearly, Sharp found no sufficient grounds to be concerned about black worship practices. He advised them to conduct themselves in "a wise and discreet manner" to avoid even the chance that someone could claim they were doing something inappropriate. Since he received no further complaints after his visit, Sharp considered the matter resolved.

While the pretext of long worship services is what sent Sharp to the black religious gathering, Sharp's observations about the black community illuminate a bit more about the dynamics in the community. Perhaps the employers were not just concerned about their workers showing up late to work; they may have been concerned about them showing up at all. Agent Sharp reported that "two thirds of the married Freedmen, whose intentions I have learned, propose next year to start farming for themselves."[88] Since many agents supported the efforts to reinforce Victorian respectability and nuclear family structures among the freedpeople, this should have been a welcome and supported goal. However, Agent Sharp noted the economic unfeasibility of this goal, pointing out that white farmers had all the land, tools, food, and money to be small farmers; freedmen lacked all of this. Instead of critiquing the systemic inequality his comments exposed, however, the agent blamed the freedmen for lacking "the capacity to reflect." Contrary to having a lack of reflection, the freedmen in Mother Howard's meeting were staging their freedom of time, labor, body, and eventually families through their religious community, something Agent Sharp purported to tamp down.

Not all encounters between freed religious communities and Freedmen's Bureau agents were so easily resolved.[89] In Staunton, Virginia, the issues were more complicated. Emily Rodney was working to establish an African Methodist Episcopal church there, but the black congregation she encountered had already begun the process of buying a church under the aegis of the Methodist Episcopal Church, South. According to Agent Tukey, it was better for the freedpeople to stay with the Methodist Episcopal Church, South, so that they did not lose their deposit. Thus, he advised Rodney to stop preaching in Staunton, especially since she had no license. When she did not stop, he brought her before the Freedmen's court, of which he was a magistrate. According to Rodney and her supporters, Tukey refused to allow her witnesses to testify. Allegedly acting out of concern for the freedpeople in his district, who stood to lose their down payment, Tukey brought Rodney before the court, which admonished her and instructed her to stop preaching in Staunton.[90]

This conflict development revealed how, like the independent freedpeople of Surry County, those worshipping with Rodney also sought to establish their independence. These worshippers and Rodney wrote directly to the Freedmen's Bureau's state commissioner, Oliver O. Brown, laying out their concerns. The worshippers asked, "Why is it that she can't hold Meetings in private houses For us and Preach." Sister Rodney described it as a matter of "Justice and Religious Liberty," having implicated Agent Tukey in interfering with the desires of the people to unite with the AME Church by asking the first minister to wait to organize the church, during which time some of the members went and joined the Washington Conference. When the agent tried to insert himself as a paternalist authority in the religious lives of the community, they directly challenged him. Though Agent Tukey thought it was best for them to remain with the Methodist Episcopal Church, South, at least to maintain their financial standing, they did not see that as the primary aim. Where the agent in the Immanuel case was called on to aid the freedpeople in negotiating with members of the Methodist Episcopal Church, South, the agent in Staunton tried to push the freedpeople into fellowship. This is a remarkable look at the dynamics that shaped black people's separation from white churches and the roles that Freedmen's Bureau agents and the pursuit of church property played in it.

Though the Freedmen's Bureau's abilities to redistribute land were limited, the agency played an important role in shaping the landscape of black religious freedom. The bureau literally helped or hindered black churches from securing land. Where the Immanuel AME Church appealed for and received assistance, the church at Staunton found little support from the bureau agent. The agent's view of protecting the freedpeople meant keeping them in league with white church leadership rather than ensuring that black church members' desire for independence would be honored. The Freedmen's Bureau also stepped into the role of mediating culture even though its main purpose was to manage labor contracts. Just as agents were concerned about the behavior of black religious people, so too were the numerous missionaries who came to the aid of the newly freed people. Not only did black women play important roles in establishing black church communities, but they were also at the forefront of black missionary endeavors and aid to the freedpeople after emancipation. While the work of teachers like Frances Ellen Watkins Harper, Charlotte Hawkins Brown, and even notable former fugitives like Harriet Jacobs and Sojourner Truth are well known, the preaching ministries of Mother Howard and Sister Rodney have been lost in the historical narratives. While Agent Sharp found no reason to interfere with Mother Howard's ministry, Agent Tukey tried to use church rules to disrupt Sister Rodney's ministry—claiming that she did not have a license. This discourse provides an alternative view to the postemancipation narratives of attempts to withdraw black women to the home. Howard and Rodney were claiming pulpits. These northern black female religious leaders occupied a space within the black community for black community uplift and support. At the same time, black people began to carve out space for black women's security by withdrawing them from the labor force and setting them at home. This push to have black women at home coincided to some degree with the missionaries' efforts to provide domestic education. Though the missionaries aimed to train a labor force, the skills they focused on reinforced domestic labor for black women. While the efforts of Freedmen's Bureau agents to establish and reinforce nuclear black families with patriarchal control and the practices around labor contracts reinforced patriarchy, interactions like Tukey's also shaped the dynamics of black gender roles.[91] Using church law to bully Rodney into ending her ministry, Tukey's efforts had the effect of depriving the community of the leadership of a woman, one whom they clearly supported.

CHURCHES WERE MORE THAN just spaces over which freedpeople had gained control for themselves. They had become powerful bases for independence in other areas of black life, which brought black people into direct conflict with white church trustees and government agents regarding land, free religious worship, and even labor. Many black Virginians, whether returning migrants from the North and West or newly emancipated people from the countryside and the city, had serious critiques of white Christianity, and they staked their claims to independent worship on those grounds. In some instances, freedmen had planned to withdraw their wives from the labor force.[92] Add to that employers' frustration that they might show up late or not at all, and the tensions increased. As a result, independent black worship became a very tense proposition. The power of community worship that involved hundreds of black worshippers and workers could not have been lost on employers. In the same way that they recognized the significance of the schools that dotted the landscape, the organizational power of the churches was becoming more evident. For the freedpeople, the convictions of their freedom to use the government to secure these rights and upturn the systems of oppression was a foundation for the larger units of organizing they established in their associations and conventions.

This first engagement with the government was no doubt also informative of black religious political strategies. As intent on independent worship as black people became, however, the bureau was ineffective in supporting it and even worked against it. The churches had to appeal to agents whose goals sometimes dovetailed with those of black church people as reinforcing family structures and the authority of parents. But other times, the agents' ideas about labor and their paternalism directly contravened freedpeople's goals.

CHAPTER TWO

Independent Black Church Conventions, 1866–1868

In 1847, Fields Cook, an enslaved man, penned his autobiography.[1] Only a small snippet of it—thirty-two pages—has survived. In those pages we learn a bit about how life in slavery shaped Cook's politics after emancipation. In narrating how his relationship with his master's son transformed from the equality of playmates to the hierarchy of slaveholder and enslaved, he identified a central fallacy in the institution of slavery: it disrupted natural human relations. Through his experience, he understood that the greatest sin of slavery was keeping him and other enslaved people bound by false teachings and from living out their true spiritual callings in life. Called to the preaching ministry, Cook was denied the chance to follow his calling because he was enslaved. He explained, "From the day that I beleaved untill [*sic*] now I have ever felt and beleaved [*sic*] that god has called me to the ministry and if I never perform that I shall ever think that I have fallen short of the work which god has assigned to my hands to doe [*sic*] the reason why I have not preached may be known by all of those who know the laws of the land."[2] Cook's relationship with his playmate was reinforced through their shared religious experience, but it was also the context in which his oppression was reinscribed.

The circumstance Cook described was particularly notable given that in Virginia, it was never illegal to teach enslaved people to read, as it was in other states. Instead, it was only illegal to gather enslaved people together to teach them—a law that precluded the establishment of schools but not the dissemination of knowledge.[3] This limitation of gathering enslaved people aimed to break down the networks of communication and community building that helped foster the Nat Turner rebellion. It extended to the churches because Virginia's laws prohibited independent religious gatherings for enslaved people. Instead, they could only meet to worship if a white person was present. Though religion brought people together in pursuit of salvation, the institution of slavery divided them. Moreover, political institutions and laws circumscribed enslaved people's ability to carry out their religious callings. Thus, Cook developed early on a deeply personal sense of the need for legally protected religious freedom. This view of the intersection of religion and politics through policy and practice was on full display in Cook's political activism and in the newly formed church associations and state conventions during the first years of freedom.

Virginia's black religious conventions emerged in the ambiguous legal context of the immediate postemancipation period. Despite the legal uncertainties under which free and freed people lived, they immediately began forming their own churches and associations. These gatherings, which included a number of black people who had been free before the end of the Civil War, drew on an antebellum legacy of independent church denominations and conventions steeped in the fight for recognition of black humanity and the abolition of slavery. With this foundation, these associations responded to the new context of freedom and independence in which they found themselves.[4] The various black Baptist associations of Virginia, the Zion Union Apostolic Church, and black people in the Episcopal Church were immersed in struggles to make freedom meaningful for freedpeople.

While the postbellum black churches continued their anti-dehumanization stance, the new political terrain of freedom allowed church leaders and members to redefine how they carried out their missions. Suffrage became a predominant concern, and the conventions became the preeminent proof of black political fitness. In addition, black people began to articulate political rights in terms of religious freedom and independence, defining their desire for cultural and social independence in terms of First Amendment constitutional rights, a marker of their political sophistication. Members of the denominational conventions understood their work to be important in the political realm, where their rights were being defined. Beyond demonstrating political capacity, these conventions were also spaces that showed the depth of the black leadership pool: it reached beyond the pulpit. In this way, the religious and political worlds overlapped.

The church conventions responded to the political context of Republican Party politics and the resultant state constitutional convention—two events that demonstrated the black political and tactical acumen and spiritual resilience the people needed to persevere. Black leaders like Thomas Bayne, a former slave, dentist, politician, and itinerant minister, and Fields Cook, a barber, activist, and minister, played key roles in black political conventions, church conventions, the Republican Party, and the constitutional convention, demonstrating not just the great variety of political activities and engagements of black people but also the interplay and exchange between the many arenas.[5] The racial animosity and political marginalization against which black Virginians fought in the years leading up to the ratification of the new state constitution in 1870 was an important and influential context for the development of postemancipation black religion. While the racial dynamics between black and white Baptists were significant foundations for the formation of southern black religious polities, what happened within the black conventions themselves and how that related to the broader political conversations developing in the immediate postwar period need further development.

The formation of independent black Baptist associations shows how black people organized themselves, developed their identities, and articulated their place within the new American freedom. Within these spaces, leaders articulated their views of the larger political and spiritual settings in which they were operating and the role that their conventions and denominations played in the freedom struggle, because even though freed, they were in the process of obtaining political rights. In addition to articulating their own views of the world in which they lived, they organized and oriented themselves to power. These leaders developed a political structure and articulated ideas about the meaning of freedom as being religious freedom, and they defined the boundaries of their communities and established the frameworks of their shared beliefs. Moreover, they began to articulate the meanings of manhood and womanhood. They articulated what their relationship to white people would be, and they did all this with overlapping involvement and engagement in the external political sphere, placing them in a position that was both creative and defensive. In essence, these new conventions and denominations helped free and newly freed people create a political world of control and of possibility.

Conventions as Models for Political Participation

Among the salient features of Virginia's early postemancipation associations were the goals and purposes they established and the structures they put in place to achieve them. Led by men with national connections and prior experience in regional associations, Virginia's black Baptists immediately began to organize their churches into regional associations and a state convention.[6] The Norfolk Union Baptist Association (NUBA), Virginia's first regional association, was organized in 1863.[7] It was quickly followed by the Colored Shiloh Baptist Association (CSBA) in 1865. The state convention, the Virginia Baptist State Convention (VBSC), emerged shortly after these two regional associations and seemed to preview the call of the Consolidated American Baptist Missionary Convention (CABMC) for black Baptists to organize state conventions and affiliate with the CABMC.

The CABMC was the result of the effort to unify black Baptists at the national level. It formed from two organizations—the American Baptist Missionary Convention and the Northwestern Baptist Convention—in August 1866.[8] The political context in which these regional and statewide gatherings emerged elevated the significance of their work to defining freedom as citizens with rights and the freedom to live and worship as they wished. The attention they paid to the structure of governance in their associations linked them to Baptist polity and illustrated their ability to participate in orderly governance. They preempted questions about whether freedpeople could exercise the franchise responsibly and not be controlled by their employers by leading aid efforts among the freedpeople.[9] They simply launched into doing the work that independent, capable people could do and were not hindered by the questions people raised. From the way they depicted themselves as having deep roots in Baptist history to the way they claimed leadership in providing aid to freedpeople, their desire for religious freedom and political engagement intertwined, illustrating the intersection between religion and politics at both a rhetorical and a practical level. Having political rights would allow others to fully realize their religious lives. In this context, the associations articulated freedom in religious terms and made their case for political participation.

The first regional associations in the state brought together churches clustered near one another. In these gatherings, they interpreted freedom and began plotting the way forward. Formed in 1865, the CSBA—Virginia's second black Baptist association—held its first meeting at Ebenezer Baptist Church of Richmond, with just seven churches representing more than five thousand members from Richmond and Petersburg.[10] The CSBA's second meeting was held in Petersburg at the Gilfield Baptist Church, where Rev. Henry Williams Jr. was pastor. By this point, the CSBA included twenty-eight churches and over fourteen thousand members. The CSBA brought together many of the leading lights in Virginia's black Baptist community, including storied preacher John Jasper, later famous for his sermon "The Sun Do Move" but then the pastor of Third Baptist Church, a small Petersburg congregation; Richard Wells, pastor of First African Church of Manchester, and its clerk, Ballard T. Edwards; Peter Randolph, pastor of Ebenezer Baptist Church; and Fields Cook of Richmond.[11] The elected executive committee included Richard Wells as moderator, Henry Williams Jr. as clerk, and Gilfield Baptist Church member James Carter Sr. as treasurer.[12]

At the Shiloh association's first meeting, members celebrated their emancipation from slavery using the Bible to interpret their experiences. President of the convention Rev. William Williams likened freedom to the resurrection of Jesus Christ: "We have long looked and prayed for this day, which has at length dawned upon us with the refulgent brilliance of that morning when Jesus, by his resurrection, unlocked the gates of death."[13] He highlighted how emancipation was like the miracle of Jesus' resurrection overcoming death. One prayer ranged across the freedom narratives in the Bible, indicating how freedpeople used a narrative theology to interpret their experience.[14] The convention recorder also reported that Reverend Bowler's prayer "bore us on the wings of imagination through the dark and dreary passage of God's people through the wilderness of slavery, over the bloody sea of war, into the Canaan of liberty." The clerk continued, "[Reverend Bowler] said the prophecy had now been accomplished—that Princes should come out of Egypt and Ethiopia should lift up her hands unto God. He invoked the blessing of God upon the infant association, and upon all its members."[15] With convention members reminded through prayer of their journey—a journey connected and made sense of through scripture—they named the association the Colored Shiloh Baptist Association and joined hands in singing a hymn.[16] The sight of this kind of unified, "heavenly" endeavor, the recorder reported, "would have melted the hearts of our oppressors."[17] Thus, as much as these delegates gathered in the midst of a new reality and new fulfillment, they still imagined the gaze of "their oppressors" and the hope of changing their hearts.

At the Shiloh association's next meeting, members shifted their gaze from interpreting the past to plotting the path forward in freedom. As suggested in their previous meeting, they thought moving forward would include some type of continued connection to white people. The association drew together the community's leadership and began to define some of their ideas for political and social inclusion, even suggesting that interracial affiliation was desirable. To that end, they sent copies of their minutes to the American Baptist Historical and Publication Society, the publishing wing of the white northern American Baptist Home Mission Society.[18] While they pushed for some type of interracial cooperation, they also held on to the idea that they needed separate spaces for black people. Thus, they affirmed that they supported black teachers and black schools. The Committee on Resolutions presented the view of the convention, first spelling out the need for ministers and preachers to be well versed in the word and then offering suggestions about race relations. They acknowledged the presence of prejudice but "believe[d] that the gospel and the church are the mediums through which God will reconcile man to man."[19] They recognized that the divided racial landscape did not yet exhibit this kind of reconciliation and so announced that they were not calling for any church to do anything differently. Instead, they wanted to prick consciences. They continued, "We do say if Christians of all colors will practice the spirit of Christ we shall soon have a different state of things in all the churches, both white and colored."[20] At the 1866 meeting of the CSBA, the association passed a resolution to remove the word "African" from the names of churches on the grounds that they—the churches and their members—were American, not African.[21] This resolution provided additional evidence of the CSBA's integrationist stance. As with so many free and newly freed people after emancipation, the promise of citizenship rights permeated their thoughts and plans.[22]

These early efforts at establishing regional associations quickly gave way to black Baptist efforts to unite *all* the state's membership into one organization: the Virginia Baptist State Convention. This new state organization emerged in the crosscurrents of ecclesiastical and political change. Black Baptists had formed a national association, the Consolidated American Baptist Missionary Convention.[23] Steeped in the long tradition of regional associations, the leaders of the CABMC saw strength in numbers and the opportunity to denounce the structures of slavery and race that had kept black people divided by unifying across state and regional lines. In its 1869 annual report, the executive board called for states to organize conventions and send delegates to the annual CABMC meeting. "By this means," they wrote, "we may concentrate our forces, bring into employment all of our resources and show our strength to our advantage as a denomination and a missionary body, who as a representative is numerically superior to any colored body of Christians in the world."[24] This emphasis on numerical strength was an idea easily shared among Virginians, who were well represented in the CABMC. Among the CABMC's life members were thirty-two Virginians, including Fields Cook, Peter Randolph, William E. Troy, Henry Williams Jr., John W. White, John H. Gains, Richard Wells, E. G. Corprew, and Burrell Toler. Indeed, many of the driving forces of the VBSC and the CSBA were also members of the CABMC.

By 1869, freedpeople generally, and free black Virginians in particular, came to appreciate the significance of numerical strength. This was particularly important in the recent election, which extended the franchise to freedmen and secured a new constitution codifying these and other rights. These advances had been far from guaranteed, which made their accomplishment all the more notable. Under President Johnson's direction, emancipation looked much like slavery, and it was not clear that black people would achieve their political goals. President Johnson's requirement of former Confederates to take a personal oath in order to have their voting rights restored applied only to a small number. The great majority of Confederates had their rights restored summarily. While Johnson had a policy for Confederates, he had no recognizable policy for freedpeople. Moreover, the quick return of Confederates to county and city offices along with the black codes that continued to keep black people disenfranchised and in a subordinate place through vagrancy and contract labor laws marked the way for continued struggle.[25] The concern for the strength in numbers might have been heightened by the beginning of congressional Reconstruction in March 1867, which called for registration of all voters for an election and a constitutional convention to incorporate black suffrage into state constitutions and to adopt the Fourteenth Amendment.[26] Virginia's black men registered in large numbers and out-participated white voters in the election of 1868 for the constitutional convention and in the election of delegates to the convention. A clearer sense of the possibilities of black political leadership and the strengthening case for black suffrage emerged. The Reconstruction Acts of 1867 effectively set aside the rejection of the Fourteenth Amendment by Virginia's reconstituted legislature in January 1867.[27] The associations took note of these developments. In the August 1867 meeting of the CSBA, Elder Sampson White offered a resolution acknowledging the work being done by the United States Congress to advance black rights.[28]

Black Baptists set about the task of demonstrating their suitability for self-governance and political participation through the ways they set up and ran their associations and conventions. Many scholars have asserted that black churches were the political training grounds, where black people learned how to participate in political debate, how to organize, and how to speak in public.[29] My findings coincide with these studies, but with a nuance: black people already had political acumen from their antebellum organizations and used the churches and conventions as exemplars of their skill. The early establishment of some of these associations before and immediately after the Civil War testifies to that fact. To be sure, there were many enslaved—now freed—people who had not participated in formal organized religion and associations, but the size of that population relative to those who had antebellum experience in churches and associations is difficult to ascertain. There were independent black churches in both the North and the South, so one cannot simply presume that southerners lacked experience but northerners did not. Still, the growth in the number of independent black churches after emancipation increased the numbers of new church members and leaders that fit the description of individuals learning skills for the first time. These individuals became more prominent as time wore on, but in the immediate postemancipation period, leadership came from individuals with experience before the war. Focusing on what black people knew and demonstrated and assertively claimed about themselves is a much more fruitful and productive way to look at and understand the transition, their frustrations, and their choices.

Within these associations, members made the case for their inclusion in the American democratic polity. Corey Walker describes how black Freemasons "redeemed the black body" through their various rituals and vestments, thereby making the case for their political fitness.[30] Along these same lines, in Baptist meetings members told their histories in order to place themselves on the American landscape and make themselves part of the narrative of religious freedom.[31] In this way, they linked freedpeople's pursuit of independent worship to colonial-era foundations. By placing themselves in Baptist and American history, they were able to make claims for political rights and ground their desire to lead the efforts to aid freedpeople. They knew they were capable; their associations in history and practice showed it.

One of the ways in which black Baptists articulated their claims to First Amendment freedoms was by historicizing themselves. They traced their lineage back to Roger Williams's revolutionary colony established for religious freedom. This practice reflected what Laurie Maffly-Kipp suggests was a widespread practice of bringing race, nation, and religion together in black histories and in black people's lived politics.[32] These largely northern-influenced black Baptists did not trace their lineage to slavery, though some, like Fields Cook, certainly had these origins. Rather, they reached back to a common Baptist past. For instance, the CSBA sent greetings to the 1871 CABMC meeting, writing: "Dear and much beloved brethren in Christ Jesus, we hail with inexpressible joy, another annual opportunity of meeting you with letter and delegate in the great work of evangelization and fostering education among our once downtrodden and bound people, and to enhance liberty, justice, righteousness, and equity. Yea, that *soul* liberty, that Roger Williams thunderingly proclaimed in Massachusetts, when the American Baptists were seeking a foothold upon American soil." The letter, which outlined how black people had been rejected by Southern Baptists of Virginia and their resolve to focus on black development, was recommended to be published in the newspaper on the CABMC's behalf.[33] In connecting their multifaceted works to the "*soul liberty*" that Williams advocated, they defined all their endeavors as pursuing religious and spiritual freedom.

Moreover, they saw the moment of their organization as critical to their own religious freedom. This was freedom of religion in its truest sense: black Baptists wanted to be able to worship freely as they saw fit, without intervention or interference by any other forces or individuals, and outside of white supremacist control. Organizing in these conventions also meant that the broader pursuit of justice, righteousness, and equity could be manifest in many different arenas, including the churches. This approach to narrating themselves had a few significant effects.[34]

First, claiming a colonial religious heritage allowed black Baptists to perform some of the racially transcendent work that religion and religious affiliation allowed, even as white Virginians pushed black people out of fellowship and black people sought to carve out independent space for themselves. In the uncertain space of Reconstruction, black Baptists were able to make sense of themselves through Baptist history. In addition to seeing themselves as part of the Baptist history, this framing included a sense of themselves as being equal to white people. Although Virginia's Episcopalians and Southern Baptists had clearly not arrived at a point of ecclesiastical equality with black people, the Baptist General Association having rejected delegates from the CSBA in 1871, black people were not moved from their belief in their own equality and their biblical and natural justification of their position. Black Baptists carried on building their own organizations and networks despite being snubbed by white Southern Baptists. They found more connections and resources from their collaborations with the northern American Baptist Home Mission Society. For the black Episcopalians, though white church leaders sought to aid the freedpeople, there was not yet a broad acceptance of freedpeople as equals. Nevertheless, black Episcopalians seized on the church's claims to catholicity or universality and used that to advocate for the dismantling of racist paternalism within the denomination.[35] Their ecclesiology—their identities as Baptists and Episcopalians—drew inclusive circles where their white fellow believers used race to exclude them. The overlapping theology was one of the key ways freedpeople merged their religious faith and the political project of defining and securing freedom. In the conventions and associations, they communally interpreted their experience from the perspective of the faith. It is no wonder, then, that they also situated themselves in the denominational history, another way they came to understand and then demonstrate their political skill.

Second, the broad narrative of religious freedom resonated with many freedpeople who also valued the opportunity to worship freely. Moreover, many fugitive slaves and freedpeople decried the spiritual and religious inconsistency of white slaveholders. Others, like Fields Cook, who would become a minister in Richmond and a delegate to the Republican state convention, found the way that slavery essentially separated enslaved people from God to be more than sinful; he saw it as a political abomination. Laying claim to a religious heritage of resistance to oppression, then, was much more significant.

In addition to linking themselves to a historic past that contextualized their current political trajectory, these black Baptists drew on denominational resources about governance and structure. In fact, the best examples of black political skill were the conventions' governance by constitution and the rules of order established in the *Baptist Church Directory*, to which they often referred as they were establishing their associations.[36] By appealing to the *Directory* to help them establish their organizational structure and to resolve conflicts, they demonstrated their knowledge of Baptist polity—something that came up repeatedly in their meetings as they discussed their concerns about how much Sunday schools and sermons could help believers understand Baptist distinctives. Moreover, the associations demonstrated their desire for order and their willingness to implement the strategies and processes adhered to in the denomination. The constitutions, presidents, elections, and committees all bespoke black political acumen and skills that would easily translate into the political arena. The constitutions established the purpose of the meetings and the general structure of leadership, while the rules determined how they would conduct their meetings. The conventions had nominating committees that proposed candidates for each executive board position, which the delegates would then vote on. The president then appointed all committee members. These organized structures of executive boards and committees mimicked the structure of the United States government. The Baptists were not the only denomination to mimic democratic structures. The Zion Union Apostolic Church convention was led by a president who was elected every four years, a configuration with overt reference to the United States quadrennial national presidential election. These black churches saw particular communicative value in the structure of their organizations, and the parallels between these structures and the federal government's, viewed in the particular postemancipation context under examination here, are uncanny.

Though well intentioned, these structures did not always serve democratic ends, one of the espoused primary values of the members. For example, the CABMC had a president who presided over the convention and a bicameral structure of delegates. The convention was divided into districts, for which the president appointed secretaries who then selected representatives.[37] The challenges with this structure were manifold, but the most obvious was the undemocratic manner of appointing district leadership and leaders within districts. There was no way for the governed to have any say in their leadership, which must have been particularly bothersome at the national level. The regional and state associations had similar processes for appointments, but the group of eligible officeholders were closer to the people and thus more representative. CABMC leadership became increasingly undemocratic over the organization's existence, contributing to its demise. Leaders who were once identified by a nominating committee came to be appointed by the president; voting once conducted by secret ballot was viva voce by the mid-1870s. Fields Cook recommended that the VBSC switch from ballot to viva voce voting on preachers to deliver sermons because balloting took too long. This rationale was also expressed later in the postemancipation period, when Richmond's black people actually favored keeping illiterate black men from voting. Cook's proposal was accepted, and by 1879, executive board elections were also conducted viva voce. Ironically, where black people sought to make voting more expeditious by using viva voce voting procedures, Funders during the early postemancipation period tried to use viva voce voting to demobilize the masses of voters.[38]

These early associations also presented themselves as de facto arguments for political participation through the models of governance and organization they presented. The agenda that the conventions set for black Baptists hewed to racial progress and stability but also to proving black political capacity.[39] One of the most immediate ways in which CABMC members tried to demonstrate their acumen was through performing mission work among the freedpeople. By demonstrating their specific qualifications for the task, they sought both to prove their own political mettle and to take a stand as the people most qualified to missionize among the freedpeople in the South.

In this regard, CABMC members were very much like members of nearly every other religious denomination that attempted to perform some sort of humanitarian work among the freedpeople.[40] Like the other denominational leaders, black Baptists felt that they had a special ability to do the mission work, but they were distinct in that they were black people themselves. Because of the competitive nature of mission work, they appealed to benefactors by professing and demonstrating what was distinctive about them as compared to other missionaries and what would ensure their success. In the annual report of the CABMC executive board in 1869, three years after the organization's founding, board members wrote, "From the fact that there are about twenty other missionary and educational societies, representing all denominations, and laboring ostensibly for our education and evangelization, it is no easy matter to raise money outside of ourselves for the support of our missionary enterprises, unless we can show our claims upon the charity of the public to be stronger than the claims of those societies professing to work for us and to do for us what we feel we can better do for ourselves."[41] The CABMC rejected the notion that black people had to wait for aid. In this regard, missionary work was about more than spreading the gospel or aiding the downtrodden. It was the means of validating black contributions to their own uplift and of placing them on equal footing with the benevolent white organizations.

Black Baptists further asserted the significance of their involvement in mission work when the executive board responded to the accusation that they were unable to govern themselves. "But our very organization is our proclamation to the world that we are able to do this work, and that we *ought* to do it. Now, we say, we are watched; and the demand is that we shall *prove* ourselves, and place our capacity beyond question."[42] The major impetus for the formation of these organizations was multidimensional.[43] On the one hand, they united in order to establish a unified network for black Baptists and to live out their view of religious freedom, but they also united as a means to demonstrate their suitability for self-government. It was out of this desire, perhaps, that these conventions took on recognizably democratic forms.[44]

As the black conventions defined community through their structures, they also defined men's and women's roles, a definition that would become central to black political participation during the latter part of the nineteenth century.[45] In the conventions, the men carved out leadership spaces for themselves as ministers and missionaries, and women's place was defined in relation to those roles. Perhaps the most significant aspect of these efforts was that the convention leaders defined ministerial leadership as male, and dependent women reinforced that view.

These religious conventions were largely theaters for the construction of black male identity. Women held no significant leadership roles in either the ZUA or the Baptist conventions for at least the first five years and, in most cases, for closer to ten years. Women were generally excluded from leadership on committees except when the committee work involved performance of traditional women's roles, such as cooking or providing accommodations. When women began to be incorporated into leadership, they were usually members of the Sabbath school or education committees. On rare occasions, women were included in committees that determined the time and place of meetings—presumably because they would be the ones to make arrangements for attendees' food and accommodations. They were most definitely excluded from committees involving missionary fieldwork and from being actual missionaries. VBSC members defined missionary work and political participation as the exclusive purview of men in the convention's constitution. The constitution asserted that "missionaries shall be men" and described the improvement in the black condition as being the transition from having to ask "am I not a man" to being free to do the work of building their churches, recognizing their own leaders, and participating in the selection of government officials and representatives.[46] While it is clear that many associations did not appoint women as missionaries, a role that was generally reserved for men, this pattern of excluding women from missionary work became more evident in Christian communities at the beginning of the twentieth century.[47]

Interestingly, though missionary positions were entirely the purview of men within the VBSC and the CABMC, they often could not complete their work without the aid and support of women.[48] Ironically, the missionaries in the Baptist Church were the ones appointed to collect funds, but the women were much more successful in raising money. In fact, in 1869, the Baptist convention first acknowledged a woman for her sacrificial gift of a gold coin, which the convention read as a mark of her faith in God, rather than mammon.[49] From that time on, there was usually at least one woman's donation to the convention acknowledged during the conference proceedings. Moreover, women became members of the convention through their roles as delegates of the religious benevolent societies that focused on charitable aid. Women were the key financial supporters in the conventions. The convention continued this process of acknowledging women's sacrificial giving by noting the near-annual $3 gift of Harriet Wells, the wife of Rev. Richard Wells, to the convention.[50] Women helped to financially sustain the conventions with their individual donations and through their work in benevolent societies.[51] Over the first three years of the VBSC, there were nearly equal numbers of male and female annual members. As the number of religious benevolent societies climbed—from two to eight between 1868 and 1870—about half of the organizations had women as presidents.[52] The near equal representation of women among the annual members and in the benevolent societies makes the recognition of Mrs. Wells's gifts all the more remarkable.

Although women's centrality as financial supporters of churches and conventions has long been acknowledged,[53] this moment illuminates why. In a cash-strapped community, male leadership positively viewed women who donated of their meager wages, thus earning women a place at the table; in the following year, women began to appear as representatives of benevolent societies.[54] The underlying economic fragility of the conventions provided a means for women to enter leadership positions within the church because they could demonstrate superior faith. It also turned out that they were able to raise money because they actually tried; in contrast, some of the missionaries, like Elder E. G. Corprew, went on missionary trips but did not collect any money to support those missions. Rather, Elder Corprew only encouraged the churches to set up missionary societies of their own.[55] Women took leadership roles in benevolent societies to begin marshaling resources and to improve the economic footing of the community.[56] Even though missionary work was initially defined as a male task involving church establishment and fundraising, it was relatively quickly shorn of its pastoral component, and women stepped into the breach.

Transformations in missionary responsibilities enabled women to be seen in terms of their financial organizing capabilities in the community and in their households, an idea that would continue to develop throughout the nineteenth century.[57] Thus, it is no wonder that women were lauded for their economic abilities. As the convention records document, women were no strangers to money management and fundraising; they knew how to do much with little. As the centers of the family and the ones who had to work in the field and then come home and stretch the rations in order to feed the family, they had a lot of knowledge of how to make do—and how to *make* do. In other words, they had learned how to stretch the little money they had to accomplish their goals. Thus, they understood sacrificial giving for the greater good. In the churches, women began to play this role as well. While it is clear that enslaved women and men contributed to purchasing church property during the antebellum period, I cannot say what percentage of the money women contributed or what specific roles they played in fundraising at that time. It is even difficult to depict what sacrificial giving enslaved women may have done, though it is likely that they played a similar role during slavery. For the purposes of this study, however, the transformation to wage labor was significant in how black women's roles evolved. Rather than attributing women's leadership in churches and the broader community to their sacrificial giving, Glenda Gilmore offers a different take on the transformation in black women's community leadership. She argues that black women became the social workers of the community in the late nineteenth century, as black men were pushed out of public political participation.[58]

Looking at the places black women exerted leadership roles earlier in the postemancipation period suggests that women's roles as leaders began in the churches and community rather than as a response to political transformations later in the nineteenth century.

Even though women were foundational to church and convention financial development, the conventions also used women's financial vulnerability as a means to define manhood and manly responsibility. In response to the biblical injunction to take care of widows and orphans, many conventions and associations established funds to take care of the wives and children of deceased ministers.[59] They reasoned that such funds would recognize and honor ministers' contributions to the conventions and community.[60] In this particular instance, recognition of the financial vulnerability of women and children reinforced ideas of male leadership and responsibility rather than highlighting women's resilience.

Religion in the Political Sphere

Just as the male gendering of ministry evolved during the immediate postemancipation period, the relationship between the ministry and political leadership was also being defined. The work of the conventions in restructuring the communities from within carried over to the work that its members did outside, in the world of Reconstruction politics. Some of the members of churches and conventions held overlapping positions in churches, conventions, and politics. Sometimes these were elected positions; sometimes they were activists or community appointed delegates. As Fields Cook's life shows, these roles could be blended, and it was not simply a matter of position; it was also about the content of ideas and context. His life also shows that the overlapping roles did not last forever, as he played an important role in the immediate political scene but did not serve in the constitutional convention. Still, Cook's narrative moves the discussion of the political involvement of black ministers beyond simply observing overlapping roles and hypothesizing about the historical or sociological roots of the ministerial role.[61] His life also shows that the political significance of individual leaders shifted over time as they adapted their views to the changing political landscape. Cook began as a radical leader but grew increasingly more willing to collaborate with white people in the political arena. In this way, the changing role of ministers is illuminated as much as the source of their influence initially coming from the people. Cook's ease with moving from the rostrum in a commemorative event to the lectern in a convention—the boundaries of the church convention and the Oval Office of the White House—illustrates the fluid movement between religious political critique and activism.

While descriptions of the relationship between black religion and politics during the postemancipation period suggest that ministers also tended to hold leadership roles in politics, a closer examination of politicians' profiles shows that the overlap between politics and religion went beyond the pulpit. Notably, of the eighty-five black and mulatto men who held office in Virginia between 1865 and 1890, fourteen were members of or affiliated with the Baptist conventions under study here—the CABMC, VBSC, CSBA, BCBA, BBA, NUBA—the ZUA Church, Gilfield Baptist Church, or the Virginia diocese of the Episcopal Church.[62] Half (seven out of fourteen) of the religiously affiliated politicians were ministers: Henry Williams Jr. (the most prominent among them), Fields Cook of Richmond, Cephas L. Davis of Mecklenburg County, Guy Powell of Brunswick County, Nelson Vandervall of Richmond, Burwell Toler of Hanover County, and John M. Dawson of Williamsburg. Narrowing the selection to just Southside counties limits the number to five politicians of thirty-three from Richmond, Petersburg, Brunswick, Greensville, and Mecklenburg counties. Of these, two were the primary pastors of congregations: Williams and Powell. The other three—Cook, Davis, and Vandervall—had other occupations in addition to the ministry. Cook, though a leader in the community and in the First African Baptist Church of Richmond, was a barber; Davis was a teacher; and Vandervall was a plasterer and storekeeper.[63] In Petersburg, politicians were more likely to have taken on religious leadership positions (i.e., attended church conventions) but not be ministers than in Richmond, where Vandervall and Cook were both ministers. Fourteen black Virginia politicians were from Petersburg, and slightly more than half (nine) of them were religiously affiliated, but only one was a minister. By contrast, Richmond had the second highest number of black politicians (twelve), and only two of them were affiliated with the religious groups studied here (both were ministers).[64] This brief sketch demonstrates that in addition to political leadership deriving from church members generally, and not just leaders, this dynamic may have been more prevalent in some areas (Petersburg) than in others (Richmond). This difference in patterns might indicate that attention to leadership roles was more pronounced in Richmond than in Petersburg, where black religious life and networks suffused the political landscape without necessarily calling attention to itself.

Some black leaders carried the influence of religious ideology into their roles as representatives as much as they carried their spiritual mantles into political office. The experience of Fields Cook, who occupied a kind of middle ground in church and political leadership as a minister without a church, who was active in the Republican Party but did not hold public office, provides a window into how religious community and affiliation in the postemancipation period affected interracial relations and political engagement. While black men were reconstructing their religious worlds and establishing themselves as leaders within the black religious community, they were also playing a role in shaping the politics of Virginia.

The spiritual alienation Fields Cook experienced during slavery seemed to animate his political activism after emancipation. Cook, who so trenchantly expressed how slavery inhibited the spiritual freedom of the enslaved, offered a robust account of how his own conversion was hindered by ignorance and how his spiritual calling and even his ambitions were diverted. Cook carried into his postemancipation political and religious leadership endeavors a strong critique of slavery, based on how it impinged on equal relations between black and white people and, more importantly, on how it derailed his religious life and expression.[65] In his autobiography, he criticized the institution of slavery that falsely created dichotomies between himself and his master's son, who was close in age to him and with whom he was raised like a friend. He described the relationship between black and white children as "all faired alike and grew on togather [*sic*] highfellow."[66] They played together and even challenged each other in their faith. But when they became adolescents, their relationship was sundered by the institution that made Cook call his playmate "Master," for "the white boy," whom Cook had regarded "as if he had been my brother," changed his demeanor and began "to feel some what a man," and "like the peafowl in the mist of a brude of chickens he began to raise his feathers and boast of the superiority which he had over me."[67] Cook described the transition this way: "If there be anything in the world that is hertful [*sic*] to one who reflects on such things it is this that after one has formed a real attachment to an individual that they should after wards appear to have forgotten all friendship and kindness and treat you with contempt."[68] Cook was deeply wounded by his friend's sudden rejection, and by how the institution of slavery interfered with natural human connections and relationships. Suffering the further entrenchment of racial discrimination when his young master was sent to school and Cook to work, Cook was not "pleased" but resigned, noting that he "had to comply with the old saying work little pig or die."[69] Despite Cook's personal disappointment in his friend's behavior, he held the institution of slavery and not his friend responsible for the breach.

The rupture that slavery caused in Cook's relationship was even more hurtful because of the religious experience he had shared with his playmate. Unlike the accounts of evangelical revivals that challenged racial divisions within religious communities, by the late antebellum period racial barriers were no longer being challenged but accommodated among evangelicals.[70] Cook recounts how he and his young white playmate encountered Christianity together but were forced down different paths. Cook found common ground with his white friend through his religious experience, and he came to understand the greatest sin of slavery: keeping him (and other enslaved people) bound by false teachings and from living out their true callings. He and his playmate had attended a revival and subsequently challenged each other regarding who would be saved first. They would pray to experience conversion. Cook believed that slavery caused him to fall under false teachings that delayed his spiritual rebirth. He had been taught that one had to see heaven and hell before being saved until his playmate told him what his grandmother would say, "Whosoever seek me early shall find me saeth the Lord."[71] This encouragement, along with the sincerity with which his playmate imparted this wisdom, deeply impressed Cook, causing him "to thing [*sic*] of it more than ounce [*sic*]" afterward.[72] As a result, Cook surmised that his young companion had achieved salvation before he had. This delayed salvation compounded Cook's frustration with the institution of slavery. It fed his critique of the institution and strengthened his analysis of the cause of the limitation in his ministerial career.

While religion was the tool by which Cook was returned to his schoolmate, it was also the context in which his oppression was reinscribed. The political system of slavery obstructed his ability to answer his religious calling. After emancipation, Cook—who did not pastor a church in Richmond—became heavily involved in the politics of Reconstruction, participating in black conventions, protests, Lincoln memorial efforts, and more. His work in the political sphere overlapped his engagement in the Baptist conventions of the state and placed him in local, state, national, religious, and political leadership milieus. Immediately following the war, Cook became enmeshed in efforts to establish black freedom. His early activism in the community reflected the communal eschatology of hope that emancipation brought about, even as the community grappled with the loss of Abraham Lincoln, whom they perceived to be a champion.[73]

Freedpeople's participation in common celebrations that extended from the antebellum period reflected how they marked time and later how they claimed political space through parades in the street.[74] When viewed through the prism of Fields Cook's life as a religious leader and person, these activities became part of the practices of worship and meaning-making that is at the heart of Christianity. They also reflect how the religious and political intersected in theology and in practice. On April 18, 1865, Cook presided over a freedom celebration at Richmond's Third Street Methodist Episcopal Church. While the initial purpose of the meeting was "to rejoice over their deliverance from bondage, and to give thanks to Almighty God for the triumph of freedom in our land," the mood turned somber when Mr. George L. Ruffin of Boston turned everyone's attention to the assassination of President Lincoln. Ruffin's speech led those at the meeting to express their "inexpressible horror and indignation" at Lincoln's assassination and their "feelings of sorrow and sadness."[75] After the resolutions were read, several attendees gave speeches, and then the meeting adjourned.

The newspaper account of the event suggests a dramatic shift in the tone and focus of the meeting, brought on by the northerner's address. What had begun as a joyous celebration was turned into a moment of mourning and sorrow. The focus on the freedpeople and their experience of liberation was displaced to focus on the death of Abraham Lincoln. Their moment of jubilation was hijacked, causing the celebration to differ significantly from the tenor of antebellum commemorations and the assertiveness black Richmonders exhibited when their desire to hold celebratory parades on the street was challenged. Opponents argued that the parades were a celebration of the demise of the Confederacy. On the contrary, black Richmonders explained, they wanted to celebrate the liberation of black people, not the defeat of the Confederacy; they wanted to celebrate black life, not white suffering.[76] Black creativity and purposes would not be long diverted, however, and future plans would reflect the needs and desires of the freedpeople.

Beyond local black people leading remembrances and celebrations of freedom, Cook became part of a national network of black people seeking to pay homage to Abraham Lincoln. Cook cooperated with the committee of the National Lincoln Monument Association, which was planning to build a "Colored People's National Monument to the memory of Abraham Lincoln."[77] Cook was a state director, along with other men from Bangor, Maine, to San Francisco, California. There were Methodist and Baptist ministers, abolitionists like Gerrit Smith and James McCune Smith, and black nationalists like Martin R. Delany among the leaders named as part of this association.[78] In effect, Cook found himself part of a national, multi-ideological group organized around a common cause. Like the state and national networks the Baptists formed, this organization drew black people together, another step toward a communal consciousness. The core purpose of the monument was to honor Lincoln, and they planned to do so with a school. They wrote that the Colored People's Monument in memory of Lincoln was to be "a SEAT OF LEARNING, dedicated to God, to Literature, and to the Arts and Sciences, and shall be held and appropriated for the education of the Children of Freemen and Freedmen, and their descendants forever, and to be called 'the National Lincoln Monumental Institute,' to be located in the District of Columbia."[79]

In addition to the church being a site of celebration and meaning-making, it was also a place where the people could identify their leaders and representatives to speak on their behalf. Cook was elected as one of five delegates from the Richmond churches and First Baptist Church, Manchester to address the governor and eventually President Andrew Johnson and the commissioner of the Freedmen's Bureau, General Oliver O. Howard, about the lack of freedom Richmond's freedpeople were experiencing.[80] The delegation of five men, introduced by Mr. Van Vleet, president of the Richmond Union League, presented their grievances of mistreatment by Union soldiers who harassed black people, demanding that they present passes, and of difficulties obtaining control of their churches from white trustees.[81] The delegation presented its very astute assessment that the failure of state laws to reflect the changes the abolition of slavery wrought kept black people from fully exercising their rights. They could not own property or testify in court in order to address their grievances, so they had to appeal to the federal government for protection and redress.[82] The delegation acted in an environment where nerves were still raw over the Confederate defeat and where Union allies had fought for the right of freedom but were ambivalent or even hostile to personal interactions with black people. Immediately following a black mass meeting in Petersburg, convened to discuss suffrage, one local newspaper refused to print any details about the proceedings, fearing that to do so "may produce evil."[83] Nonetheless, black people and their representatives persisted in pursuing political equality with an emphasis on suffrage.

Cook's role as appointed representative of the Richmond community continued into the fall of 1865. Just a couple of months after participating in the delegation to the president, Cook attended one of Virginia's black conventions in Alexandria, Virginia. He captured the sentiments of the attendees, and so they adopted his carefully worded appeal that affirmed the existence of white allies while pointing out that "we have among the white people of this state many who are our most inveterate enemies; who hate us as a class, and who feel no sympathy with or for us; who despise us simply because we are black, and more specifically because we have been made free by the power of the United States Government."[84] In such a context, the only sure political protection black people could hope for was the right to vote. Then they could vote for people who would support their interests. After some extended discussion, the address was "unanimously adopted by a rising vote."[85] Cook contributed much to the convention, and though he was twice offered an opportunity to address the convention directly, he declined both times due to logistical concerns: first it was too late, and then he did not consider himself to be a fitting replacement for General B. V. Butler, who was unable to address the convention in person as had been planned.[86] Despite his somewhat demure presence there, he was singled out by name in a terrorist threat sent to the convention: "Beware! Beware! Fields Cook, you and other negroes will die before the autumn leaves fall upon the unavenged graves of the many Southerners who are buried through our land," the missive began.[87] Recognized both in and outside the black conventions for his leadership, Cook presented an evenhanded and practical argument for black suffrage and participated actively in the organized political work of the community. His presence in these representative spaces pointed to the democratic principles and practices of church communities. They selected individuals to represent their ideas and concerns, and they collectively chose what documents would best argue their case. These democratic practices also carried over onto the landscape of electoral politics.

A leader in articulating black pro-suffrage arguments, Fields Cook held this role at a point when the Republican Party was on unsteady ground and when black political awareness was severely questioned in the media. By 1867, the state Republican Party had become more organized than it was immediately after emancipation. At that point, federally recognized governor Francis H. Pierpont essentially allowed former Confederates to regain control of the state legislature when he called a special session to amend the 1865 state constitution and remove Article III, which disenfranchised white former Confederates.[88] With the disenfranchising issue on the ballot in the October 1865 election, Virginians agreed to allow former Confederates to hold office. And those who were elected set about creating black codes and doing everything they could to circumscribe black power and possibilities.[89]

When Fields Cook was elected a delegate to the 1867 Republican state convention, he had to represent what he believed was best for black people in these uncertain circumstances. Just weeks before the April 17 convention, the First Reconstruction Act made Virginia Military District No. 1 and placed the state under military rule.[90] In this context, the Republican Party organized a state convention that managed to advance a pro–black freedom platform. Cook was among 160 black delegates to the convention. In total, there were 210 delegates from forty-nine counties.[91]

Cook and his fellow delegates supported the Republican platform that provided for "equal protection of all before the courts, . . . the right to hold office, . . . education at public expense, equitable taxation, new usury laws, and the recognition of all men as free and equal."[92] Though there were shades of disagreement over the full extent of measures to be enacted to secure black freedom and political equality, black people were unified in the pursuit of suffrage and equal treatment under the law. By contrast, their white allies were plagued by divisions over how to define black freedom, causing rifts in the party that made the prospect of interracial coalition difficult. A combination of black people and radical and moderate white people, the Republican Party was divided over the full scope of Reconstruction.

Though the Republicans had adopted a reasonable platform advancing black freedom at the April convention, a faction of conservative Republicans, led by John Minor Botts, desirous of stemming the tide of rights to black people, sought to hold another convention to revise the party platform. This conservative faction understood that to regain control of state affairs from military control, they needed only to meet the federal government's requirement of allowing black suffrage.[93] The conservative faction of the Republican Party mobilized and secured agreement of the national party leadership to hold another convention in August.

When the meeting was held, the radical white Republicans and black people packed the First African Baptist Church in Richmond, leaving the conservatives out of the discussion and out of the readoption of the platform presented in April. The convention also rejected the proposal that Botts address the convention.[94] And before John Minor Botts and Governor Pierpont—representatives of the conservative faction of the party—could participate on the second day, Dr. Thomas Bayne, the black delegate from Norfolk, "outgeneraled" them by motioning to close the meeting, the work of the convention—adopting the platform—having been completed.[95] Outnumbered and outmaneuvered, the conservative faction lost. The Republican platform was moved forward into the 1867 election, and delegates for the constitutional convention were elected. Whereas Cook's role as an elected delegate from the churches and black community illustrated the democratic nature of church-based leadership, with clear goals and lines of accountability, the world of electoral politics and policy making through coalitions and constitutions was more complicated.

Fields Cook, Thomas Bayne, and their fellow black delegates had an intimate view of the fissures within the Republican Party made evident by the actions of John Minor Botts and Governor Pierpont. Even within the ranks of their political allies, there was dissension and those who sought to limit black freedoms. With more than three-quarters of the delegates to the convention, these black people could have some confidence in their voting power within the Republican Party. When the delegates to the state constitutional convention were elected, however, the dynamics shifted, and Cook, a favorite among black people, was not elected to the convention.[96]

Still, black people formed a significant contingent in Virginia's 1867 election and the state constitutional convention that resulted. Among Virginia's counties, fifty-two had white majorities, and fifty had black majorities. Overall, the majority of registered voters were white (120,101 to 105,832 others).[97] In the election, more black people (93,145) than white people (76,084) voted in favor of having the constitutional convention, and 25 of the 105 delegates elected to the convention were black men.[98] Though a minority, black delegates formed part of a coalition of 72 radicals against 33 conservatives. With the numerical majority, the radical coalition was able to pass a new constitution that ended slavery and secured the vote for the freedmen.[99]

Once convened, the Virginia constitutional convention addressed the same issues that other state conventions did—black suffrage, civil rights and education, taxes and disenfranchisement. Black representatives advocated for the principles of equity and justice in all areas regardless of whether their comments addressed specific legislation. Eric Foner generalizes about these congressional Reconstruction constitutional conventions, noting that they were characterized by varied negotiations and alliances between native southern Unionists, northern migrants to the South, black people, and former Confederates. The conventions differed in how they determined the authority of a governor, whether imperial or keeping more power for the people.[100] Much of the discussion about the conventions continued in this vein. Attempts to get a finer picture of convention participants tend to limit views to race, origins (northern or southern), and a small but significant set of salient issues.[101] And yet the issues raised in the convention and on which black people weighed in were much broader and much more assertively argued than most general studies acknowledge. Such was the case with delegates Thomas Bayne and Willis A. Hodges, who raised concerns about black people being turned off the land by their employers as punishment for their support of the Union and voting for Republican delegates to the convention. Hodges, a minister from Norfolk, was known for his wire-rimmed glasses and for calling out his colleagues for their procedural mistakes in the convention.[102] Bayne and Hodges were concerned about the ways in which black people's independence and political freedoms were being impinged on, a recurring theme from the religious landscape. They demanded that the convention do something to address those immediate issues even as they worked to reframe the constitution.[103] Hodges also raised the strong critique of the Freedmen's Bureau and its exploitation of black labor.[104] In many ways, black people asserted themselves, their goals, and their views well beyond the set of issues that made their way into the constitution, and yet this thoughtful and adept black participation was denigrated.

Alongside the negotiations about political inclusion and access to resources lurked base racist perceptions against which black people contended. The significant representation that black people had with one-third of the conventions' delegates raised the ire of Virginia's white people precisely because, though a minority, black representatives held the balance of power in the convention, and debates leading up to that year's elections solidified black people's anti-coalition stance, opinions of certain salient black leaders like Fields Cook notwithstanding.[105] Consequently, black people had to deal with the racial backlash that led to the derogatory naming of the convention as the "Mongrel Convention," the "Convention of Kangaroos," and the "Black Crook" and the stunningly offensive description of eloquent and intelligent Thomas Bayne as "the ape-looking Negro Bayne."

Despite the racial animus black people faced, the Underwood Constitution—named for Judge John C. Underwood, who moderated the proceedings—provided for black suffrage by giving the right to vote to all men over twenty-one years of age who met residency requirements; instituted various tax changes, including a $1 poll tax; established free public schools and voting by ballot; granted equal civil and political rights to black people; and called for disenfranchisement of Confederate supporters, requiring an "iron-clad" loyalty oath be taken by all office holders and jurors.[106] This constitution achieved much of what black people desired.

THE WAY BLACK PEOPLE attained the suffrage they sought was very much influenced by the backdrop of racial tension with former Confederates and by the tumultuous, uneven, and uncertain relationship with white allies in the Republican Party. In such a setting, emphasizing political capacity by demonstrating it became necessary, and black people did so in their religious conventions and in the realm of party and constitutional politics. The state freedmen conventions and the church conventions reinforced the importance of the vote. While the participants demonstrated a good understanding of the need for suffrage in order for freedpeople to have some say in their governance, black voters experienced the strength of their numbers and of their swing vote status, two dynamics that would continue to shape black political participation over the next two decades. In this context, community cohesion and identity were important themes, but at this early stage of emancipation, these identities were newly forming and allowed for religion-based political critiques. As these black religious and political leaders stepped into the fullness of political participation and possibility after the ratification of the constitution, they continued to shape a conception of gender and women's roles that was internal to their organizations and faith. In chapter 3, the role and place of women moves to center stage.

CHAPTER THREE

Religion, Race, and Gender at the Congregational Level

In January 1870, Fanny Myers, an unwed pregnant woman and member of Harrison St. Baptist Church in Petersburg, Virginia, accused Montgomery Randolph, of the Gilfield Baptist Church, of fathering her unborn child—or, as the church described it, he was "her seducer." This was not an unusual case to be handled at Gilfield's biweekly business and discipline meeting, but it did mark a watershed in how the Gilfield church would handle issues of sexuality for its male and female members. As the congregants waited for the birth of Fanny's baby to determine the disposition of the claim and then initiated a discussion about the handling of cases of unwed pregnancy, they codified a model of minister-centered leadership that contrasted with the pre-emancipation traditions in southern black religion.[1]

The Myers–Randolph case occurred at a critical juncture in the history of free and freed black people in the South. Only four-and-a-half years after the end of the Civil War, four years after the ratification of the Thirteenth Amendment, and two years after the ratification of the Fourteenth Amendment, Petersburg's freedpeople were constructing and reconstructing their lives as a new community. Churches were one of the key sites for this development.[2] The churches became independent bodies under black leadership, and they helped forge community norms and ideas of gender and sexuality in even more intimate ways than the denominational conventions had. In this process, black southerners initiated a new phase of institutional church history, one oriented around the political black minister.

The story of the Gilfield Baptist Church reveals the results of using religion as a proxy for political participation in the early postemancipation period. This approach rests on the tautology that religious leadership leads to political leadership, which is rooted in the recognition of the centrality of the church in the postemancipation period and an analysis of the educational biographies of many leaders. Rather than accept this framing, this chapter charts the evolution of the relationship between a minister and a congregation.[3] In so doing, the establishment of the authority of the church pastor and ministerial leadership can be seen as the result of a process rather than as a fact. Additionally, the notion that black ministers were inherently radical or "organic intellectuals" engaged in community uplift should be tempered and the variety of political positions more carefully established by acknowledging ministers' diverse interests.[4] Few studies capture the contingent nature of black religious leadership. Moreover, privileging the role of ministers over that of congregations has dominated the literature, and the diverse factors that propelled black ministers into leadership—education, opportunity, spiritual authority, circumstance, and individual ability—exist within scholarship on black politics and black religion without systematic explanation or exploration.[5] Thus, there remains a sense of inevitability of ministerial political leadership.

In contrast, this chapter depicts how the transformation of pastoral leadership took place in church meetings as members and leaders grappled with church governance and social interactions. In particular, the way the church handled out-of-wedlock pregnancies revealed communal struggles both with defining family, marriage, and sexuality and, more importantly, with ministerial authority. Gender roles and norms were contexts in which the pastor's authority became established within the community. Male freedom and authority meant female constraint. The pursuit of religious freedom, righteousness, equity, and justice that often pointed toward independent churches and to self-determined leadership also carried with it gendered ideas and limitations.

Discipline Cases in the Church Community

The establishment of black ministerial authority in the Gilfield Baptist Church of Petersburg in the immediate postemancipation period from about 1868 to 1870 was a process. This depiction rests on the notion that antebellum black religious experience, which was incredibly diverse, had more fluidity and flexibility regarding leadership and decision-making than one might think. Interpretations that uncritically assert ministerial political leadership may draw too much on early twentieth-century narratives in which black ministers, as had been the tradition, held positions in the labor force that made them not just pastors but also brokers of economic and material opportunities. In an urban, industrialized context, wielding material resources was an understandable marker of political power. But it is important not to conflate this later development with what was happening during the late nineteenth century, when communal support was more indicative of a pastor's power than any political office or occupation he might have held.[6] A chronicling of the changes in the postemancipation period precludes the need for an extensive discussion of antebellum religion. The various kinds of issues the church meetings addressed and the changes in how decisions were made in the meetings capture the evolution.

The Gilfield leadership model represented a break from antebellum church practices, and this model came about *because of the intersection between religion and politics,* not just because of the social and economic standing of ministers. My analysis is largely based on the notion that the transition to freedom brought increased emphasis on the need for respectability within the religious sphere as well as in the public sphere.

The postemancipation black church—and Gilfield in particular—had elements of the open communal dynamics evinced in the antebellum period. This was reflected in the diverse religious experiences of enslaved people and of black leadership within organized denominations. Most significantly, within racially mixed congregations, there was a fair degree of negotiation and exchange, as reflected in land ownership, preaching, and leadership responsibilities.[7] In the context of freedom, Gilfield initially continued the tradition of community-based decision-making, while threads of gender and political conflict began to emerge.

In the landscape of freedom, most but not all freedpeople opted for independent black churches. Gilfield, an urban congregation, fit the mold of black churches that opted for independence after emancipation.[8] Despite the independent leadership, the church carried on practices of discipline that had been established during the antebellum period.[9] Now, however, they were no longer under the surveillance and scrutiny of white co-religionists. Instead, they decided on what issues to address. In this context, their emphasis on temperance, sexual purity, and model social behavior echoed the Victorian values of the day and the uplift ideology that rested on these ideals.[10] Gilfield operated on a very independent framework. Though the Freedmen's Bureau had an office in Petersburg, there was not much interference between the agent and the church, as was the case in Staunton and Surry County previously discussed.[11]

Church meetings were a staple component of antebellum and postbellum Christian religious life. In fact, the meetings of the Methodist Church have been credited with helping to form the class consciousness of the English working class.[12] In the United States, these small group meetings at once set the Methodists apart from broader southern society but also facilitated close bonds among members.[13] Baptists also held these meetings, as a means of establishing accountability among church members. Even the duty of reporting infractions devolved on church members, who earned reproach if they failed to live up to these standards and expectations.[14]

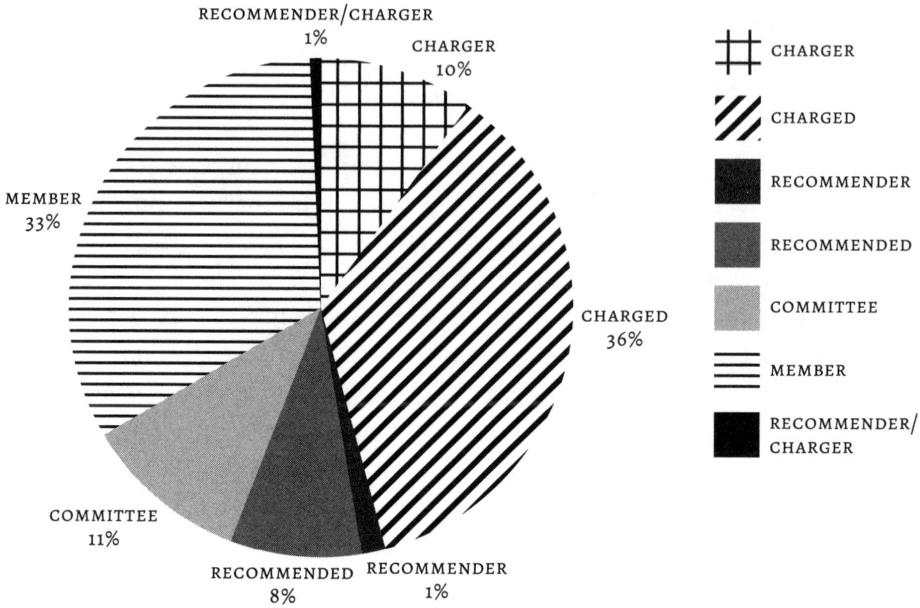

GRAPH 3.1 Roles of Gilfield members in church records. Of the 131 members whose names were found in the census, 43 (33 percent) were just members listed in Henry Williams Record Book; the remainder (88 or 67 percent) were involved in discipline cases in some capacity. Source: Gilfield Baptist Church Record Book, 1868–71.

At Gilfield, the church meetings were held biweekly and had a regular attendance of about thirty to fifty people—a respectable number when you consider that there were only about three hundred active members in good standing at any given time. These meetings had an even broader reach when one considers that hundreds of members were involved at one point or another by charging someone with an infraction, being charged, or being part of a committee. Between June 1868 and January 1870, there were 97 individuals charged with infractions. Sixty individuals brought charges against members. Eleven of these "chargers" had also been charged with an infraction, leaving 49 unique individual chargers. There were 38 unique individuals who served on committees. A total of 184 people were involved in the church meetings in some way over the eighteen-month period. A few hundred more people were involved in baptism and restoration proceedings.[15]

It is possible to get a tentative sketch of the church's membership from the list of members in Rev. Henry Williams's papers and the names of individuals included in the church's meeting minutes. Of the more than 1,000 people in these sources, I was able to locate 131 in the 1860, 1870, or 1880 U.S. Census, or the Petersburg or Dinwiddie County Registers of Free Negroes.[16] Of these 131, more than half were women, and more were born free or manumitted than not. A significant portion (43 individuals or 33 percent) were members from Rev. Williams's list and not involved in the proceedings in any way. Just under half could be identified as black, and about 20 percent were mulatto. The race of the remainder could not be identified. About half of these individuals were in the census, making information about literacy available. Forty percent could not read, and just over half (35 out of 68) could not write. What is most striking about this group is the wide diversity of jobs they held. There is barely a critical cluster of jobs, and they range from skilled to unskilled. Nevertheless, by 1870, the majority of black Petersburg residents were in the lowest-paying jobs, with few individuals occupying positions that paid well or garnered much social or political esteem.[17] The profile of the Gilfield Baptist Church represented here is largely free black, literate, and a mix of skilled and unskilled.

Within this diverse grouping of Gilfield Baptist Church members, community building continued as congregants began to work out new procedures of self-governance and for ensuring acceptable behavior—for example, determining whether women could hold meetings in their homes or whether members in good standing could partake in the increasingly more popular recreational activity of excursions.[18] While Reverend Williams was a strong figure in this process, members participated in dialogues about these standards in their biweekly church meetings.

Communal Decision-making in the Church

Church meetings were sites of great collaboration between members and leaders. Church members began to organize themselves both as a business and as a religious body. They made motions to rent a post office box and to have the doors of the church closed after the sermon or after the Lord's Supper was served until the benediction was given.[19] The goal was to preserve order and decorum in the worship service, and such proposals met with unanimous agreement.[20] These recommendations sound like the modernizing organizational tendencies that came to predominate in postemancipation churches, but perhaps more significantly, these matters were brought before the community for ratification.[21] The church meetings often incorporated issues pertaining to courts and legal matters, like securing property and handling mortgages.[22] This business brought freedpeople into the courts and cultivated a deeper knowledge of the judicial system.[23] Dylan

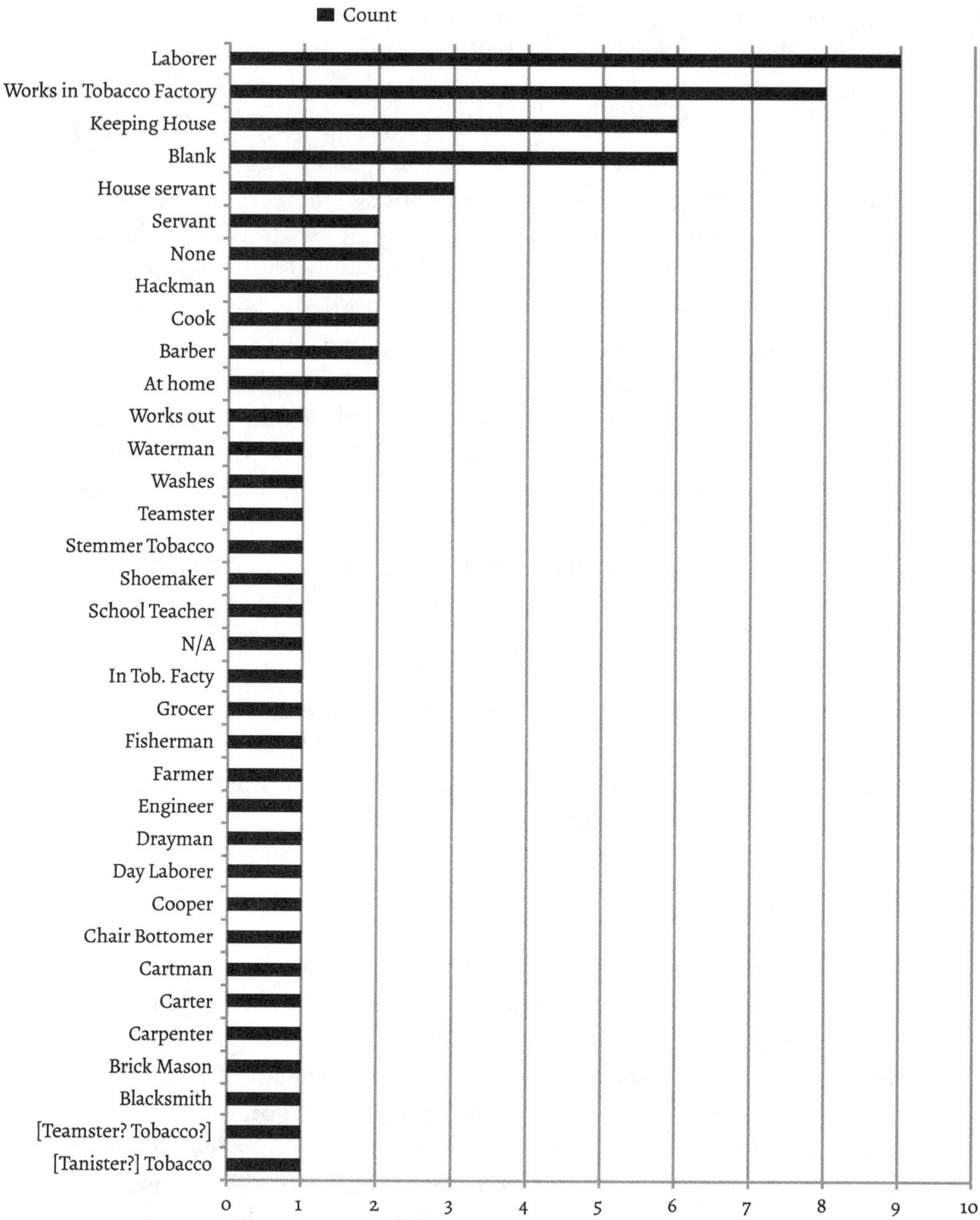

GRAPH 3.2 Occupations of select Gilfield members. Of the sixty-eight individuals whose occupations could be identified, about two-thirds were unskilled laborers, and many (twelve) worked in the tobacco factory. Sources: Gilfield Record Book, Henry Williams Record Book, and 1860, 1870, and 1880 U.S. Census.

Penningroth explains, "When black worshippers went to their local court and filed the paperwork to incorporate or appoint trustees, they took for themselves several important rights and protections, not just property rights, but also tax-exemption and the standing to sue and be sued as a collective rather than individually."[24] Church trustees and leaders represented the community in the courts and, in so doing, underscored how vulnerable freedpeople were in the legal system. Without the ability to testify in court, they could not secure justice if their rights were violated.[25] However, through churches and through "the vernacular histories of violence" recorded in women's testimonies to congressional investigation committees about the sexual violence they suffered, freedpeople laid claim to their citizenship.[26]

In addition to addressing the logistics of church management and worship procedures as communal negotiations, the churches also addressed the matters of community accountability, authority, and gender roles.[27] A couple of cases illustrate these trends, beginning with the case of Henry Woodley. In studying these early meetings, one gets the sense that some members were parsing the meaning of freedom and how they were supposed to exercise their own volition, balancing those expectations against church community values and expectations. Henry Woodley was one such individual. Members were asked to vote on whether to approve candidates for baptism and restoration. In 1868, Woodley opposed the baptism of George Davis. The church called on him to explain his vote, and Woodley stated that he simply "thought he had a right to Exrcise [*sic*] his vote as he please[d,] for or against."[28] The church determined that Woodley was too cavalier in his response and censured him for the "trifling maner [*sic*] of voting against a candidate for Baptism."[29] Perhaps there was a mismatch in Woodley's expectations of his voting and veto power within the confines of the church and what he believed participation in the democratic electoral politics of the state meant. Certainly in local, state, and national elections one's vote required no justification or rationale. It was a man's possession to do with as he saw fit.[30] In fact, as much as planters and other white southerners attempted to confuse freedmen about their rights and the franchise specifically, black people—with the aid of the Union League, the Republican Party, and each other—came to appreciate the value of the independent vote. And many of them exercised it.[31] But in this church community, there was a much broader frame of accountability and set of standards for participation in decision-making. This did not mean that one could not disagree or oppose restorations or baptismal candidates, because other members certainly did and were persuasive in their efforts, but one was still accountable to the community and its standards for decision-making. In this case, then, the emphasis on belonging and the community superseded the emphasis on the individual and individual freedom.[32] There was a clear mismatch between the prevailing attitudes about voting in the public sphere and voting on church membership and community discipline.

A second case—that of Henry E. Johnson—reveals the community grappling with expressing values around leadership and gender roles. Church members were concerned about who could be leaders in the congregation and in the church. At one church meeting, a member raised the question of whether members were approved to preach in and establish churches in the country. Questions raised in these meetings were rarely if ever theoretical considerations but rather responses to actual events and concerns of the membership. It turned out that Henry E. Johnson was the offending party, and he was called before the church to answer the charge. Johnson reported that he had been permitted by the church to exhort in the past and that what he was doing in the country churches was not preaching. Johnson could make such a distinction because ministers had to be ordained to preach by a presbytery established by the regional Baptist associations, which did ordain black men. The responsibility of "taking a text" and expounding on it or "preaching" was reserved for ordained ministers or preachers. Exhorters were also spirited speakers (doing something often indistinguishable from preaching because of the use of scripture), but the position did not come with the pastoral responsibility a minister or preacher might have. The coexistence of preachers and exhorters likely extended from the antebellum period, when a church, prevented from ordaining black preachers, would make them exhorters. This particular case also reveals how strenuous ordination proceedings could be and how urban churches usually chose educated ministers.[33]

Upon being confronted, Johnson apologized for calling and leading meetings and asked forgiveness. The church forgave him and instituted a rule that no one could go around preaching or leading public meetings without being licensed.[34] But "no one" apparently did not include women, because a separate discussion on whether women could hold public meetings in their homes was brought by George Taylor at the very next regular church meeting. The committee appointed to address the question found that women holding meetings was inappropriate according to 1 Corinthians 14 and 1 Timothy 2. Whereas by rule no one—read "no man"—could hold meetings, by scripture no woman could either. Rules were subject to interpretation and to change; the Bible was not.[35]

This ruling against women holding meetings in their homes struck a blow against women taking spiritual leadership roles in the community. This was so despite the burgeoning movement to carve out domestic space as the spiritual purview for women, which white southern missionary Joanna P. Moore's newsletter espoused.[36] In the postemancipation Gilfield Baptist Church, black women were not permitted to hold meetings. This may not have extended to the roles they might play for their families, but it did limit what they were permitted to do in the church community. Restricting women's roles in the church contrasted with other instances of broadened inclusions of black women in public political space. Black women teachers like Charlotte Forten and Frances Watkins Harper were welcomed into southern communities as leaders and role models for educational pursuits among freed children and adults.[37] Women were allowed to vote in the AME Church.[38] Despite broadening democratic participation of black women in education, church governance, and even politics (participating in voice votes, for example), formal church leadership from the pulpit was denied black Christian women.

Nevertheless, both cases show continued appeals to community approval, democratic decision-making, and community-based issue raising. Following Henry Johnson's case, he petitioned the church to be ordained, and his request was granted. On September 7, 1868, Johnson was accepted into the ordination track. Despite the concerns initially raised about Johnson's informal ministry, his ordination went off without a hitch. At the same time, attempts to restrict women's power in the church—a matter that came into clearer focus in the Myers–Randolph case—began to arise.

Leadership and Decision-making in the Church Community

The communal decision-making process began to break down as a leadership–laity hierarchy began to emerge. The tracks for change were laid in the immediate postemancipation period when Gilfield called Rev. Henry Williams to the pastorate, and he immediately turned his attention to organizing the Sunday school and later to church decision-making processes. Williams's story provides an opportunity to understand efforts to lead his congregation and shape the church's leadership paradigm.

Williams's first attempt at shaping the Gilfield community was made through the Sunday school. Under the cover of the immediate postemancipation fervor of religious and secular education through missionary and Sunday schools, Williams began his project of shaping the people to submit to the authority of the minister. The Sunday school was one of the first places that the relationship between laity and leadership was worked out.[39] This work of community transformation through adults could be achieved because at this time, the Sunday school served community members of all ages.[40]

Williams laid a firm foundation of order and discipline in this space in which the superintendent—the post that Williams held—was the head of the school, and all other adult leadership fell under him. William Henry Johnson, historian of the Gilfield Baptist Sabbath School, commented on the leadership model that Williams established:

"Many organizations fail because of the multiplicity of heads upon one shoulder. It has been the policy of this school to recognize one head and that head, be it long or circular, is the superintendent. It has been the policy to place the leadership in the care of one man; to give him an open field, a clear view, a loyal support from grandstand to door, and hold him responsible for the success or failure of the performance. With this as an outstanding policy the organization has been free from serious misunderstandings and disintegrating turmoils. The head has regarded the other members of the body as necessary to the correct functioning of the structure, and the members regard the head as the conducting power."[41] Johnson provides some important clues to the community's views of leadership. He depicted the church community as one that readily consented to the centralized leadership and "care of one man" and to support him even as they held him accountable for the broad responsibilities they had given him. Moreover, Johnson acknowledged the community's concern about preserving order and unity by noting how effective Williams's structure was at preventing disorder. The community had invested in centralized leadership for the sake of order, and while the adult leaders sometimes disagreed with Williams, they eventually fell in line.[42]

Reverend Williams might have ruled with an "iron hand," but he also had a good bit of compassion and concern for his members, and he instituted practices that acknowledged their particular circumstances and motivated their participation.[43] He tried to promote attendance by giving out beautifully designed cards, gold-plated reward pins, certificates, punch cards, and other trinkets to reward punctual attendance.[44] The Sunday school also held gift days, which Reverend Williams strategically held on Wednesdays to avoid conflicting with wash day on Monday, ironing day on Tuesday, the preaching service on Thursday, and the fact that "Friday presented the possibility of depleted purses."[45]

Through his punctilious leadership and considerate ways, Williams built a strong Sunday school and a very loyal cadre of leaders and supporters during his early years. William Henry Johnson claims, "Elder Williams came, saw, and conquered in the might of the conqueror."[46] In so doing, he built a devoted following that did not always agree with him. Johnson writes admiringly of Williams: "Elder Henry Williams was a mastermind. His unerring foresight has been demonstrated. Notwithstanding some [of] us hot-head fellows felt aggrieved at times, at what in our conception was severe treatment by him, we loved him. His discipline had for its purpose the establishing of sound, sturdy principles but we [could] not see it in our moments of passion. Nevertheless, there was not one of us boys with a conscience, who would not have fought for him as long as we could stand, in word, and in physical prowess, and woe be to the fellow on the outside who had anything other than a bouquet for him. He was urging us to build on the Rock, and he surely injected a bit of his kind of fire in us that may be witnessed today in a few of his boys, and of which they are proud."[47]

William Henry Johnson's remembrances of Williams's leadership testify to how central ministerial leadership had become by the early twentieth century. Johnson succeeded Williams as superintendent of Gilfield's Sabbath school upon Williams's death, so he may have had a vested interest in depicting Sabbath school leadership in a certain light.[48] It is more likely, however, that Williams established a model of assertive leadership to which the community subscribed. Another of Williams's contemporaries, Rev. William Henry Sherwood, feted the leadership of Rev. Charles B. W. Gordon in a biography of the young pastor of First African Baptist Church. In this narrative of Gordon's life and ministry, Sherwood argued that ministers needed to be disciplinarians. He wrote, "Probably there is no qualification of ministers more important among the African churches than this. Church government almost entirely depended upon the minister's disciplinary management. Where every member is allowed the same authority as any other, some one will try to carry that authority too far, and general disorder will naturally result. . . . If the moderator is lacking in knowledge [or] manhood, it is a drag."[49] Sherwood pointed to the calming roles strong centralized leadership played. Without it, members, enthralled with democratic spirit, would jockey for position, or "disintegrating turmoils" would ensue. Concern for maintaining order and community by decreasing conflict was evident. Having a strong central leadership figure helped achieve and sustain such order. Some people valued this. When memorializing Williams's leadership, Johnson and other members emphasized not only the solitary nature of Williams's authority but also the extent of support that church members gave him. In particular, the men had cottoned to Williams's leadership no matter what challenges may have been raised. "Us hot head fellows" became "his boys" over time, suggesting that the men at Gilfield Baptist Church attached particular salience and meaning to Williams's leadership.[50]

Williams came to Gilfield and immediately made an imprint on the Sunday school. Then he turned his attention to the day-to-day business of the church and, with the same steady and firm hand of discipline, shaped the community.

AS TIME WENT ON, it became clear that the exchange between leaders and laity became less interactive, and the power came to reside in the pulpit. This sharp distinction between the powers of the leadership and laity was more formally developed over the early years of Reverend Williams's pastorate and with specific reference to his relationship to his members. That Williams was and remained involved in church meetings marks him as part of a class of ministers whom Carter G. Woodson describes as conservative. Other ministers, like Rev. Anthony Binga Jr.—who became pastor of First Baptist Church of Manchester—were considered more progressive and stayed out of church meetings.[51]

One instance where this was evident was in the handling of excursions. Reverend Williams displayed his persuasive powers when he raised the issue of members going to military drills at the fairgrounds on Sabbath evenings and asked the church if it approved of this practice, to which the church replied no. So they required any member who participated in these activities to be "Delt [*sic*] with by the church."[52] These excursions and drills were quite popular, and some members questioned the church's authority to make such rules and were expelled for refusing to submit to them or censured for complaining.[53] Standing outside the consensus and questioning the authority of the pastor and deacons was not allowed. A similar note was struck when the ordaining presbytery determined that church members did not have the right to inquire into the particulars of the ordination process.[54] By quashing the inquiry, the council made a clear distinction between the powers of leadership and the laity.[55]

Once Reverend Williams established the precedent of orderliness through his structuring of the Sabbath school for both adults and children, he moved on to providing order and structure to the life of the congregation and taking a much more pronounced role in the leadership and hierarchy of the church. Even though the laity played an active role in posing questions and voting on rules and punishments within the church, there was a limit to that power, and Reverend Williams was it. When the church began to dig even more into the relationships between members, especially sexual relationships between men and women, the tensions between laity and leadership would reemerge, and the place of women within the community would be defined even more sharply.

Changes in Discipline Practices

Gilfield Baptist Church functioned as a moral guardian, and one of the key methods of this role was the periodic church meeting.[56] Gilfield's biweekly church meeting was the place where behaviors and community norms were articulated and members' expectations shaped. Though other church business (financial planning, collections, points of order, restorations, baptisms, and candidate nominations) could be part of the program, most of the time was spent on discipline. Of the ninety-eight cases handled between January 1861 and February 1862 (an average of seven cases per month), nearly three-fourths pertained to issues of marital or sexual relationships, suggesting that this was one of the major concerns of the church's constituency. During the antebellum period, the dominance of these cases indicated the increased role of the church in social discipline and surveillance.[57]

These meetings were also largely male-dominated spaces, where the meting out of justice and discipline tended to favor the male participants. Whereas Elsa Barkley Brown depicted the postemancipation church as a democratic space of political engagement, where all members of the community—women, children, and men—could participate in political decision-making, the case at Gilfield suggests that the democratic nature of black church spaces was more varied. Brown writes, "Central to African Americans' construction of a fully democratic notion of political discourse was the church as a foundation of the black public sphere."[58] What becomes evident by looking at the developments in Gilfield's decision-making practices is that women were clearly kept from participating in the democratic processes of church governance. Where the church members attempted to adopt more democratic processes, the pastor rejected those practices. Only males could bring charges against members (except in cases of unwed pregnancy) and serve on committees. And men were more likely to be excused from a charge or restored to the church fellowship once expelled. Expulsion or censure seemed to involve temporary separation from the community. Restoration occurred at the recommendation of a member and with an apology from the expelled person, who would then be accepted back into fellowship. There were thirty-one restoration cases between January 1861 and

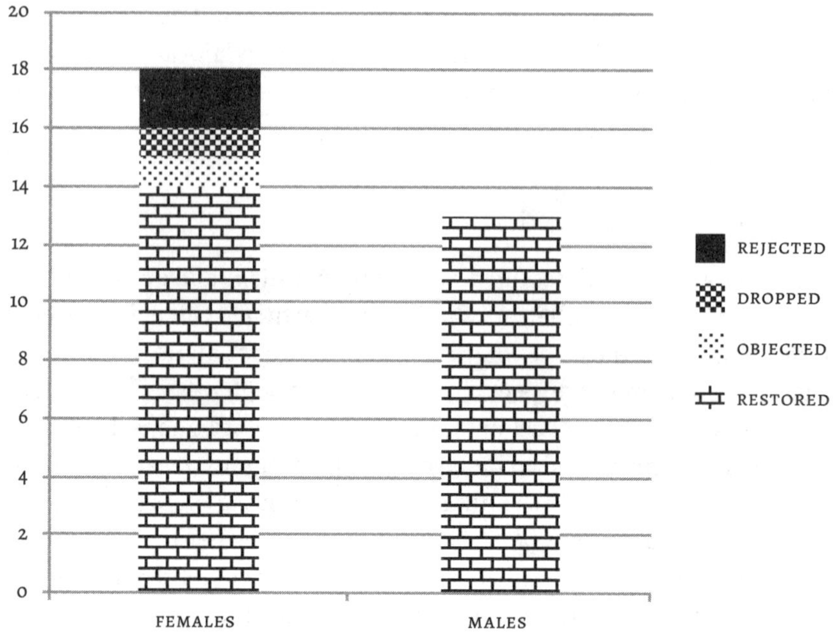

GRAPH 3.3 Gilfield restorations, 1861–1862. As this graphic makes clear, men had an easy walk toward restoration, but women did not. Source: Gilfield Baptist Church Record Book, 1868–1871.

February 1862, distributed more or less evenly between males and females, though all the men were restored, while two women were rejected and one woman's restoration was objected to. Of the nineteen women whose restorations were placed before the church, only three cases were listed in the church minutes, and thus the offenses for only these cases are known; all of them involved fighting. Similarly, a majority of the offenses of the men are not known, but the ones that were listed in the disciplinary minutes pertained to public offenses, like disorderly conduct, being publicly whipped, and making false charges.[59]

Men were also at times successful in challenging the charges brought against them. Brother George Taylor accused Frank Glenn of marrying another man's wife, and the majority of the members present at the meeting concurred with the finding of Glenn's guilt until one outlier, Brother James Z. Matthew, the church clerk, was asked why he disagreed with the majority. He replied that the church was not following a biblical path with this decision. When he gave a scriptural explanation for his position, the substance of which was not recorded in the minutes, the church was persuaded, and Glenn was acquitted of the charge.[60] It bears noting that without scriptural justification for an acquittal, the ravages of the institution of slavery made such cases of perceived adultery more prevalent and unintentional, but perhaps unavoidable.[61]

While challenges worked on some men's behalf, women sometimes took a different tack. At times they were contrite enough to bring themselves before the church, as Harriet Johnson did. Johnson submitted a letter to the deaconesses, who were sometimes (but not often) brought into the process of handling charges of unwed pregnancy. But instead of the deaconesses' involvement bringing any kind of moderation to the handling of such cases, their involvement inevitably led to expulsion. One could argue that the indiscretion of unwed pregnancy told on itself and secured the punishment for the woman, and thus the failure of women's involvement to temper or otherwise vary the outcome in these cases is no commentary on the women's participation. But if being pregnant out of wedlock carried its own natural consequence of discipline, then what was the point of involving deaconesses? It did allow women to have a more vocal role in these cases, but the moment was so short lived, it is hard to know whether in more time there would have been other results. The case of Fanny Myers and Montgomery Randolph suggests so. Deaconesses were as much invested in the respectability politics of policing black sexuality as anyone else. And the outcome for Harriet Johnson was no different. After her case was brought by the deaconesses to the general session, Johnson was expelled for "being in the family way without a husband."[62]

While the term "unwed pregnancy," when used to describe situations like Harriet Johnson's, captures the general issue being dealt with, the more commonly used terminology makes the concern of the community with marriage more explicit. They used terms like "being in the family way without a husband" and "having an illegitimate heir." The emphasis on marriage and property encoded in such terms reflects some of the disjuncture between experience and the values encoded within. Under slavery, marriage was a tenuous proposition, as any partner could be sold away at the whim of the master. Solemnizing unions through churches became a way to secure whatever measure of stability such recognition afforded.[63] After emancipation, many freedpeople sought governmental recognition of their unions or were forced into it in order to secure labor contracts or pension benefits from the federal government. Even still, having a child out of wedlock under slavery did not carry the shame that was heaped on it after emancipation because this status was not within enslaved women's or men's ability to control. Still, some enslaved women did try to secure a measure of chastity and control over their bodies.[64] Linking childbearing to marriage also had implications for property inheritance. Due to the existence of progeny of white men and enslaved women, keeping those children from making legitimate cliams to their father's property was a key concern.[65] Having an "illegitimate heir" penalized the woman for conferring a status on her child that did not allow the child to lay claim to property rights of the father.

For enslaved families, there was no such status as illegitimacy. Thus, the entire discourse suggests that this church was engaging in important conversations about marriage, family, sex, and property that reflected the new landscape of freedom and a redefinition of roles and terms. There are certainly insights about the construction of family life and values to be gleaned from a close analysis of the language of unwed pregnancy cases, but for the sake of clarity, focus on the relationship between these cases and leadership development in the churches directs the remainder of this chapter. Suffice it to say that these cases reveal how black-run communal organizations played an important and understudied role in shaping and informing black ideas about family and marriage both in the antebellum period and especially in the postemancipation period. But this concern with marriage status and, by extension, family, was not the only issue that the churches sought to regulate.[66]

Throughout the early years (1861–62), women were routinely charged with unwed pregnancy. But toward the end of the decade and well into the beginnings of freedom, some members began to question the propriety of charging only female members with the offense of being pregnant out of wedlock, and they began allowing women to name their "guilty partners."[67] In the summer of 1868, Gilfield handled two such cases of unwed pregnancy in which the pregnant woman was allowed to name her "guilty partner." These cases generally followed the same process: The woman was charged by some male, often a deacon, joined occasionally by the "Deaconist sisters," of "having an illegitimate child" or "being in the family way without a husband." Upon her admission of guilt, the woman was expelled and was allowed to name her partner, who, if present, would be called, charged, and then expelled. If not present, he would be ordered to attend the next meeting to face the church. If he failed to respond, he would be expelled on the strength of the woman's testimony.[68]

After the initial two cases of joint discipline, there were no more such cases for more than a year. During that time, eleven women were expelled for being pregnant out of wedlock.[69] But beginning in October and continuing throughout the fall of 1869, three couples were expelled for the social impropriety.[70] One notable aspect of these developments is that prior to these incidents, only men could make charges in the church meeting. During this period (which would be short lived), individual women also wielded the power of disciplinarians within the church. Previously only select women acting as a corporate body—the "Deaconist Sisters"—and represented by a male could partake in the process and only for this select group of cases.

Fanny Myers's case might have focused attention on this developing power dynamic. Fanny, you will recall, had charged Montgomery Randolph with fathering her unborn child at the January 1870 church meeting. Unlike most any other case, there were several men who testified that Fanny had also accused other men of being the father of her child, thus calling into question the reliability of her claim against Montgomery. Rather than immediately expelling Montgomery, the church decided to take a wait-and-see approach, believing that "time and its developments would prove his Inocense [*sic*]."[71] And wait they did, for five months.

In May, the church revived Montgomery Randolph's case, appointing a committee to investigate. All tensions came to a head at the June 20, 1870, meeting, where women seemed to be gaining more of a voice in the proceedings. Two of the cases debated that day help draw out the tensions between men and women.

The first case involved a mother who objected to the restoration of a man who had impregnated her daughter because both had been expelled for the same offense but her daughter had not been restored.[72] When the church members voted, a majority of those present sided with the mother in opposing the restoration of the male on the grounds of unequal treatment. This case was particularly notable because the male was the son of a deacon.[73] One year after the offense, the church attempted to continue holding the charge against the woman but not the man; the woman's mother called out the inequality. Women's voices in these meetings were gaining strength.

In the Myers-Randolph dispute, Fanny's claim against Montgomery was found baseless. Five months passed, and Fanny produced the child before the church. Based on the testimony of two experienced women, the church determined that the child was not Montgomery's. The church minutes do not explain the process by which these two women determined the paternity of the child. Some contemporaries even deprecated the influence of the "old church mothers" as being disruptive. In 1868, northern black minister Charles Satchell wrote, "In addition to the vices and irregularities inseparably attendant upon the state of slavery, there have been the 'church mothers,' 'gospel mothers,' and 'old shepherds,' officials [of the congregations] quite outside of the New Testament arrangement, but who nevertheless claim to be under the special influence of the Spirit, and exercise an authority, greater in many cases, than that of ministers. If a member can keep on the right side of these gospel mothers, he need *not* have *no* fear of church displeasure; but woe to that disciple who is so unfortunate as to be out of their favor. Then, again, there are bad men under the garb of preachers, who go around imposing on the ignorance of the people, baptizing them for a fee of five dollars, or performing some other spiritual service by which they can rob them."[74] These critics believed that as long as you were in good standing with the old church mothers, everything was all right, even if what you were doing was not scriptural or in keeping with the doctrines of the church. While members of Gilfield may have shared this critique, it is not evident in the disposition of this case, at least not at the start. In Gilfield, then, it appears that there might have been this kind of body of women endowed with decision-making authority. One can imagine that these two old mothers of the church looked at the child, looked at Montgomery, and determined that the baby did not look like Montgomery and thus that Montgomery had not fathered the child. The church voted to acquit Montgomery of the charge by a vote of thirty-nine to ten. Fanny showed herself to be an unreliable witness, in the view of the church community, and Montgomery escaped the fate of other (guilty) males who had been charged and expelled. More importantly, however, the church took the time to listen to and consider her claim.

This period of women's participation in disciplinary efforts was to be short lived, for at the same meeting Reverend Williams argued that trying to find the guilty male party was "unscriptural and injurious" to the church and proposed that they leave the discipline of the guilty male to their "all seeing God." He appointed a committee of five men to consider the proposal and report back.[75]

The committee Williams appointed went quickly to work, presenting its findings at the very next church meeting, at which Reverend Williams was not present. The committee described the process as one in which the deaconesses gathered evidence in the "female case" or accepted "the Females Individual Evidence against any male member of Guilt with the Female." Essentially, the committee highlighted what would seem to be the one real issue with the process when compared to the handling of other disciplinary issues—the issue of evidence. As the process stood, all that was required was testimony of the pregnant woman to identify her "guilty partner." In most any other case there could be other witnesses to the infraction, whether it be drunkenness, dancing, fighting, or gambling. But in this most delicate matter there were most likely only two witnesses and perhaps some speculators. The committee therefore decided that to remedy the inequity of justice and reliability, a pregnant woman could name her guilty partner, but she also needed to have witnesses to substantiate her claim.[76] No longer, however, would the church "act upon the individual charge or Testamony [*sic*] of one Female member to the Exclusion of any male member."[77]

But when Reverend Williams returned at the next meeting, the committee's decision was reversed—or, more appropriately, overturned. Williams said that they "went beyond what was intended by him in Bringing the matter before the church" and further stated "that the matter had better be [altered?]." They "reconsidered the matter and decided to leave the policy at Deaconist Sisters not being allowed to [even] ask the woman who was 'guilty' with her." So ended the practice of shared responsibility for unwed pregnancy. The door for women to be the moral and spiritual burden bearers of perceived sexual impropriety was reopened and reinforced. Male policing of female bodies through the deaconesses was restored. And, most importantly, by establishing an indemnity for men in illicit sexual relationships, the church stepped into the role of tolerating male sexual impropriety. This move countered the transformations in the broader landscape, where freedmen and women were being encouraged and nearly forced to marry in order to ensure that freedmen would become responsible for their dependent women and children.[78] Freedpeople placed a high priority on reuniting their families and solemnizing their marriages after emancipation.[79] In the courts, more rights were being established for freedpeople to marry and for them to secure control over their children in order to avoid their children being forced into apprenticeships. Additionally, freedpeople petitioned the courts to establish paternity for children in order for them to lay claim to their father's property. Admittedly, these cases were few, but the political landscape had shifted to reinforce the authority of freedpeople's family relationships so long as they conformed to the Victorian nuclear family model.[80] Thus, the church's reversal of its decision stands out all the more in contrasting with the political values around forming and reinforcing nuclear families among the freedpeople.

The whole process of discipline was very male dominated because, as I have noted, the only instances when women could exercise any say was in these few cases of unwed pregnancy, and now that was being severely curtailed. What remained in place was that any man could make a claim against another man or woman and have it considered by the church. Women remained in the position of the disciplined. Moreover, the church yielded to the instruction of the minister even though it differed from the community's sentiments. This was a marked contrast to how decisions had been made just ten years earlier.

The transition to a minister-centered leadership framework occurred through the various decisions the community made rather than in response to later political exclusions at the advent of Jim Crow.[81] Regarding issues of leadership credentialing and inter-member relations, the minister became the central figure despite the democratic underpinnings of these meetings. Rev. Henry Williams's adept handling of the Sunday school set this process in motion.

WHY DID REV. HENRY WILLIAMS become the central arbiter of community life though the church had played that role for so long?

One can only imagine the spectacle created by the prolonged case of Fanny and Montgomery—a sort of test case for an instance in which a man disputed the charge of being a guilty partner. In prior instances, the accused man conceded to the charge and was summarily expelled right along with the woman. But in the case of Fanny Myers, the church disbelieved her charges and so they waited for five months to see—literally—if the child was Montgomery's. One can imagine the amount of talk and speculation that occurred during those five months. Such a circumstance could have informed some of the practical reasons why Reverend Williams—quite the disciplinarian—arrived at his recommendation to leave the discipline of the male in God's hands. The situation merited an address, and Reverend Williams had to do something to stop the noise.

Baptist churches were noted for their democratic underpinnings and for being independent congregations for whom the preacher served at the people's will.[82] The congregation did not have to submit to the minister, so why did they? It's possible that the claim that the church's new procedure violated scripture was a compelling reason. In previous instances, scripture-based arguments had prevailed over the decisions of the church. Another possible explanation is that Reverend Williams's charismatic leadership persuaded the church to change their position. Reverend Williams was a ubiquitous figure in the black Baptist community of Virginia, holding posts on nearly every Baptist convention in southeastern Virginia.[83] Highly esteemed among the black and white communities of Virginia, he was a leading preacher often consulted on principles of the Baptist tradition and frequently sought out to sermonize and instruct on these topics. And while Reverend Williams's reputation would be hard won over a much longer period than just the first five years of his pastorate, he clearly laid a strong foundation in these early years for the accolades and praise that his members would heap on him thirty years later, at his death.

Elder leadership in the Baptist tradition establishes the elder as the pastor and preacher for the congregation, charged with teaching the congregation and leading by example. The relationship between the pastor and other leaders within the church and congregational decision-making authority has been more complicated. According to pastor and Southern Baptist Church historian Robert A. Wring, the practice of having a board of ruling elders—a body of church leadership between the pastor and congregation charged with legislative and decision-making authority for the congregation—was not a distinctive practice of Southern Baptists, and though he documents some discussions of a board of ruling elders among northern Baptist associations prior to 1845, there was no discussion of such leadership among the Southern Baptists after 1845, and the use of the ruling elder died out due to lack of clarity over the role and because there was no biblical basis for the role.[84] Though Wring focused exclusively on the Southern Baptist tradition of the late nineteenth and early twentieth centuries and tried to discredit the use of the board of ruling elders as unscriptural and potentially harmful to the church's unity, because allowing it to persist could lead to schisms within the Southern Baptist Convention, his study is informative of how the elder was viewed as a leader for the congregation and that although he was the leader, the congregation in a congregational model still bore some authority for making decisions that affected the body. In the case of Gilfield, however, the congregation's decision-making was deemed "unscriptural and injurious," and its decision was effectively overturned by the pastor. This case does not by itself suggest that the pastor's authority was always higher than that of the community, but that was what this case represented in that moment. The question is whether or not that pattern of leadership and decision-making continued in the church.

Though the members of Gilfield were not explicitly debating the role of the elder in their church, the developments around these cases of unwed pregnancy illuminate how they grappled with this matter implicitly. The fact that the members of Gilfield participated in this practice of debating and discussing how to handle questions of unwed pregnancy, developed a strategy for how to address them, and then had it overturned by their elder reflects how they were trying to establish the boundaries of decision-making and leadership. These developments were not unlike those in the early Christian church of the first and second centuries, when the role of the elder had to be developed and defined. And while it is not entirely clear exactly what the elders did or how it looked in practice, the role was clearly a new one in need of definition, but the authority of the role for leadership and the responsibility of the role for care of the followers was clear and biblically supported.[85] And it was in between these two characteristic responsibilities that Reverend Williams inserted himself into the postemancipation developments around family, marriage, and sexuality.

The work that Williams did to establish the Sunday school endeared him to the people in ways that they would express in their remembrances of him. The particular exigencies of the moment, the desire for order and education, placed Williams (and other ministers) in good stead to a people seeking validation. He provided the means for them to achieve the social and political acceptability they sought. They enjoyed his stringent leadership and the order he brought to his community. Of course some of what they wrote has to be considered with a bit of caution, because they were memorializing a leading figure in their community who had served their church and community for nearly forty years. But it wasn't just church members; white community members also held Williams in high esteem.[86] He was well regarded in many circles, including those of city merchants and other church leaders.[87] This stability and even fraternity that Williams helped establish seemed to be particularly appreciated by men who felt that Williams helped reinforce their manhood.[88]

It was just this desire for respectability that brought the religious and political worlds together and that led to the third reason why the community followed Williams's lead to the rejection of their own intuition. Since the churches and religious worlds were proxies for politics, religious spaces were de facto arguments for the strength of black political participation. In chapter 2, I discussed how church conventions were spaces where male religious identity was defined and submitted as evidence of freedpeople's fitness for political participation. Since the committee's decision seemed to honor the larger concerns of freedpeople with fair participation in legal proceedings, Williams's decision is all the more jarring. Freedpeople fought for the right to participate on juries and to be able to bring their claims before courts. With the recent passage of the Fourteenth Amendment, which secured due process and equal protection of the laws, ensuring that everyone would get what was coming to them in a fair and equitable way made sense. The larger political and social context is instructive. Reverend Williams asserted that how the cases were handled was "unscriptural and injurious" to the church, which he likely meant in a theological as well as a political sense.

First the theological sense. The discipline meetings involved the process of taking gospel steps to resolve an issue; there was no place for naming guilty partners or investigating such cases. Instead, gospel steps involved directly confronting the party with the offense, and if no resolution could be reached, taking two witnesses to establish the facts; if resolution remained elusive, the offender would be brought before the church and expelled.[89] Following a process outside this framework could have been considered "unscriptural."[90] Williams's admonition turned the community away from the democratic political principles of the world toward the Baptist biblical principles of community admonition and conflict resolution. He was also likely concerned about respectability and community unity. Such processes of naming guilty partners injured community relations and created tensions over restorations, as in the case referenced earlier.

Now to the political sense. While the religious concerns were dominant in this case, the political context suggests that the injuries could have been broader. At the same time that these cases were going on, men had been voting and participating in public governance since the 1867 election of constitutional convention delegates. In 1870, black men received the constitutional right to vote, the final codification of black political belonging. At the same time that the church was waiting to find out if Fanny's baby was Montgomery's, three church members—John K. Shore, Richard Kennard, and James Carter—ran for and were subsequently elected to the Petersburg City Council. Christopher B. Stevens, another member, was elected keeper of the powder keg.[91] The need for respectable men during an election season in which several male members were running for office may have been at least as influential as the biblical and ecclesiastical concerns. The issues they advocated for while in office shed light on the kind of organizing they had in mind. Kennard presented a motion to get a map of the city, and John Shore presented a motion to change the location of the voting precinct in his ward.[92] These early politicians tried to move the organizational aspect of their city forward. Moreover, the attempts to conform the church's judicial proceedings to that of the state echo the efforts of the church associations to emulate government structures and processes. The need for unified community and respectable church congregations colluded to make the concern for church order about more than just church order, even as Williams tried to pull his members back from interpolating worldly values into the Baptist realm. The "politics of respectability" in which black women engaged at the end of the nineteenth century is a helpful idea here. As women attempted to become respectable in the larger community by changing their behaviors (how they dressed, talked, took care of their homes), they also imposed such standards on one another in ways that eventually became limiting. The concern for respectability among black male church leaders with regard to the political realm influenced how they dealt with one another in the church.

Freedpeople did not fully accept the state's constructions of marriage and rights, though they used them to secure what they wanted. Freedpeople might not have agreed with the idea of household heads, the limited rights of wives, the separation of the public and private spheres instantiated by government laws about marriage, or the definitions of the terms for effecting a divorce, but they used these constructs for their own ends.[93] This way of relating to the overarching structure of marriage, family, and rights suggests that the dynamics around unwed pregnancy cases were determined by the values and interpretations that the Gilfield members set for themselves rather than some kind of capitulation to the state standards—at least at first. The church members make a gesture to adopting some of the legal terms set forward by the court system, but under Reverend Williams, this idea did not prevail. This suggests the need to look more carefully at the gendered dimensions of the conflicts within the church.

ON THE GROUND IN PETERSBURG, the evolving intersection of religion and politics is more clearly seen. Periodization of changes in black church leadership and explanations of why they occurred look different from the pews of the Gilfield Baptist Church. Some studies see black people's closing ranks in their churches as an end to a nineteenth-century phenomenon and a response to political disenfranchisement and violence. The developments at Gilfield suggest that the process may have begun earlier and lasted longer, so that changes at the close of the nineteenth century were the result of a longer struggle over the relationship between religion and politics in the black community.

With little coverage of Gilfield in the local, largely conservative white newspapers to provide a sense of how life was changing for black people in this congregation during this period, my interpretation of the pursuit of political respectability meshes with existing interpretations of the broader goals of Baptist and ecclesiastical orders. What this case suggests is that there is more to be gleaned about the intersection of religion and politics in the late nineteenth century. Yes, there were ministers who were political leaders, and those roles often overlapped, but church leadership was based on the specific exclusion of women from equal participation—the downside of politics and religion intersecting.[94] Behind the narrative of centralized black ministerial leadership is the backstory of the suppression of dissent and the marginalization of women.

CHAPTER FOUR

Theological Education, Race Relations, and Gender, 1875–1882

In 1878, members of the Zion Union Apostolic Church voted to unite with the Episcopal Church. At least, that is what white Episcopalian missionaries Rev. Robb White and Mrs. Martha "Pattie" Hicks Buford believed, and that was what they reported to the Annual Council of the Diocese of Virginia.[1] ZUA bishop and convention president James Howell had a different impression of what transpired, but since the minutes of the convention were lost, no record of the church's actual decision survived. When the dust settled, Howell was asked to step down from the presidency, and the ZUA Church reorganized itself as the Reformed Zion Union Apostolic (RZUA) Church. The RZUA Church had a set of policies and practices distinct from that of the ZUA. Around the same time, the Virginia diocese created the Branch Theological School to educate black ministers, especially those of the ZUA Church, so that they could be ordained to the Episcopalian diaconate and eventually the priesthood. James Solomon Russell, a ZUA Church minister, became the first student.

Did ZUA members vote to unite with the Episcopal Church? This is a matter of contested narratives, and the evidence is unclear. Reverend White and Mrs. Buford reported to the Annual Council that a merger between the two churches was imminent. Yet there is no formal record of a vote, or—if there was—how the ZUA members voted, and one cannot definitively deduce from the diocesan reports and subsequent developments what the ZUA Church members wanted.[2] In fact, those diocesan records leave quite a bit of room for interpretation. The extant report produced by representatives of the Diocesan Missionary Society (DMS), who had been appointed to investigate, indicated that the Zion Union ministers—when asked how close they wished to become to the Episcopal Church—responded rather inconclusively, "As close as we can get." This ambivalence in the archive—the sparse ZUA records, the lost minutes of the ZUA members' vote, undocumented oral histories, and the printed minutes of the Annual Council of the Diocese of Virginia—captures the dynamics of power and resources that animate this narrative of how black religious politics of the postemancipation period emerged as a discourse about race, education, and the cultivation of black manhood.

ZUA members did not control the archive of the discussion; the Episcopal Church did. The Episcopal Church apparatus was organized enough to create and retain records and to create and sustain a school in response to the ZUA proposition. While the records offer conflicting and even inconclusive documentation of the ZUA Church's decision, the establishment of the Branch Theological School (BTS, later the Bishop Payne Divinity School) by the Virginia diocese and the Protestant Episcopal Theological Seminary points to some sort of organizational resolution, even as it raises more questions about black religious politics. One of the first issues that arose from this discussion was what kind of relationship to the Episcopal Church the ZUA Church members—and black Christians more broadly—wanted. What was the place of theological education in the black community's goals? While the BTS was one of two seminaries and one theological department in Virginia that educated black ministers, the reach of theological education was much broader.[3] Its reliance on the emerging common school curriculum structure to prepare and produce students, as well as the dominant role that churches played in providing secondary and college educational opportunities for black men and women, extended the significance of seminary education beyond just the students who enrolled. The establishment of the BTS opens up questions about how theological education contributed to the development of a politicized black minister, and especially the gender dynamics of this creation.

Among the first BTS students were James Solomon Russell and George Freeman Bragg Jr., a member of the founding family of Petersburg's black St. Stephen's Episcopal Church. Russell went on to become an Episcopal minister and to open his own school. Bragg spent some years working in politics and then returned to his Episcopal Church roots to become a priest and historian of black Episcopalians. Together, these men's experiences point to broader narratives of education, leadership, and religion—demonstrating how black religious politics overlapped religious and political spaces and created a politicized black ministerial leadership. The establishment of the Episcopal seminary to educate black ministers marked an important moment in the development of black religious politics because it highlighted how black ministers brokered relationships with white church leaders and missionaries in order to facilitate black advancement in education, and how and why black men as ministers became the central figures in politics more broadly. Thus, in this moment, black religious politics shifted toward minister-centered leadership and a politicized black religious manhood, forged through education and negotiations with white church leaders. Because the school was dedicated solely to the instruction and cultivation of ministers, the limitation of opportunities for religious education to men only created a situation where black manhood and religious education became conjoined. The moment also illustrates how black religious politics in theological education was premised on the pursuit of religious freedom and how education complicated that goal. Black people sought more equity and justice for themselves and for black women, while also maintaining the integrity of their religious institutions and communities. These goals overlapped with white co-religionists' racially motivated goals in interesting and complicated ways. Developments in theological education mirrored the political landscape in terms of how black folks had to negotiate racial dynamics while pursuing the fullest expression of soul liberty.[4]

Politics of Education and the Trained Ministers Debate

Just how close was close? When the ZUA ministers responded to the question of how close they wished to get to the Episcopal Church, it was clear that they had some potentially connective institutional elements in mind—educational opportunities being one of them. But they also did not mean to lose their autonomy. This was reflected in their resolution: "That [while] holding firmly to our church organization as now constituted and with no present desire to change the same, we feel the deepest gratitude to the P. E. Church for the Christian love and charity which has been extended to us by the same in teaching and disciplining our people, aiding them to embrace a pure Christian faith, and to lead Godly and Christian lives."[5] Still, by introducing the prospect of unification, they invited this discussion in a moment when education was politicized. By 1878, when the ZUA ministers initiated this discussion, black people in Richmond, Petersburg, and Southside had begun demanding more black teachers and leaders in schools. Thus, having schools generally, and seminaries for training ministers specifically, involved marshaling educational resources and opportunity, something freedpeople had a legacy of doing.[6]

Increasing educational opportunity for black people and increasing employment opportunities in teaching and administrative positions had become critical issues because Democratic fiscal policies actually diverted funding away from public schools, which black legislators had fought to establish after emancipation. Social and cultural practices instantiated in hiring policies kept black teachers out of public school classrooms and black leaders off the school boards.[7] While racial policies limited black education and leadership opportunities, discussions between the ZUA Church and the Episcopal Diocese of Virginia began to open up religious educational opportunities and, along with them, leadership opportunities for black male preachers and female teachers.

When the ZUA Church requested a closer relationship with the Episcopal Church, it entered a national discourse about race, education, and opportunity. Underlying this discourse was the struggle for control of the lives and minds of freedpeople. Northern industrialists reinforced the power dynamics of education. Industrialists tried to circumscribe educational opportunities and the mental and intellectual horizon for freedpeople by offering them a curriculum designed to prepare them to be laborers in the southern workforce in roles that would not disturb the racial paradigms of the South.[8] Becoming welders or line workers wouldn't disrupt; becoming the faces of education could.

Between 1880 and 1915, the number of private secondary and missionary schools available to black people tripled. The American Baptist Home Mission Society (ABHMS) increased the number of schools it ran from eight in 1880 to thirteen in 1892 and nearly quadrupled the number of students it served, from about 1,191 to 5,167. Given the potential real power and symbolic danger attached to teaching such large numbers of people, it is perhaps unsurprising that education increasingly became figured as female. Because white missionaries came to see educating black men as a dangerous proposition, educating black women was perceived as less threatening. The changes at the American Baptist Theological Seminary bear this out to some extent. At the same time, black people increasingly chose to send their girls to school in order to protect them from field labor. This, too, contributed to the feminization of education. And, concurrently, black church preaching leadership became more definitively masculinized. During the same epoch of secondary and missionary school growth, the ABHMS also flipped the ratio of male to female students from about 2.5:1 to 1:1.3, serving 852 men and 339 women in 1880 and 2,219 men and 2,948 women in 1892. The shift in the number of women being educated reflected the increased number of women being trained to become teachers—about two-thirds of trainees were women. The remaining third, nearly all men, were studying for the ministry.[9] On the whole, higher education for black people and especially black ministers was limited. The Southern Baptist Convention had the American Baptist Theological Seminary, the American Baptists had Richmond Theological

Institute, and by 1879, the Episcopal Church had the Branch Theological School.[10]

THE VIRGINIA Diocesan Missionary Society's emphasis on developing a trained ministry overlapped with and even propelled debates and discussions about the need for trained ministers in black churches. As black churches became independent and northern black missionaries clashed with southern black church leaders, tensions about the structure and tenor of worship emerged.[11] These conflicts often hinged on practices like ecstatic worship and extended to discussions about what kind of ministry was best for the churches. The debate has usually been framed as a tension between free black people who preferred a trained ministry and freedpeople who favored an inspired ministry.[12] The developments around the Branch Theological School suggest that other factors also influenced the conversation. The debate was amplified by the emphasis that white missionaries placed on providing educational opportunities to develop a trained black ministry.

The debate about having educated church leadership was most pronounced in the African Methodist Episcopal Church, which had a history of being committed to a literate leadership and laity. Accordingly, it had a trenchant sense that it was particularly suited for mission work among the freedpeople, which compelled it to reestablish itself in the South, from which it had been ousted.[13] AME bishop Daniel A. Payne vociferously opposed practices like the ring shout and hymn lining, calling instead for ministers to be trained so that they could lead worshipful services in a refined style.[14] It was not just northerners like Payne, however, who called for educated, literate, or trained ministers for black churches. In the associations and conventions of the Baptist Church, the attempts to close ranks around recognized and ordained ministers reinforced the education debate. Some Baptist associations adopted rules requiring ministers to be able to read.[15] This was one of the ways that the debates about educated ministry emerged. And within the ZUA Church, the debate raged: the majority favored inspired worship, but notably, James Solomon Russell advocated for a trained ministry.

Russell, a representative of the ZUA-affiliated Penuel Church, differed from his peers on the major issue of having a trained ministry. At Zion Union's 1876 annual convention, he asserted his support for the church to have a trained ministry, proposing that only literate ministers be allowed to preach.[16] Russell was part of a faction within the denomination that favored a trained ministry, orderly development of the denomination, and alignment with the Episcopal Church.[17] Church historian James Oliver Allen attributed

Russell's position on literacy to his alliance with his patron, Episcopal missionary Mrs. Pattie Buford. Russell had already aligned himself with Buford over establishment of Sunday schools for the ZUA Church.[18] Russell's position on literacy was just an extension of his growing affinity for the Episcopal Church and his relationship with Buford.

The Virginia diocese's turn toward black ministerial training has important implications for understanding black people of postemancipation Virginia. Locating the origin of a focus on black ministerial education in these missionary efforts differs from the established narrative about religion and education. Debates within the African American community about inspired versus educated ministerial leadership often came out of concerns about how black people were perceived. However, efforts by the Episcopal and Baptist churches to promote an educated ministry illustrate how the politics of black religious institutions were shaped by internal struggles as much as they were external judgments about black uplift. The pursuit of an educated black ministerial elite also came from the desire of these various white-led denominations to develop leadership for the black communities that would allow black people to remain contained in their own churches. In the same ways that these missionaries sought to train a cadre of teachers to educate the masses of black people, they also sought to cultivate a group of ministers to carry on the work of the church.[19] In both instances, black leadership was the price white organizations had to pay in order to continue their containment of black Christians.

Intricacies of Race Relations

Though the ZUA Church did not initially call for increased educational opportunities for its ministers, more discipleship, Sunday school classes, and a trained ministry, initiating the conversation about changing their relationship to the Episcopal Church brought all of these issues into play. The discussion between the churches highlighted the debates about having a trained ministry in black churches and furthered the development of politicized black church ministers. Though the specific details of the discussion are occluded in the ZUA records, the big picture of the power dynamic between the independent denomination and the Episcopal Church is more accessible. The ZUA Church initiated a conversation from the standpoint of maintaining religious freedom while pursuing closer collaboration. While the benevolent paternalism of the Episcopal Church made the furtherance of the discussion untenable for the ZUA Church, Buford secured money and donations to run the school and provide nursing services that the freedpeople needed but were unable to secure for themselves because of the limitations in the emancipation process.

The politics of theological education echoed the dynamics of early schooling efforts because the Episcopal Church had the money and human resources to develop schools and other services that freedpeople needed. These dynamics were best captured in how Pattie Buford funneled resources to the freedpeople and helped foster relationships between the freedpeople and leaders of the diocese. The church also sought to reinforce black religious communities through education and leadership development but, in so doing, raised concerns about control and power both within the black churches and between black and white church folk.

Having access to the various resources offered by the white missionaries was an important motivation for the ZUA Church. But the church also understood that education opened up discourses of control. This was especially true in the case of trained ministers, which was a major source of anxiety and debate in the ZUA Church. The Virginia diocese's approach to unification focused attention on the development and control of leadership through formal training. The diocese suggested creating a school based on its belief that the Zion Unionists wanted to unite with the Episcopal Church. From what we can tell of the existing record, the ZUA Church initially accepted this offer because its members wanted closer ties to the Episcopal Church; unfortunately for them, however, education requirements for the ministers and loss of autonomy were not what they ultimately had in mind.

Because the ZUA Church had enjoyed the education and nursing ministries of White and Buford, it sought to strengthen the bonds between the two institutions.[20] White was assigned to St. Andrews Church in Lawrenceville, Brunswick County, Virginia, where he ministered to a small congregation that included few black people.[21] Buford built a school for teaching; led a team of twelve nurses; and coordinated donations of books, clothes, and money.[22] She practically ran a social service agency under the aegis of the Episcopal Diocese of Virginia, and the fledgling Zion Union Apostolic denomination angled to create an even closer bond with the Episcopal Church that she represented. Even Reverend White, who was the formally recognized missionary, credited Buford with being the actual force behind the efforts. White acknowledged as much at the 1879 Annual Council of the Diocese of Virginia when he reported, "Mrs. Buford is the only person in this great work. . . . Of course I am heartily in sympathy with her, and do all I can to help, but hers is the work and hers be the praise."[23] Buford's ministry was like Mary Miles's in Halifax County. Miles's ministry included a school that served between seventy-five and one hundred students. She used the liturgy of the church to teach literacy, and she used materials that students could then take with them to teach sewing.[24] In Miles's school and others like it, the teachers taught the women to sew and allowed them to keep and even sell the products of their lessons.[25] These kinds of classes provided education and material resources that students needed and that ZUA Church members may have desired.

THOUGH BUFORD AND WHITE reported at the 1878 Annual Council that the ZUA Church had decided to unite with the Episcopal Church, the ministerial delegates that met with the Diocesan Missionary Society's representatives—the Reverends Alexander Weddell and Grayson Dashiell—had a more ambiguous interpretation. After initiating the discussion, fifteen ZUA ministers and more than 1000 members met with Weddell and Dashiell on April 30, 1879, at the Chapel of the Good Shepherd in Lawrenceville, Brunswick County. The committee chairman met with the ministers and members inside the church while the other representatives preached to the rest of the members outside. After the service concluded, they held a meeting. When asked how close they wished to become, the ministers answered, "As close as we can get." The DMS representatives left the meeting understanding that "by an unanimous vote the organization puts itself into the care of the Protestant Episcopal Church, giving their assent to our doctrine, discipline and worship."[26] The delegates believed that the ZUA members were not motivated by ecclesiastical concerns, for they had not experienced any change in belief about the episcopacy, but had "been led to desire such a union for reasons which in our judgment are more to the glory of God and to the credit of our church." The delegates explained the reasons more precisely:

> In their poverty and friendlessness, along with their yearning for a better condition, these people have been helped by our church through one of its female communicants. . . . Through her they have gotten to some extent education for their children—care for their sick and their aged—religious books, such as Bibles, Prayer Books, and Catechisms, for their Sunday schools and commentaries for their ministers. They have learned something as to the theory of the church from books and papers, but they have formed their opinions rather from kindness that has been shown. They have said just about this—"We wish to go with you for we believe the Lord is with you."[27]

According to the DMS representatives, the Zion Unionists sought to unite with the Episcopal Church because they had received much assistance from the Episcopal Church through Mrs. Buford. Through her service, they came to believe in the presence of God among the Episcopalians.

The DMS, Buford, and White chose to interpret the ZUA's motives as emanating from admiration, but the coterminous debate in the ZUA Church suggests that not all ZUA members had such a feeling. Despite the report of a unanimous vote in the ZUA Church, the extant records reflect an explicit desire to remain independent.[28]

Though the ZUA Church initially proposed a closer relationship, the diocese took the lead on defining the terms of unification. At the 1879 Annual Council, Bishop Francis Whittle affirmed that the ZUA Church was to be absorbed by the Episcopal Church. He said, "In Brunswick county a devoted lady, by simply manifesting the spirit and following the example of the blessed Savior, has so gained the confidence of the colored people that, by means of her influence[,] an organized body, composed of a number of preachers and of several thousand members, has asked to be received into community with our church."[29] Concerned about preserving the church and its members, the diocese turned its attention to training ministers, which required a school to prepare them for ordination. Whatever the Zion Unionists envisioned, the Episcopal Church missionaries interpreted its leaders as requiring additional education.

The ZUA Church wanted to test the waters of comity but pulled back when the terms of unification revealed plans that did not promote equality but rather segregation and control. The initial invitation, however, triggered a series of choices that led to black ministers being politicized in the process of training for the ministry. The ZUA Church placed black self-determination at the forefront of its goals and turned away from the Episcopal Church, which overlooked the invitation to fellowship for a more simplistic and self-congratulatory assessment of spiritual righteousness. While the ZUA chose not to unite with the Episcopal Church beyond receiving the missionaries and their services, the Virginia diocese moved forward with planning a school that would affirm its own view, even if it could not fully control the results and subsequent actions of the students. Despite their racism, the context for interracial cooperation that theological training schools and seminaries established opened the way for future political mobilization for their students.

THE VIRGINIA DIOCESE'S APPROACH TO EDUCATING black ministers stemmed from a different concern than that of black church leaders who advocated for a trained and literate ministry. Instead of pursuing respectability and an organized worship style that would secure it, the diocese pursued community cohesion, coherence, and endurance through racial segregation. What the diocese offered through establishing a seminary for black men to be ordained as Episcopal priests was an opportunity for the development of the ministry. Ironically, the proposition also opened the way for black ministers to be placed on equal footing with white ordained ministers in the Episcopal Church even though they were eventually segregated into churches and missionary districts. Thus, when the Virginia diocese created the BTS, focus shifted from the benevolent paternalism of the church to the social and political significance of black ministerial leadership. Black ministers enrolled in white-run seminaries faced the racist attitudes of their co-religionists and teachers as they pursued common aims of learning the material needed to minister to people of faith. In this context, black church convention members tried to define the terms of their interactions and maintain a sense of autonomy and self-determination even though they required assistance from white church associations to achieve their higher education goals. As white Christians shaped schools like the Episcopalian Branch Theological Seminary and the Baptist Richmond Theological Institute, they laid the foundation for black ministerial activism and for contesting racial paradigms that paralleled the political alliances that would later emerge in the Readjuster movement.

The relationship between white-run theological schools and this emerging community of black religious leaders was fraught with tension. The issue defined breaks within the Virginia Baptist State Convention and the Zion Union Apostolic Church. While a faction of VBSC members remained affiliated with the American Baptist Home Mission Society and the Richmond Theological Institute, another segment separated into the Baptist General Association. In the case of the ZUA Church, it formally reorganized as a result of differences spurred by the discussion of uniting with the Episcopal Church. The failed negotiation between the Episcopal and ZUA churches illustrates the political dynamics that informed such interactions. The Episcopal Church played an important role in black education during the immediate postemancipation period, and the experience of its affiliated school—St. Stephen's Episcopal Church and School (later, St. Stephen's Normal and Industrial School)—illuminates one of the little discussed elements of postemancipation black education: the involvement of white southerners.[30] Focusing on these white-run educational institutions and their development helps shed further light on the political culture of the South, especially with regard to interracial cooperation in education.

As black church members pursued potential educational collaborations with white co-religionists, black church members proceeded with caution relative to the white denominations in which they found themselves. Black churches were careful to guard their own sense of autonomy even as their leaders may have been receiving valuable education from those same umbrella organizations. Church members established their authority by directly challenging any racist ideas or expressions they encountered. At their 1880 annual convention, Virginia's black Baptists had already begun to hone a hermeneutic of suspicion about the intentions of white reformers. In a hot confrontation with Samuel Chapman Armstrong, the principal of the Hampton Normal and Industrial School, the ministers called Armstrong to task for publishing "some uncharitable remarks" about black people. Several of the convention leaders, including the Reverends Henry Williams Jr., Fields Cook, and W. H. Brooks, discussed the issue, and the convention accepted Brooks's motion that Armstrong's invitation to visit Hampton be declined.[31] The day after the convention rejected the invitation, Armstrong appeared and "made some explanatory remarks" in an attempt to absolve himself of the claims made against him, complaining that the charges were erroneous and attributing the comments to his brother.[32]

The convention members, dissatisfied with Armstrong's disavowal, grilled him on his views about black people. They asked him whether he thought "that God has made the Negro inferior to the white," to which he replied, "No. They are capable of as high attainments as whites."[33] Their question revealed the essence of their claim—that black people were equal to white people because that was how God made them. Equality between the races was innate. In their question, they called for Armstrong to affirm both a theological idea and a sociopolitical one. Upon hearing his explanations and affirmation, they decided to visit Hampton after all. Nevertheless, the confrontation caused them to maintain a critical posture toward white-led educational institutions and informed their decision to support and open their own educational institution, the Virginia Seminary. To launch this institution, they would need resources and independent leadership to serve the seminary.

This was not an isolated instance of black Christians grappling with the costs of interracial cooperation. Black churches in Texas and Kentucky also debated whether to continue to allow white missionary organizations to provide schools for them or to develop their own.[34] Likewise, the ZUA Church evaluated and ultimately rejected the possibility of unification and cooperation, preferring instead complete independence from the Episcopal Church.

INTERACTIONS LIKE THE ONE with Samuel Chapman Armstrong and those with southern white missionaries and teachers indicate that black folks had good reason to be cautious in their dealings. The ideas that the missionaries held about black inferiority and the purposes of education directly conflicted with the ways black Christians saw themselves and the ways the first generation raised in freedom sought to live. The new postemancipation dynamics of black religious independence depleted the Episcopal Church's black membership, which gave rise to open discussions about why the church would specifically and intentionally take up mission work among the freedpeople. Giles Cooke, principal of St. Stephen's Normal and Industrial School, articulated the racist ideas about the freedpeople that were echoed in the diocesan discussions about education.

The Episcopal Church was prompted to consider uniting with the ZUA Church as a result of the latter's inquiries but also as part of an effort to increase black membership. After emancipation, the Virginia diocese saw a precipitous drop in the numbers of black members. While the black exodus from white southern churches was substantial, in the Episcopal Diocese of Virginia, it was almost complete.[35] In 1865, the diocese had just 67 black members; five years later, that number had doubled to a still small 144 black members. This growth was paltry compared to the 8,500 black people who had been baptized and were being catechized by the church before the Civil War.[36] The postbellum decline in membership paired with the increasing efforts by northern churches to conduct mission work among the freedpeople compelled the diocese to develop a missionary project. The decrease in black membership was pronounced and of particular concern for Episcopal churchmen in Virginia, who had been among the largest slave owners in the state.[37] Though the national convention of the Episcopal Church Board of Missions created the Protestant Episcopal Freedmen's Aid Commission (later the Commission of Home Missions to Colored People) to aid the freedpeople, by 1879 the commission had been disbanded, leaving the state diocese, which was rooted in a culture of former slave owners, to spearhead and direct the efforts.[38] These developments placed the members of the Virginia diocese in a situation in which they had to figure out strategies to attract black people to their church.

The Virginia diocese saw unification with the ZUA Church as a way to increase the numbers of black people in their church. The Branch Theological

Seminary became the primary method for achieving this increase. There is no doubt that in conceiving this plan the diocese was influenced by racialized views about black people and by a keen sense of the need to "preserve" the black community as intact and distinct from white Christian life. In constructing the school, the diocese honored the policy of racial exclusion adhered to by the Protestant Episcopal Theological Seminary (PETS), which did not admit black students. Instead of admitting black ministers to PETS, the diocese decided to locate the BTS at St. Stephen's Episcopal Church, where there was already a church school that white rector Giles B. Cooke had turned into a normal school. Initially, the school was not equipped to train ministers. John H. M. Pollard, the first black man ordained to the diaconate, began as a student of Cooke's. After taking his education with Cooke as far as he could, Pollard trained privately for the ministry and was ordained in 1878 at PETS.[39] However, St. Stephen's Normal and Industrial School was responsible for training a number of Petersburg's black teachers.[40] When Cooke became rector of St. Stephen's Episcopal Church and principal of the school, it had three black teachers: Thomas Caine, Emma Morgan, and Miss Brown of New York City. Cooke fired these teachers and replaced them with white ones.[41]

Cooke's firing of St. Stephen's black teachers seemed to reflect his derisive views of black people as dependents needing guidance. Black teachers undermined this perspective. Cooke's interest in educating freedpeople stemmed from his paternalistic views of black people and his desire to shape post–Civil War relations in accordance with them.[42] Many former Confederates in Petersburg took paternalistic approaches to postemancipation politics, actively participating in the education of freedpeople in order to rebuild the South. In this way, white southerners played important roles in the development of black education alongside the white northern missionaries and local black people; together, these three constituencies forged black education in the Reconstruction South.[43] Cooke's first seminary student, James Solomon Russell, explained Cooke's interest this way: "Both before his entrance to the priesthood [in 1871 at the age of thirty-three] and after, he was impressed with the fact that the end of the War left a greater struggle to be fought and won—the struggle against the ignorance and poverty in which the newly freed found themselves, and against the quite as disturbing ignorance and prejudice in which the masses of Southern whites were steeped. He chose as his special field, therefore, work among the ex-slaves and taught and preached, being pastor of St. Stephen's Church until a colored rector could be secured."[44] Like North Carolina's Episcopal leadership, Cooke's evangelization and teaching of freedpeople were motivated by the belief that the uneducated were like children, and freedpeople were children needing guidance.[45] Even still, there were some white people who rejected altogether this idea, and there were black people who left a record of knowing better.

While Russell depicted Cooke's goals as directed toward both freedpeople and southern whites, one of Cooke's speeches indicated that he was primarily interested in freedpeople. He set out to describe to his listeners his "experience amongst them [colored people] before and after the late civil war and then to consider their present condition—spiritually, politically, [illegible], and socially."[46] Cooke then went on to describe the freedmen using adjectives and anecdotes to illustrate their qualities. At the top of his list: "ignorant—illustrated by 'the case of suicide &c.'" At the bottom: "Religious" and "grateful," which he found the freedpeople to be "almost universally." While religiosity and gratitude were presumably positive traits, they were the only positive traits the freedmen possessed. All others left them vulnerable to misdirection. They were, he wrote, "Credulous . . . Superstitious . . . [Delict?] . . . [with] a slavish fear of one another . . . Deceitful . . . [and] Emotional."[47] In the best sense, he may have been concerned with improving the conditions of the freedpeople so that they could improve their own lives. But his depiction of the freedpeople shows that his attitude toward them was not far from what antebellum southern white people thought about enslaved people or what many thought about the freedpeople. As Bond and Gundersen note, "Cooke was no egalitarian. He believed blacks should be educated to fill a subordinate role."[48] Cooke was also able to serve the church community because some other southern white people saw these efforts as a means to keep outsiders, or Northerners, from taking the lead in what they considered miseducation of black people.[49]

Cooke's ideas about dependent black people were echoed in the diocese's discussions about the needs of the black community they sought to serve. This vital and rich mission field's existence appeared to the diocese at a time when they had begun to consider more seriously the church's missionary role. The robust group of ZUA Churches looked ripe for helping the Episcopal Church live out its spiritual mission to preach the gospel to those who did not know it. At the 1879 Annual Council, Bishop Whittle noted that the "colored population" was "becoming more and more accessible to the teaching and influence of our church," and he suggested that every minister should consider it his duty to preach the gospel to every creature on earth.[50] Thus, the church began to view black people as needing and being open to its spiritual guidance.

The diocese further reinforced and lauded Cooke's attitudes and, in the process, exposed its sensitivity to black desires for independence and to the complicated relationship between black independence, white racism, and resources. When the diocese acknowledged the work of Rev. Giles B. Cooke in Petersburg, it explained its rationale: Another vast field (the colored population of this State)—a field as yet very partially occupied, claims our attention and culture. Furnishing as this class does the labor best adapted to our particular wants, and at the same time the least turbulent, most orderly, and on every account most desirable, which capital anywhere controls, it is little to expect, and, to say the very least, impolitic and unchristian to withhold provision for their spiritual as well as temporal necessities. . . . A ministry of their own race is one of their most imperative needs—a need which schools like Mr. [Giles B.] Cooke's are best calculated to supply.[51]

The diocese considered this work to be important because it recognized black people as laborers that society needed and because it would be remiss in not doing something to aid black folks, especially as it pertained to the Christian call for ministers. Thus, the white rationale for conducting mission work included a cacophony of racial ideas rooted in a sense of black inferiority and white dominance. Despite the diminished view of black humanity that the church leaders evidenced, their paternalism produced a need for black church leadership to sustain "orderly" black church communities. Even more, without black ministers, the diocese would not have been able to achieve its goal of increasing membership; black religiosity proved to be a demographic boon to the diminishing membership rolls.

Against the backdrop of these racist ideas, the black church associations strove to maintain racial autonomy as they tried to secure schools for themselves. ZUA Church members, in discussions about the possible merger between the ZUA Church and the Episcopal Church, assumed they would be able to access the resources of the Episcopal Church and maintain their autonomy. They wanted to continue to profit from the resources—educational and ordinational—of the Episcopal Church but aimed to retain their own denominational name; their own president; and the president's powers to assign preachers to their posts, to committees in conventions, and so on.[52] During the early years of their convention, then, the ZUA Church saw the potential benefits of cooperation with the Episcopal Church.

THE NOTION THAT the ZUA ministers required formal education emerged from conflicting goals. Though the ZUA ministers initially sought a close relationship with the Episcopal Church and desired to become communicants, the DMS committee members did not think this was a good plan. The committee believed that if the ministers and members became communicants, the churches would have to disband because they would not have an ordained minister. In order to avoid such disruption and possible scattering of the congregations, the ministers needed to be trained for ordination. Thus, the committee recommended "establishing a school of higher grade near the center of the territory occupied by their congregations, so that the ministers can, without giving up their charges, attend school, and when capable, study theology there."[53] In proposing to establish a separate school for the ZUA ministers, the committee sought to accomplish two goals: to use ministerial education to extend its missionary aims by training black ministers who could lead black congregations, and to preserve the unity of the ZUA congregations. The committee knew the community needed to have its own indigenous leadership and to possess relative organizational sovereignty.[54] At the 1879 Annual Council, the Special Committee on Colored Work made several resolutions that affirmed the church's desire to support developing leadership in the ZUA Church, including that it should allow the ministers of the ZUA Church to assist priests as catechists.[55]

Yet even as the diocese tried to preserve black leadership and black congregations, its plans reinforced the idea of racial segregation and did not fully address the autonomy that many black people sought. Instead, the diocese planned to impose an education requirement on the ZUA Church's leaders and restrict black leadership to black congregations. Through the BTS, the diocese began to see even more clearly the possibility of establishing a "substantial and lasting superstructure" through its work with the people in Petersburg and Brunswick County.[56] This idea of a "superstructure"—or overarching control—was put forth by the Committee on the State of the Church, which pointed out that the students at the Branch Theological Seminary had begun fanning out in the community and teaching among the "colored people," resulting, the committee believed, in increased numbers of confirmations and baptisms.[57] The diocese described the growth in the black churches through educational initiatives in the same way that it described increases in youth adherents cultivated through the secondary schools. The diocese believed that the schools introduced young people to the traditions of the Episcopal Church.[58] Moreover, the diocese's policies for educating priests began to fall in line with the Episcopal Church's national agenda. Three years after emancipation, the missionary arm of the General Convention—the Protestant Episcopal Freedmen's Commission—began advocating educating ministers in order to establish churches rather than supporting common school education, which did not often translate into membership increases.[59] So when the diocese began to see how educating black men for the ministry could turn into more communicants in the churches, church leaders were pleased. Perhaps even more significantly, the committee read the increased "interest" of the "colored people" in the Episcopal Church as evidence that they were "beginning to realize that our church not only welcomes them gladly, but is eminently fitted to meet their religious wants."[60] In short, the interest ameliorated some of the spiritual crisis that the church was experiencing due to postwar attrition because black participation affirmed that the church's missionary work was succeeding.

While the Episcopal Church interpreted black interest as indicative of black people's appreciation of the spiritual work of the church, it made no mention of the value that black people placed on education. In the background, however, the church had some sense that education was a recruiting tool because of the growth it saw from Mrs. Brent's school in Gordonsville.[61] Mrs. Brent's school was akin to Pattie Buford's in its outreach to the freedpeople. The church also worried that freedpeople would avail themselves of the education but not join the church.[62] Still, though the Episcopal Church used education to "recruit" members, it dismissed the validity of these desires. It acknowledged that there was no doctrinal interest on the part of the black people, and diminished the significance of meeting the freedpeople's practical needs. The church's spirituality blinded it to the needs of the people it aimed to serve. Instead, it attributed the interest to spiritual value obtained from fulfilling practical needs. Further, the diocese's self-interested stance, reflected in the DMS missionaries' assessment of the religious landscape, was that "the responsibility now upon our church we think is a most serious one. It *may* be a crisis with these negroes; it *is* a crisis with us."[63] The representatives articulated the notion that mission work among the freedpeople could serve as expiation for enslaving black people.[64] The diocese's limited view of black people's needs and wants opened it up to negotiating with the ZUA Church and created a very limited concept of what unification would look like. This created a bind that the ZUA Church decided to avoid.

After several months of conversations with the DMS Committee and some internal upheavals within the church, the ZUA Church resolved to keep its independence and to continue to receive Buford and White as missionaries. The church members wanted Buford to continue to run their Sunday schools, but they did not wish to become part of the Episcopal Church if it meant losing the ability to "[hold] firmly to [their] church organization as now constituted."[65] The ZUA Church's rejection of Episcopal Church leadership centered education as a potential site for negotiating the terms of freedom. Initially, the ZUA Church sought to unite because of the spiritual, educational, and material resources Mrs. Buford shared. But the same concerns about church autonomy and leadership that led the diocese to propose a school for training ministers caused the ZUA Church to reject unification altogether.

The institutional structural concerns of the ZUA Church stopped the possible merger and highlighted ministerial education as a potential nexus for interracial cooperation. The ZUA Church maintained its relationship with the Episcopal Church but declined to require formal training as a requisite for its church leadership and communities. The ZUA Church's rejection of unification also exhibits the church's self-determination. The give and take between the ZUA Church's pursuit of resources and the diocese's efforts to fulfill its mission of evangelism, especially across racial lines, opened a space for negotiation—a space in which black people's imagined futures might be pursued and where their goals for independence might be achieved. In this space, black people were able to reject the overtures of the Episcopal Church, seeking instead to maintain their autonomy, thereby fully realizing the power and authority that they sought. This example of the Virginia diocese's failure to expand its membership demonstrates how contingent interracial cooperation was on local dynamics and not something that could be reasonably seen from the national level.[66]

Black churchgoers had good reason to be skeptical of white religious overtures for cooperation. In the case of the Episcopal Church, though one of its concerns for the unity of black religious community caused it to create a school, its unresolved striving around aiding black people while maintaining a segregationist posture was revealed at almost every turn of its process of creating black educational opportunities—from the normal school to the seminary. Against this backdrop, black ministers' evolution as politicized and gendered leaders becomes clear.

Gender in the Education of Black Ministers

Black people and white missionaries created politicized black religious manhood by establishing gender bifurcated school curricula. These educational agents laid the foundation for gendered school curricula in Petersburg and Southside. In addition to addressing the desperate need of freedpeople for education, the curriculum that these missionaries and educators created reinforced bifurcated educational opportunities for black boys and girls based on the Victorian ideals of the time. These schools also implicitly provided additional benefits for boys and men, even though they were open to both boys and girls.

Missionary and black educational efforts to promote Victorian domestic ideals required special tools, because domesticity was an ill-fitting ideal for just about every black person of the era: free and freed, northern and southern, male and female. Most black people did not experience the market revolution in the same ways that white people did.[67] They did not experience the transition from home-based production to a separation of the business and domestic spheres and the attendant need to justify men's external work and women's newfound control over the domestic sphere. As Jim Cullen notes, before the war, there was no gendered division of labor for black people.[68] Free black men and women worked outside the home. In fact, patriarchal control characteristic of the southern plantation household was predicated on the existence of enslaved men and women.[69] So when postemancipation efforts to integrate freed and free people into the national body of citizens were put in place, black people's family relations and educational opportunities were shoehorned into the ill-fitting ideal.

By the end of the nineteenth century, black manhood was a complicated notion, and black men subscribed to a producerist vision of black manhood that emphasized respectability, thrift, and moral uprightness. Black manhood was constructed in response to white racist chauvinism, and so it was not able to overcome the sexist elements of the idea.[70] For black ministers attending to issues of black church leadership and securing educational opportunities to reinforce their efforts, the racial component of defining black manhood was certainly there, and ideas about black respectability were key to black separatism and black people's pursuit of autonomous institutions. In the case of black Episcopalians and Zion Unionists, these opportunities were crafted in relationship to black women's opportunities. And even though they did not explicitly argue that ministerial education should be for men and teaching for women, that is exactly how it played out, especially in the case of black Baptist men. Thus, the construction of a black religious manhood incorporated producerist, bourgeois values of manhood as moral, upright, and protector of women.

In some instances, freedpeople pursued the Victorian ideal because it was how they could best establish their distance from the limitations of slavery. Having a nuclear family and control over one's children, with a wife who stayed at home, away from the threats of sexual and physical violence, was very much attractive to a people for whom all these protections had been denied. This was particularly the case in Durham, North Carolina, where these aspirations were also colored by the dynamics of class, in which black people who participated in the practice of "upbuilding" the black community could obtain enough financial stability to secure the Victorian ideal for themselves. But it was also the case that there were working-class and single black women for whom this ideal was not possible, thus exposing a fault line in the Durham black community based on class and gender differences. In this way, black women's experiences also provided a way of understanding some of the choices and ideas, critiques and criticisms, that black people in Durham held.[71]

White missionaries and free black educators crafted specific curricula for black women and men that conformed to Victorian domestic ideology. This was the first step in creating gendered educational opportunities for freedpeople. Some scholars have highlighted the coeducational classroom of the postemancipation period as evidence of egalitarianism.[72] Indeed, with an entire race going to school, it would have been nearly impossible to have sex-segregated education. Thus, at the common-school level, such co-ed classrooms prevailed.[73] However, Baptist missionaries and other education agents placed emphasis on educating male students after emancipation.[74] Though agents' explicit approaches to male and female students shifted over time, the structure of the curriculum they taught yielded to domestic ideals nonetheless. During the war, American Missionary Association chaplains argued for gendered black education when advocating for black soldiers to be taught, on the grounds that literacy and other training would make them better men and better soldiers. Steeped in the idea that slavery debased the humanity of the enslaved, chaplains thought that education could help black men to become more fully men and to demonstrate their manhood on the battlefields of war.[75] After the war ended, numerous missionaries who went to the South took with them ideas about the toll that slavery took on black family life and domesticity, which caused them to focus more directly on women's roles in the home in their educational efforts.[76]

While separate educational opportunities for black men and women gave rise to a black ministerial elite, it also politicized these ministers in the struggle for black autonomy and for black women's educational opportunities. In both instances, the sequence of events that created advanced theological educational opportunities for black men also reinforced the black church pulpit as a male-dominated political space. This first became evident in the separation of ministerial education opportunities for men and women, and again when black people began to struggle for independent educational institutions, like the Virginia Seminary and the St. Paul Normal and Industrial

School. The founding of these schools coincided with the fight for black teachers to be hired in Richmond's and Petersburg's black schools and for the provision of education for black women through what became Hartshorn Memorial College. In line with Elsa Barkley Brown's explanation of how the narrative of the black freedom struggle became oriented around black men, this sequence of events illustrates how black ministers became central to that freedom narrative.[77]

THE BOUNDARIES OF MINISTRY were further drawn around men by the schools that the ABHMS and the Episcopal Church established. At this time, education for the ministry was limited to males by the established educational institutions. Richmond Theological Institute was one of two ABHMS male-only educational institutions, and the Branch Theological Seminary, a school for training ZUA ministers, had only male students.[78] Other educational institutions, especially the common schools, were open to both males and females; but higher education, particularly courses that constituted ministerial education, was limited to black men. It may come as no surprise that black women were excluded from ministerial training, but it bears noting that the exclusion was palpable. Anna Julia Cooper recounted her experience as a young girl attending the Episcopal Church–affiliated St. Augustine's Normal School and Collegiate Institute in Raleigh, North Carolina. Capable of taking and succeeding in classes in Greek and Latin (languages she went on to teach at the prestigious M. Street School in Washington, DC), she was marginalized by her teachers, who acknowledged her academic achievement by constantly calling on her in class. Despite these moments in which the teachers engaged Cooper, they ultimately made clear that the main focus of their teaching efforts were the black men training for the ministry and that her presence was merely tolerated.[79] Virginia's black Baptists eventually called for extending higher education opportunities to women. When they did, however, the opportunities for women were specifically tailored to their place within society—outside the pulpits and religious leadership of churches.

According to Cooper, women's education was subordinated to men's in the theological school curriculum. In an 1883 speech to black Episcopal priests, she said, "Indeed, to my mind, the attitude of the Church toward this feature of her work is as if the solution of the problem of Negro missions depended solely on sending a quota of deacons and priests into the field, girls being a sort of *tertium quid* whose development may be promoted if they can pay their way and fall in with the plans mapped out for the training of the other sex."[80] Cooper's statement appears biographical, as she paid her way through school and was only suffered to be in the classes geared toward the male ministers.[81] The church's view of mission work as male work subordinated women's education. Black women would only be educated insofar as their education could be subsumed under the mantle of ministerial training. And even when that occurred, women were often excluded from some aspects of the curriculum, as it was divided into the "gentleman's course"—which prepared men to undertake later theological training through offering classes like Latin and Greek—and the "Ladies' Course."[82] Their educational prospects were further limited by low expectations.

While theological education created a male-only space for black ministers, it also politicized them in the fight for independent schools and for educational opportunities for black women.[83] Black Baptist ministers became part of the public discourse about education, and their participation reflected a shift in their thinking about the role of education in securing manhood for black men to ensuring a place for nurturing children for black women. The VBSC focused on the education offered at the Richmond Theological Institute, where a majority of its leaders were educated.[84] The VBSC asked the ABHMS to expand its offerings to include educational opportunities for black women.[85] Initially, the ABHMS was reluctant to do this on the grounds that increasing enrollment would entail the need to raise additional funds, but VBSC members offered to help raise the money to accomplish these goals.[86] It took the ABHMS a few years to comply with the request, finally graduating its first woman in 1882, and then opening Hartshorn Memorial College for black women in 1883. The VBSC also discussed the possibility of opening an autonomous school.[87] The discussions about creating educational and teaching opportunities for black women coincided with those about developing independent black educational institutions. Evelyn Brooks Higginbotham describes the Kentucky Baptist Institute's development as an expression of the black nationalist ideologies of black ministers, arguing that black women helped advance this dynamic through their fund-raising capacities. Black women's gender consciousness provided the framework for advancing the black nationalist project.[88] In Virginia, the establishment of black women's schools seemed to have been not only part of the advancement of the black nationalist project but also part of the attempts to inculcate gender roles for black women. Rev. Anthony Binga Jr., a prominent black Baptist minister and pastor of the noted First African Baptist Church of Manchester, advocated hiring black women as teachers in Richmond's public schools, a central issue of the day.[89]

One moment of politicization of black male ministers in regard to education happened when some of Virginia's black Baptists decided to sever ties with the northern white Baptists and establish their own school. Their plan was for this independent educational institution to represent their self-determination. The Virginia Baptist Seminary, located in Lynchburg, Virginia, was founded in 1886 and opened its doors in 1890, and it is still in existence today. The black Baptists who opted to remain affiliated with the white Baptist General Convention did so in part because they wished to retain access to the educational institutions established by the ABHMS, notably the Richmond Theological Seminary. The VBSC reached its decision to create an independent school in part because of the work that the Sunday school committees and conventions, along with the education committees, did to frame the discourse about black education. At its 1882 annual meeting, the Bethany Baptist Sunday School Education Committee asserted, "We do [not] believe in that system of education which fills the head with knowledge, but leaves the heart uncultivated by the grace of God, and the hands avoiding labor."[90] Where the missionaries early on conflated religious training and academic training, the different committees made a strong distinction between Christian discipleship or the education of the believer and education for ministerial leadership. The schools that the black Christians created eventually fell into the trap of the industrial versus liberal arts debates and, in the case of James Solomon Russell's school, used the discourse about black women and domestic education to advance the school.

In 1882, James Solomon Russell left the Branch Theological Seminary, "placed his books upon the upper shelf," and went to minister to the freedpeople of Brunswick County.[91] A few years later, he founded what became St. Paul Normal and Industrial School. After several years of running St. Paul, Russell described his work as being about doing the work rather than complaining about the circumstances: "Some by agitation and complaint think that they must be heard for their many words and loud talking but my plan has been to solve the problem by applying myself to the work. I think I can safely say that my work is a success, while it has made me a perfect slave."[92] Russell appeared to be a man of action, and he noted how his work, his focus on getting things done, ironically turned him into a slave, so dedicated was he to the work of educating the masses of black people. Russell's school exemplified how male-centered theological education was turned into gendered educational opportunities for black women. By the end of the nineteenth century and just four years into the running of St. Paul, Russell affirmed the need to focus on educating black women, arguing that "it is equally important to send out teachers acquainted with the Church as to educate and send out ministers."[93] Russell made this statement as part of his plea to raise more funds for his school, which was increasing its efforts in the direction of black women's education. The need for black women's education to be central had been a running conversation in the pages of the school's *Southern Missioner* for several months.[94]

The focus on educating black men was a way in which black manhood came to be constructed: black men were the ones worthy of education. By 1893, the Bishop Payne Divinity School had maintained a connection to the normal school in order to allow men of promise to pursue theological training without the impediment of being denied due to lack of academic preparation. Of the school, it was reported: "In addition to the Divinity course it is also the object of the school to admit to the academic instruction of the school a limited number of promising male students, making good character the chief requisite for admission and continuance, and aiming to build up in connection with the Divinity School a High School of a high order, fitting scholars to enter a first class college or professional school."[95] Just two years later, Bishop Payne was reported as thriving by Rev. J. Wesley Johnson, an instructor at the school, whom Russell happened to meet in Manchester. Johnson reported that the school was doing well and that there was even a Roman Catholic student at the school. He hoped that more people would send their men to the seminary to be educated regardless of denomination. The school was apparently still receiving students from different denominations, as it had when it was first founded.[96] Notably, the students they solicited were male ministers. When black women came to be included in the educational missions of the black community (as an explicit discourse), the claims were based on their role in the family as mothers who needed to be educated in order to lead their children.[97] Alternatively, the inclusion of black women could have been a means of protecting them from exploitation by white men by providing another professional avenue for them and thus preserving a sense of respectability for them.[98] Essentially, by the 1880s–90s, education for women became subsumed under the racial project of freedom and of a masculinized freedom struggle. By the early twentieth century, however, black women in the Church of God in Christ tradition, such as Mother Lizzie Robinson, began to carve out teaching as a female space in order to relieve male concerns about women becoming preachers.[99] Within the latter part of the nineteenth century, however, black men and women were still negotiating the power dynamics between them, and preaching and teaching roles were at the heart of those debates.[100]

THEOLOGICAL EDUCATION CRYSTALLIZED some of the race and gender elements of the evolving black religious politics. Just over a decade after emancipation, freedpeople attempted to reconfigure the aid model that organized educational opportunities and distribution of resources in their negotiations with white church people. Taking additional steps toward securing religious freedom of belief and a homegrown leadership cadre revealed the incompatibility of black autonomy and racist paternalism. Even if uniting with white co-religionists meant securing black communities, submitting to segregation was simply untenable. Hence, black church independence and collaboration foregrounded the struggle and established a paradigm of black church leadership that was gendered male.

In the ZUA, Episcopal, and Baptist churches, race relations between black and white Christians determined the success of each educational venture. While racial tensions often shaped the formation of black educational institutions and struggles over incorporating black people into the leadership and faculty ranks, educational institutions also shaped gender roles and ideas in the black community. The initial push for education of black ministers that occurred during the immediate postemancipation period reinforced the pulpit as a black male space while limiting black women's religious ministry to teaching. Theological education for ministers became a de facto kind of gender training for black men. Available only to recognized leaders of black churches, theological education reinforced the ministry as a male domain. While Evelyn Brooks Higginbotham credits the turn toward education for black women to white Baptist missionaries' growing sense that educating black men was a "suicidal policy" because educated black men challenged social structures of the South, the development of the BTS extends this depiction.[101] Educating black men was not just suicidal in the postemancipation context; educating black men was also a policy that generated a homegrown resistance to racial bigotry within the denominations and a vocal advocacy for black women's educational opportunities.

CHAPTER FIVE

Politics of Engagement

In 1882, forty-one of southwest Virginia's most prominent black citizens submitted to U.S. senator William Mahone a letter of endorsement for Captain G. McHenry Gish of Roanoke County. They requested that Mahone find a position in Washington for their "highly esteemed friend." Gish, a white man, found favor with these black citizens because, in addition to being "eminently qualified in every respect for almost any position the department could give him," he was faithful to the Readjuster movement. Most importantly, however, he was supportive of the endeavors of the black religious community. "With the exception of Col Wm Watts," they wrote, "he was the only man in this county for a long time when we had no churches that was willing to furnish us grounds for our camp meeting associations[,] Pic-nic excursions &c—his groves have always been free & open to any & all & have been largely enjoyed by our people from nearly every town along this line of Railroad while he has aided us with means as far as able in our every effort at advancement." The petitioners acknowledged and appreciated Gish's support of their nascent attempts at establishing religious freedom and independence by providing space for their church meetings when they had none. Gish, they attested, also recognized their equal humanity by defying the growing tradition of segregation and providing places for black social gatherings when other white people had closed them out.[1] He supported the social and cultural development of the community, and for that reason, black and white people in the community respected and supported him. They solicited Mahone's aid in securing a position for Gish because it would "redound to the good of our people & the state in general."[2]

During the early 1880s, black political and religious networks were strengthening and expanding. This letter captures the breadth and depth of such networks among "the freedmen of South west Va." In addition to the forty-one signatures, the letter noted: "We could [have] furnish[ed] a solid list of all our race for this man but the leading and most enlightened we presume will suffice." The signatories were ministers, newspaper editors, deacons, elders, teachers, and barbers from Botetourt and Roanoke counties, Fincastle, Lynchburg, and Big Lick.[3] These forty-one people were not just family members, not just party chairmen and city officials, but individuals whose network crossed counties and encompassed some of the largest cities in western Virginia. While the signatories were all of a certain class, they presented themselves as representative of the community to a person. The presence of church leaders on the list further indicates that church people engaged in political action.

This letter illustrates how religion and electoral politics began to intersect more directly through organizing two decades after emancipation. The primary reason the endorsers supported Gish was that he had provided meeting grounds for their churches. Like the cross-county network depicted in this letter, church conventions included cross-county connections that drew black Virginians into communication of even greater breadth and depth. Over the four years of the Readjuster movement's success, the Baptist and Reformed Zion Union Apostolic (RZUA) associations grew in the number of people and counties they reached. These growing church networks fostered the spread of the gospel message and increased the sense of community identity. Through these statewide and regional associations, religious, racial, community, and collective identities formed. The Gish endorsers considered themselves to represent all the black people in their region. In this way, black churches were becoming the communal and race organizations that "provided the new basis of social cohesion" and later fostered the development of "a church with the soul of a nation."[4] This chapter reveals that these robust and unifying networks were also evidence of more diverse communities and churches. These churches emerged with the struggles of a nation's soul, and by that I mean they also faced the challenges of mediating electoral politics. Black church associations between 1879 and 1885 structured community and identity across counties and cities, onto which politicians easily mapped political strategies, and those structures influenced how black people entered the political arena of patronage so prevalent during this period.

This letter captures the overlapping and reinforcing effects of strengthened black religious and interracial political networks during the lead up to Mahone's 1883 attempt to harness that power for the Readjuster movement by canvassing Virginia's black churches. More significant for the evolution of black churches' and conventions' relationship to the political sphere was black people's growing self-awareness of the strength and vitality of their own connections, evidenced in the successful 1888 congressional campaign of John Mercer Langston. This expanding sense of community filtered into the process of engaging in patronage requests based on their own interests and strengths, the very process in which the Gish endorsers were engaged. The Gish endorsement, Mahone's 1883 church canvass, and the Langston campaign reflected the potential for an interracial coalition that would threaten white supremacy and the "Solid South." Indeed, these events have largely been interpreted in this framework. However, this chapter reinterprets them to reveal the strengthening of black religious political networks, a development that has largely been overlooked. That is the central narrative of this chapter.

Political Context of the Readjuster Era

In the background of the growing black religious networks was a shifting political terrain. As the 1870s wore on, black Virginians' political and racial alliances shifted from staunch support of Republicans to factions that supported either straight-out Republicans or Readjusters. Because they could no longer clearly identify their political friends, black political alliances were propelled into disarray. When the Republican Party weakened its support of black people's rights, black support for the party also declined. Prior to the Compromise of 1877, which gave Republican Rutherford B. Hayes the presidency in exchange for relinquishing federal control of the South, the Republican Party had a stronghold in Virginia state party offices. But for the three years following the Compromise, the Republican Party did not have a state central committee in Virginia,[5] meaning that there was no centralized entity to pull together any of the party's efforts. Republican Party officeholding declined during this period, from a high of fifty-six state legislators in 1872 to only fourteen in 1878.[6] Moreover, black people questioned the value of their allegiance to Republicans like President Hayes and started asking what he and the party were doing for them.

In the midst of these developments, several black people from a variety of states wrote to John Mercer Langston, one of Virginia's black leaders, asking why he supported Rutherford B. Hayes despite Hayes's failure to appoint any black people to office and his lack of responsiveness to his black constituents. As much as these inquiries reflected cracks in the veneer of the black-Republican alliance, Langston's response showed that some black people remained loyal nonetheless. Langston attempted to placate black voters' concerns by pointing out that Hayes had promised to protect black interests, had appointed some black people to posts already, and ultimately was a member of the Republican Party, "which saved through blood American freedom, and which now seeks to conserve and sustain it." Langston linked the noble past of the Republican Party to its future support of the advancement of black freedom and affirmed that the party would hold the president

FIGURE 5.1 Professor John Mercer Langston, Howard University. Langston's wealth and social status allowed him to secure political support from black voters in Virginia's Fourth Congressional District. Courtesy of the Library of Congress Prints and Photographs Division, LC-DIG-cwpbh-00690.

accountable to ensure "that protection, promotion and recognition shall be accorded those whose emancipation was decreed in the hottest battle and subsequently by the national constitutional rectification."[7] Republicans' legacy bound them to the future progress of the emancipated, Langston proclaimed. Yet that was not to be the case for black Virginians, neither at the federal nor at the state level. The national Republican Party had brokered a compromise to diminish protection of black freedom, while Virginia's white Republicans found common cause with the state's Democrats.

Black people's support for Virginia Republicans deteriorated in 1877, when the party fielded no candidate for governor. This moment marked the beginning of an ideological realignment of Republican Party leaders with the Funder Democrats, who had always favored paying the state debt in full and who had been aligned with the wealthier segments of society. This realignment was further evidenced when Republican congressmen John F. Dezendorf and Joseph Jorgensen reportedly threatened to vote with the Democrats in the U.S. Congress if William Mahone, elected senator in 1879, was given control of state patronage. They denied having made such statements, but a later alliance between Republicans and Democrats in the gubernatorial campaign of 1881 suggests otherwise.[8] In fact, as Eric Foner suggests, shifts in Republican alliances with black people came about because of changes in the attitudes of white Republicans. They came to prefer alliances with southern white men of class and distinction over alliances with what they perceived to be ignorant black people.[9] In this context of decreased strength of black-Republican alliances, the Readjuster movement redrew the lines of interracial cooperation. The mechanics of that transformation illuminates just how powerful black religious networks had become.

Former Confederate general William Mahone revamped the Readjuster movement to embrace a new interracial politics, one that engaged the growing black religious networks. Mahone's election to the U.S. Senate in 1879, to the eventual dismay of the state Democratic Party, set in motion the first step to realigning black and white political coalitions.[10] An alliance of Republican and Readjuster state legislators had gotten Mahone elected, with an evenly divided Senate in Washington putting him in position to control the dispensing of federal patronage. Taking his seat in March 1880, Mahone compromised with the Republicans in the Senate.[11] He promised to vote with the Republicans, giving them the majority (thirty-eight senators and the Vice President's tie-breaking vote). In return, the Republicans gave him choice committee assignments, a chairmanship—an appointment practically unheard of for a freshman senator—and control of the patronage.[12]

Backed by a legislative coalition and the power of patronage, Mahone led the Readjuster Party into the 1881 election with the means to effect an interracial political movement that could secure the governorship for the party. Its 1879 campaign produced no significant legislation, though the party did pledge to provide quality education, increased sharing of patronage positions, "honest elections, and an end to the political 'color line.'"[13] By 1881, the Readjuster movement made considerable progress, especially with expanding its coalition from the legislature to the ground-level ranks of voters. The party increased its base in the 1881 election by expanding its platform to include issues of greatest concern to black people: civil rights, education, and social welfare reform.[14] In effect, the party became more receptive to, and a champion of, black political equality, and the 1881 Readjuster convention reflected this shift.

At the Readjuster Party convention in June 1881, one-third of the delegates were black men, representing the shift from Readjusters' ambiguous efforts to include black people in the party during the lead-up to the 1879 elections to concerted attempts to bring black voters into the movement.[15] Observers described the June convention as spirited and full of energy and camaraderie. The convention was packed to the rafters with delegates, so much so that there were no seats for the general public, causing them to have to mill about outside the theater. Inside, there were no clear race divisions: black and white delegates mingled freely. Another remarkable aspect of the convention was that its attendees appeared to be poor. This was not a convention of Virginia's rich and staid elite but one of black and white manual laborers and farmers.[16] The Readjusters, with their amended campaign platform and limited interracial outreach, gained the election of William E. Cameron as governor and control of the state legislature in 1881.[17]

The tally of black votes in the 1881 gubernatorial election ought not be taken as the full measure of black political support of the Readjuster movement. Instead, it reflected the political assessments black Virginians made in the tumultuous political climate in which enemies and old friends began to look uncannily similar and in which enemies' enemies had no real track record of support of black equality to speak for them. There was no way to have known for sure at the time that this alliance with former Confederates would redound to the good of black people and be reflected in the many legislative acts of the 1881–82 legislature.

Besides reflecting the political calculus of black voters, this moment also portended changes in the formation of black and interracial alliances. Many northerners celebrated Mahone's victory as a harbinger of the demise of the

FIGURE 5.2 "Virginia—the Readjuster State Convention at Richmond—Mr. Massey Moving to Make Unanimous Nomination of Col. Wm. E. Cameron for Governor June 3d—From Sketch by Walter Golfer—See Page 287." *Frank Leslie's Illustrated Newspaper*, 25 June 1881. The illustrator depicted the attendees as better dressed and of higher status than the newspaper accounts indicated. Courtesy of the Library of Virginia.

Solid South. If Mahone could muster a coalition of black former Republicans and white people lured away from the Democratic Party, it could happen in other states, too.[18] Other contemporary observers saw the breakdown of white racial alliances and either lamented it or celebrated its potential to liberate the South from race prejudice. The breakdown of racial lines would be for the good of the Democratic Party, too, some said, for it would provide the opportunity to redefine the party according to real political ideas rather than the irrationality of racism, and would allow the South to be reconciled to the North.[19]

While much of the discussion of the Readjuster movement centered on the potential demise of the Solid South, an even more significant outcome of the politics of the Readjuster era was the emergence of strengthened black religious networks. White observers denigrated black people and the racial politics of their political coalitions when they celebrated the demise of "emotional," unthinking black support of the Republican Party.[20] The extent of black rejection of straight-out Republican tendencies and the diversification of the black vote, however, went nearly unremarked, even though that was probably the single most salient ramification of the 1881 election. Black people broke racial ranks and their alliance with the Republican Party to vote for the Readjuster Party. Black voters were hardly unthinking agents before then, however, and the racial myopia reflected in this assessment prevented white people from seeing the developing church-based political culture of black Virginians. The coalitions that catalyzed this change and the further evolution of black political strategies of patronage are the subjects to which we now turn.[21]

Growth of Black Religious Networks and Church Conventions in the Era of the Readjusters

In 1882, Rev. Henry Williams became the major statistician for the Virginia Baptist State Convention and for the Bethany Baptist Association.[22] A record keeper by nature—reflected in the lists of church members, baptisms, weddings, and deaths kept in his own notebooks—Williams turned his skill and interest in enumerating and tracking black church members to the service of the associations. The associations used this data to represent themselves to themselves, but the developing political machine of the Readjuster movement soon saw the value of this information for political purposes. The party's interest underscores just how valuable and significant these networks and knowledge of them were. However, the value that black people placed on documenting and knowing who was counted among them and the strength they derived from gathering and publishing this information were more central to this moment, marking a major shift in black religious politics at the end of the nineteenth century. The roots of this shifting politics can be found in the rapid growth of the regional and state associations during the Readjuster movement.

One of the primary ways that the conventions parlayed the strength of their religious gatherings into political influence was through discussion. In some meetings, members offered political analysis and critique, as Richard Wells, president of the Virginia Baptist State Convention, did in his 1879 annual address. He congratulated the Exodusters and U.S. district court judge Alexander Rives on his decision that exclusion of black people from jury service violated the Fourteenth Amendment rights of equal protection of defendants.[23] Wells's message was echoed by the Committee on Resolutions, which lauded the emigrants and felt prompted to "hail with joy the spirit that has prompted them thus to show the world that they have the spirit of men." And they rebuked "that spirit among the ruling classes of people of the South," who created the situations that made black people want to emigrate, calling the world's attention to "a condition of barbarity unknown in the annals of history among a people who profess the Christian religion." The Committee on Resolutions also acknowledged that though the primary aim of the convention was "to forward our Master's cause," they were "citizens of this State and also of the United States" and therefore felt they should be able to comment on the condition of their people and issues relevant to them. They went on to laud Judge Rives's actions.[24] This was a key moment for these Virginia Baptists, directly engaging in developments in the political sphere. They were bridging their identities as Christians and black U.S. citizens by claiming citizenship in two worlds—Christian and American. Notably, they did not claim that their faith informed their politics.

The conventions also addressed matters of racial representation, deciding as a body in 1880 to reject Samuel Chapman Armstrong's invitation to visit Hampton because of disparaging remarks he had made about black people. They withheld fellowship until Armstrong came and addressed the convention, submitting himself to pointed questions about his racial attitudes.[25] These conventions also addressed numerous issues of interracial alliance over education, leadership, and foreign mission work, and President Wells even mentioned religious and political turmoil in 1880–81.[26] The conventions also brought up the issue of having black teachers in public school classrooms.[27] One of the key areas in which they began to shape a race consciousness that placed black people on equal footing with white people was in education. At the 1878 VBSC meeting, the Committee on Education put forward a proposal that "a committee of three brethren take into consideration the propriety of establishing an institution of learning for both sexes to be conducted under the auspices of the colored Baptists of this state."[28] This proposal was the beginning of what would eventually become the Virginia Seminary, a black Baptist school run for black children. VBSC members decided to take education into their own hands. At the 1881 VBSC gathering, the Committee on Education—which consisted of Fields Cook, J. A. Taylor, W. H. Miles, and J. W. Patterson—advised "the patrons of all such schools to never be satisfied with white teachers if competent colored ones can be found. The reasons for this are many and obvious and unnecessary to be given herewith."[29]

Another area of discussion was the need for a Baptist newspaper, an issue that had been raised with an appointed time for discussion in 1880, which seemed to follow several years of tentative conversations about establishing a newspaper.[30] Although the minutes do not record the substance of these arguments, members argued that a newspaper would provide the means to foster community and guide education in doctrinal matters for Sunday schools.[31] Rev. Richard Wells proposed that they meet these needs by reviving the *Baptist Herald*, which was started in 1872.[32] The convention did not seem to get the newspaper off the ground in 1880, but the goal remained. By 1882, the VBSC had a committee on newspapers to address the issue.

In addition to discussing political issues of representation and rights, the conventions expanded their geographic reach and their networks. Committees on Mission Fields regularly identified areas unrepresented in the convention for missionary outreach.[33] In this way, the evangelical mission of the church fostered the expansion of the political network as well. In 1882, the VBSC held its annual meeting in Staunton, Virginia, where the then convention president, Elder R. H. Porter, resided. Holding the meeting in the western part of the state, away from the eastern counties of its founding, from whence its leaders largely hailed, reflected the opportunity to expand the geographic reach of the convention. VBSC members also considered opening leadership opportunities on many of their geographically based boards to individuals from different regions.[34] While these later measures did not become permanent practices in the VBSC—no other conventions were held out west, and its boards remained regional and eastern—these efforts at expansion and broad-based networks were still quite impressive. Even before hiring a statistician in 1882, the rich data VBSC members gathered about themselves revealed the tremendous reach of black conventions.

The Colored Shiloh Baptist Association (CSBA)—one of several broad-based regional gatherings of congregations—further illustrates the growth of black religious and political networks. In addition to increasing its number of churches and regional scope, the size of CSBA churches grew during this time, as more people were counted as church members. CSBA membership grew nearly 16 percent between 1881 and 1884, increasing from 32,640 to 37,824 members and from 94 to 101 churches. The VBSC also experienced marked growth, going from 40,741 members in 1881 to its apex of 54,417 members in 1885. Between 1880 and 1889, the footprint of the VBSC also expanded, from thirty counties to seventy-two, more than doubling its size.

What is remarkable about the growth of these associations is the sustained building of networks and their expansiveness. One explanation for this growth is that they were fulfilling their mission to evangelize. In addition to creating the Foreign Mission Board in 1882 to support black Baptist mission work in Africa, the VBSC also promoted the work of missions by appointing missionaries to travel throughout the state, conducting services and raising money.[35] Eventually the VBSC recommended less emphasis on the peripatetic aspect of the work so that the missionaries could help the new churches become sustained communities. This new emphasis seems to have contributed to the growth of the convention.

Whereas the Baptist churches experienced and documented their growth in numbers, the RZUA Church focused less on size and more on substance. The RZUA Church was much more modestly sized in general, and the individual churches tended to have fewer members. The church was less consumed with marking numbers of baptisms and dismissals and other details of church growth, which the Baptists tracked more carefully. Instead, church records evidence the kinds of ideas that likely kept the members out of political engagement while strengthening their communal bonds. Church minutes include the questions for character examination to which all attendees submitted, revealing the emphasis on moral guidance.[36]

The growth of black religious associations during the quarter century following emancipation is significant because of the foundation that they gave to black community organization. In most cases, membership in churches and associations constituted a minority of black people. Only in rare instances did black Baptist Church members make up more than one-quarter of the black population in any given county.[37] Nevertheless, these churches and associations represented a hardy contingent of networked and connected black people within their communities and counties.[38] In places where an election could turn on vote margins of a few hundred people, these church networks would come to be even more significant. As had been the case since the early stages of the formation of these associations, conventions were spaces where communal dialogues about church life, governance, and values ensued. These conventions were also timely gatherings and often explicitly engaged the political issues of the day (if not discussing specific party alliances). This was likely encouraged by the fact that the meetings were held in May, around the time of municipal elections, and in August—the heart of revival and homecoming season for the churches but also the time when political canvassing for fall elections began to heat up.[39] Additionally, these meetings were often held with some of the most prominent churches of the host community, like the Zion Baptist Church of Portsmouth, which hosted the Colored Shiloh Baptist Association in 1881, and Gilfield Baptist Church in Petersburg, which hosted three different conventions over the decades following emancipation.[40]

Though the VBSC aspired to be the state-level association of black Baptists, it never fully attained that status, due in part to the geography of the state. Its ambitions were eclipsed by regional associations formed to enable more frequent communion and communication between the churches and to reduce the travel burden on delegates.[41] While some churches from great distances maintained at least letter representation at the VBSC annual meeting (and thus also received copies of the minutes), the VBSC remained largely an eastern association of churches with delegates from the regional associations. The VBSC had church representatives from Tidewater and Valley but not Southside. The Southside churches instead affiliated with the Bethany Baptist Association (BBA) and the Bluestone Colored Baptist Association (BCBA) and sent delegates to the VBSC meeting. This arrangement not only intensified regional identification among black Baptists but also connected larger networks of black Baptists through the practices of sending delegates to the other associations and the annual meeting. For RZUA churches, the entirety of the church remained in one region, and so the RZUA Church had a regional distinctiveness all its own.

Not only were the churches belonging to these associations significant to the groups' political evolution, but they were also important parts of community formation. Like the Gilfield church described in chapter 3, the churches represented in the association were local ground-level leavening forces. And the associations became regional leavening agents, each one developing its own distinct character. As Evelyn Brooks Higginbotham and James M. Washington describe, the churches and conventions became central places for a rising black consciousness.[42] Like the Baptists, the RZUA church members negotiated the terms of race within their convention and did so largely over the issues of education and self-determination, as discussed in chapter 4. At the same time that these networks strengthened, so, too, did a race consciousness and a sense of communal power that would become the basis of negotiations within the patronage process, as the Gish endorsement in 1882 reflects. When Gish's endorsers claimed to be representative, they could do so with some credibility. William Mahone and the Readjusters were about to find this out.

Black Religious Virginians and Patronage

If the 1881 election bespoke a black political tactical decision more than an actual shift in political allegiance, black political behavior after the election reflects how black people understood themselves and their place within their political alliance with the Readjusters. As the Gish endorsement shows, black people engaged in the patronage process as broad-based communities. One of the most critical aspects of the Readjuster movement's brief success was not the politics of party but of the churches.

Mahone's use of patronage has dominated both historical and scholarly analysis of the moment. When Mahone became a U.S. senator in 1880, he gained control of the state patronage in spectacular fashion. Through savvy political negotiations, he used his vote to give the Republicans the majority in the Senate and, in exchange, received four committee appointments, including the chairmanship of the Agriculture Committee. His additional appointments were to committees with significant patronage potential: Naval Affairs, Post Office and Postal Roads, and Education and Labor. Not only was Mahone the first freshman senator to be granted a committee chairmanship, but he also, more significantly, gained control of the patronage that Virginia Republicans once controlled and now coveted.[43] From his post in the senate, Mahone dispensed the patronage, sending requests to party leaders at home for recommendations of individuals who could fill positions in Washington and in the navy yards. At the state level, too, Readjusters shared the spoils of victory in what seemed fulfillment of the promise to share patronage between white and black people.

When the party successfully captured the governor's post and the state legislature, George Freeman Bragg—a young black member of St. Stephen's Episcopal Church—became a beneficiary of the patronage politics of the party; he was appointed as a page in the state legislature.[44] Bragg listed other black people who received appointments in his memorial tribute to Mahone, but these posts were neither as numerous nor significant as they would come to be. The black people in the auditor's office, in the state legislature, and even on the governor's household staff could have been seen not just as the fulfillment of Readjuster promises of inclusion but as signs of more to come, which attracted even more black people to the Readjuster coalition.[45] It was this broader significance of Mahone's patronage that drew the ire of and condemnation from the Readjusters' critics.

According to James Tice Moore, Mahone's contemporaries saddled his legacy with claims that his bossism caused the demise of the party. In their view, Mahone undermined white supremacy, the civil service, and the state through patronage.[46] If Mahone's contemporaries saw his use of patronage as one of the most deleterious effects of his leadership, historians have celebrated his use of patronage and argued that through this means he was able to cement his alliances with Virginia's black people. Jane Dailey chronicles how the Readjuster Party got its members to vote. The Readjusters secured and doled out jobs like postmaster, judge, and other appointments through the Virginia General Assembly at a far higher rate than the Republicans had.[47] Further, patronage, when dispensed to black men, challenged white supremacy when it placed them in positions of authority over white people and "distributed the material and honorific benefits of patronage to black Readjusters."[48] Readjusters also realigned the Richmond School Board when Governor William E. Cameron fired the existing school board under an 1882 law that required officials to take an oath. The board members refused. The removal addressed black people's demands for greater representation in educational leadership and classrooms.[49] Jane Dailey also notes that black involvement in the Richmond School Board issue demonstrated the political autonomy of black people.[50]

This focus on Mahone's control and use of patronage tends to obscure the roles played by individuals who advocated on their own behalf and groups of voters like the Gish endorsers. It was true that many people's allegiances were bought and sealed through being appointed to jobs in the navy yards, post office positions, and other posts.[51] Yet distribution of patronage was more than a top-down dispensing of working papers from Mahone to his grateful supporters. Instead, it was a negotiation through which supporters petitioned for and obtained patronage posts, for themselves and for others, in exchange for their political participation.[52] Mahone's dispensing of patronage revised racial relations. Because churches, black people, and women participated in this process, and because of the various positions they held within it, patronage was the foundation on which the biracial political coalition was built. But it was not just a quid pro quo proposition directed by William Mahone, nor were black political goals submerged to the enticements of patronage.[53] Indeed, participating in patronage politics was not at odds with black political goals but rather a reenforcement of community networks and understandings of black political power. A closer look at how patronage posts were distributed helps to illuminate how black churches and church networks supported the development of a black political culture.

The development of patronage networks and processes had a significant contextual counterpart—the organization of black religious networks. Black

FIGURE 5.3 James M. Gregory. Professor Gregory was a noted leader among black people. He was featured in the compendium *Men of Mark: Eminent, Progressive & Rising* by William J. Simmons. Courtesy of the New York Public Library.

people's attempts to engage the patronage process highlight the influence of church conventions on the political process. Understanding the structure and development of patronage within the Readjuster movement is important, because it helps interpret how black people relied on networks to secure patronage. For black people writing to Mahone during the height of the Readjuster movement, patronage involved mobilizing cross-county networks very much like the ones cultivated in the church conventions. They did not make claims based on individuals, like women whose brothers, husbands, and fathers were party faithful. And they did not draw on local, city, or county service, as some men did. Instead, they used their religious networks to trade political support for the advancement of black political and social goals. The endorsement sent by Howard University students on behalf of Professor James M. Gregory, like that of Captain G. McHenry Gish, bears this out.[54]

Virginia residents who were students at Howard University in Washington, DC, organized a petition in support of an appointment in the diplomatic service for Professor James M. Gregory, professor of Latin, language, and literature. These students held Gregory in high regard and claimed that this was also true of the "scores of young men now located in different parts of our own state . . . [and also] the Faculty and Trustees [of Howard]."[55] They requested that Gregory be assigned to a "European port of such rank in the diplomatic service as would be suitable for him." The students understood that they held political sway despite being schooled outside their home state and that their voting power could influence Mahone's decision. They concluded their letter with the explanation: "Should you find it consistent to think favorably of our request, we shall be grateful to you, and shall esteem it as a personal favor; moreover, we shall return to our homes in the summer and fall to take part in the coming state campaign, which we believe will be one of the most memorable in the history of political parties in the state, we shall make proper acknowledgment of your kindness and appreciation of our claims as voters and citizens of Virginia." They were leveraging their appointment request with their political participation. The letter was signed by twelve men from eleven different cities—among them, Portsmouth, Fredericksburg, Lynchburg (2), Hampton, and Christiansburg. Their political savvy in recognizing their bargaining power is notable. Such a broad-based network could be beneficial in a gubernatorial election year. This letter represents how church networks influenced political claims-making as part of the performance of soul liberty expressed through selecting representative leadership. The letter also intimates how participation in patronage politics reinforced black people's connections across county lines.

What exactly these referrals yielded bears consideration. I have not tracked down the disposition of every referral letter and appointment request, which would presumably be possible as well as interesting. However, there exists in the Mahone papers a listing of appointments from an unspecified year—perhaps compiled in 1881, since the latest appointment date on the list is May 6, 1881. This might be a fragment of the entire document, because it ends on the Ninth District with just one appointment, and there were ten districts in Virginia at the time. There are eighty appointments listed from September 1867 to May 1881. The largest number of appointments were made in the Fourth and Eighth Districts, to white men, though there were also appointments made to black men and white women. There do not appear to have been any appointments made to black women, according to the list. Eighty appointments over thirteen-plus years may not seem like a lot of appointments on which to base claims of community, connection, and accountability, but we must keep a few points in mind. First, these were fairly tight-knit communities, where one appointment could hold a lot of weight—not just for the appointees and their immediate networks of supporters (active endorsers) but also for the larger communities of which they were a part. In fact, the conventions also practiced having a few people stand in for the larger whole. In those church conventions and meetings, a very vocal minority usually expressed the ideas and positions of the majority, which then participated in voting and choosing the prevailing view.[56] So the idea that a select few could represent the whole was not foreign to black voters of the day. Moreover, just as enslaved and emancipated people built community and kinship through property holding and through mediating claims about property—a process in which their ties were more explicitly rendered—participating in the patronage process simultaneously reinforced and exposed these community connections.[57] This notion of claims-making can also be applied to the patronage process, where community attestation to a candidate's appropriateness for a position reflected the bonds of that community.[58] Second, the notion that requests needed to be fulfilled in order for network connections to be cemented does not undermine the fact that people expected these kinds of negotiations and that they understood themselves to have some political leverage by virtue of being voters or being connected to voters.[59]

However, the broad-based support of the Howard students did suggest another way that black people's networks were more expansive than Mahone and the Readjusters had previously considered. Two elements stand out from the students' request: what the petitioners wanted and how they sought to achieve that end. These students sought employment for Professor Gregory not because of his destitution—a notable theme in patronage request letters. Instead, these petitioners sought recognition of Gregory's stature within their community. A distinguished appointment in the Foreign Service would benefit and befit him. Such a request suggests that these students viewed Gregory as being on the same level as another noted black Virginian—John Mercer Langston, who had served as interim president of Howard University, founded the law school there, and served as chargé d'affaires and consul general of Haiti at the time of their request.[60] Gregory, a leader in black politics, had founded a chapter of the National Equal Rights League in Ohio; served as secretary of the Republican Central Committee of Washington, DC, for four years; and encouraged black people to maintain their allegiance to the Republican Party.[61] Essentially, the students sought an appointment befitting their leader's status and reflecting their own importance. In holding up Professor Gregory for nomination, they sought ratification of their own evaluations of merit. In this way, Gregory's endorsement is like that of Captain Gish, the only distinction being that Gish's contributions affected the material conditions in which black people lived, while Gregory's affected their social and political standing.

The second substantial component of this referral is that the students used tools of negotiation premised on the grounds that they had some political sway. They used the upcoming election to entice Mahone to entertain their request, for they would be returning to their homes to participate in the upcoming Virginia election—one destined to be of monumental proportions. A paltry eleven votes could have little effect, but eleven well-connected activists from places linked by expanding religious networks could certainly have an impact. Like Gish's endorsers, these men's hometowns were linked by the VBSC, the BBA, and the CSBA, which had recently held or were holding conventions in the coming months. They would be returning to hometowns where residents had been connected through annual meetings of delegates from throughout the state. In fact, they note the broad reach of their own networks with reference to "scores of young men now located in different parts of our states."[62] This way of engaging in politics on the basis of broad-based networks was made credible by the expanding religious networks, even though no associations or conventions actively participated in elections as a body.

Readjusters' Attempt to Corral the Black Religious Network—the 1883 Election

Religious and political networks strengthened during the 1881–82 election cycle even though they ran along what seem like separate paths. By 1883, these paths began to converge. Black people, like those who referred Gish and Gregory, had come to see their networks as broad-based and effectual, with political potential. These networks began to mobilize, with racial progress as an important component of their political programs, and just and equitable political participation as their aim. Mahone, recognizing the potential, attempted to exploit that.

In the run-up to the 1883 election campaign, Mahone had sensed the need to increase interracial cooperation, had shared spoils with black people, and hoped for the votes enough to secure victory. The black legislators of the 1881–82 session helped appropriate funds for a normal school in Petersburg and for the renovation of the Central Lunatic Asylum.[63] These developments, which included repealing the poll tax, went a long way toward enhancing the black-Readjuster alliance. The result of the 1881–82 legislative session was an increase in the number of black people serving in the state legislature to fifteen for the 1882–83 legislative year.[64] Black people began to demand more representation. They threatened to boycott "discriminatory merchants" in Petersburg, and they took over municipal government in Danville.[65] In Richmond and Petersburg, they demanded black teachers for black schools, and with the aid of Readjuster governor William Cameron, they got them.[66] Mahone also began to reject racialized rhetoric by the early fall of 1883 and called for full integration of the machine.[67] So by 1883, it seemed that black men in Virginia were being included in the political process on the same footing as white men. More significantly, Mahone viewed the churches as the primary vehicle through which to increase his engagement of black voters. The canvassing of black ministers continued the revolution begun in 1881.[68] In this circumstance, Mahone turned to the black churches of the state to advance the political party. In so doing, he illustrated the impressive power of these church networks, which knew so much about themselves when he and the party knew so little.

Mahone's canvass was like seventh-century Japanese fudoki books, in which people in each region of the country were to list all the locations, names, and characteristics of the region, and to do so in hierarchical order, from the largest political unit to the smallest. These fudoki books were efforts of the state to map itself, only in narrative form, and took the form of lists.[69] Mahone's canvass books along with his requests to his campaign operatives mimicked this idea, in that he often required certain kinds of information about people to be referred—upstanding, party supporters, without alcohol issues—and he also required them from the various counties. Mahone attempted to map the potential universe of his political power through lists, and he tried to turn those lists into Readjuster territory. Party operatives—canvassers and county chairmen—also wrote of their spaces in these terms, mapping the boundaries of the party's influence and noting where the Readjusters were strong and where they lacked support.

On March 24, 1883, Mahone sent a circular letter to the county chairmen in the state requesting that they gather and send to him "a list . . . of the colored churches in [the] county and the full names of all the colored preachers and the Post office address of each."[70] It appears that Mahone had gotten the message, sent some years earlier, about the need and benefit of organizing through the black churches.[71] Perhaps the canvass also represented a more systematic way of mobilizing black voters despite having already garnered their increasing support in the 1879 and 1881 elections. Moreover, many of the political goals that black people sought had been achieved: the whipping post had been abolished; the poll tax repealed; schools established, albeit on a principle of separate but equal; black teachers hired; and black people empaneled on the city school board in Petersburg. One-quarter of Petersburg's teachers were black.[72] Nearly all of the goals of Reconstruction, save land reform, had been accomplished in the scant few years of Readjuster leadership.

Perhaps the suggestion that churches be organized for the Readjusters began to resonate with Mahone as he contemplated the success of Ross Hamilton of Mecklenburg County, who had held office for fourteen consecutive years, beginning in 1869.[73] As Harold Forsythe suggests, it was the church networks that allowed Hamilton to win office so handily and so frequently until 1883. Mahone's move was strategic, but the execution of his canvassing of black ministers revealed how far outside the loop he and the party were. The reports returned by the county chairmen revealed that they had little knowledge of black voters as members of black churches.

While the majority of the respondents replied with lists and little commentary, a few indicated some of what they had to go through in order to obtain the requested information. Some had difficulty gathering the information, as J. P. Schermerhorn of Richmond reported. Apparently, he had to ask black people in the city who their preachers were, and he exasperatedly reported that "no one scarcely knew who their preacher was & some churches have got near ½ Doz."[74] Still other churches failed to respond to the county chairmen's inquiries regarding "organized name[s]," leaving the chairmen to provide what little information they could of what they deemed to be "leading col'd churches and preachers in the Co."[75] Others clearly had to ask for the information and reported difficulties in gathering the information as well.[76] W. E. Craig of Staunton made one of the latest dated replies to Mahone's request. He apologized for the delay in responding but noted that it had taken him a while to gather the requested information. Amendments, like Henry Wale's addition of two more churches to his report, followed the initial reports as new informants provided additional information.[77] Still others had trouble gathering all the names and promised updates with more information.[78]

These expeditions forced the Readjuster Party chairmen to encounter and dialogue with black people in a way that they might not otherwise, as suggested by Schermerhorn's difficulties in gathering clear information about the churches in Richmond. To be sure, some of the respondents, like J. A. Tankensby of Bedford County, were "personally acquainted with most of the [colored] preachers."[79] Still, other county chairmen provided more detailed accounts of the churches, including numbers of male members or membership generally.[80] V. Jainer of Greensville County not only provided the list of "colored Baptist churches & pastors in Greensville County" but also included membership numbers. He noted at the bottom of his response that [Rev.] E. Royalls was "very prominent & highly influential." Guy Powell, who pastored two churches in the county and served in the state house and senate during the previous six years, was already known to Mahone.[81] C. Lane, pastor of two churches in the county, was, by Jainer's estimation, "young—but growing."[82] Jainer perceived that the real request was for information about networks, not just lists of names.

The reports reveal the view of black religion from the perspective of white political organizers. In some counties, there were preachers without churches.[83] Conversely, there were also churches without preachers.[84] In other counties, some preachers pastored more than one congregation, and sometimes they pastored churches in different counties.[85] In a few of the counties, there were either no black churches or the black people remained members of the predominantly white churches and denominations.[86] Recognizing the idiosyncrasies of black religious institutions could have had some bearing on how the white political organizers used this information. At the very least, they would have had to know if a minister had a church in one county but pastored a congregation in another county or city, where their sphere of influence would likely have extended. John R. White of Portsmouth was keen enough to note which churches had the largest memberships. Through their work, the chairmen ascertained the purpose of gathering this information, leading them to include not just preachers and churches but also people influential in the black community or who had other notable characteristics, such as John Bell in Fairfax, who was "Editor of 'Plain Truth,'" according to respondent Job Hawxhurst.[87] Some of the county chairmen showed themselves to be quite savvy and informed about the black churches (or at least more adept at gathering the information). One county chairman simply sent the statistics page of the church convention for the county.[88] The statistics page listed the names of the churches, their pastors' names, post offices, numbers of members, and other miscellaneous data. This is the best example of how organized black churches were and how much Mahone had to learn.

These records provide insight into how Mahone and his committee leaders sought to educate themselves about black political networks and how those networks might be mapped onto the religious networks of churches and even conventions. Although it appears that Mahone never directly used the information from this canvass in the 1883 election campaign, it likely informed his and his committee members' understanding of the reality of black political networks in a more concrete and tangible way.[89] The churches had built impressive administrative and social networks, with meeting halls that served as polling places and campaign headquarters and that involved both men and women.[90] Through these canvasses, churches, leaders, and their networks became visible. Mahone and his committee members could see that the networks crossed counties and encompassed large numbers of black people, who were also voters. Examining the pages from reports of the existing church conventions, they could deduce just how formidable black religious organizations already were.

In the same year as the 1883 canvass, Mahone opposed Ross Hamilton's reelection to the Virginia House of Delegates. Hamilton, of Mecklenburg County, was ultimately the longest-serving black politician in postemancipation Virginia, holding his seat from 1869 to 1889 save for three years: 1883, 1885, and 1887.[91] Hamilton's career suggests just how robust the church-based political networks were. Harold Forsythe argues that in addition to the other agencies of political engagement, like the Republican Party and the Union League, churches provided organization for such support. He notes that Hamilton was closely affiliated with the Boydton Academic and Bible Institute, a Baptist educational institution in Mecklenburg County.[92] In 1883, Mahone favored Amos A. Dodson for Hamilton's seat.[93] Perhaps Mahone was interested in mobilizing the black churches in order to undermine what had been pretty staunch support of Hamilton by Mecklenburg County black people. His efforts were unnecessary, however, because black people turned against Hamilton, and he was not reelected. The significance of these networks and the information-gathering expeditions becomes even clearer when Mahone's reports are contrasted with the reports of the Baptist and RZUA conventions for 1883.

The VBSC held its 1883 meeting in May at the First African Baptist Church of Richmond.[94] Henry Williams Jr. of Petersburg, the convention's statistician, made a record of church statistics and published them in the minutes. His report included specific information on the numbers of "Colored Baptists in the United States so far as Reported, 1882," from which VBSC members would have seen that only Georgia, North Carolina, and Mississippi had more Baptist churches than Virginia (with 578). Virginia reportedly had the most Baptist Church members, with just over 128,000, out of the report's accounts of twenty-one states and the District of Columbia.[95] Statistician Williams qualified his report by noting that some associations did not report their information for the year 1882 and that there were still some black people and black churches that were members of white associations.

Beyond reflecting the broad regional and national scope of the black Baptists, the convention minutes also revealed granular details about Virginia. The VBSC minutes recorded information for black Baptist churches in thirty-three counties. Lists of life members and annual members showed that they came from thirty-four different cities, Washington, DC, and New York.[96] The VBSC's reach encompassed a broad swath of counties in the state, and its networks were profound, as reflected in the delegates sent to other conventions in the state and beyond. The convention sent delegates to twenty-four different associations throughout Virginia, Maryland, Tennessee, and New England.[97] Regional conventions also demonstrate the depth of these church-based networks. The Bluestone Colored Baptist Association, for which 1883 minutes are not extant, held its August, 1884 convention with the Bethlehem Baptist Church of Mecklenburg County and its minutes reveal something of the breadth and strength of the networks.[98] They reported churches in five counties as part of their connection, with a total of thirty-six churches and more than seven thousand members. Bluestone members made up 25 percent of the black population in Mecklenburg and Charlotte Counties—a substantial portion.[99] The Bethany Baptist Association's 1882 convention reported churches in thirteen counties and seventeen thousand members.[100] In counties like Dinwiddie (24 percent), Greensville (39 percent), and Southampton (24 percent), BBA members made up a significant portion of the black population and of the total population, too. In fact, black Baptists were as much as 26 percent of the population in Greensville, 13 percent in Dinwiddie, and 14 percent in Southampton.[101] The churches had become expert at tracking their own numbers and members. By contrast, Mahone and his committee members had only superficial information about these networks.

Mapping Black Religion and Politics

Like Mahone, black religious people engaged in mapping the political and religious terrain of Southside, Virginia, in such a way that laid their spiritual networks over the political topography of the state. Maps of the conventions, canvasses, and election results underscore two important points about black religious politics in the era of the Readjuster movement. First, the maps, because of their ability to illustrate comparisons and thus relationships, show how religious folks' epistemology of community superseded the information gathering efforts of the Readjuster party operatives in 1883. Relatedly, religious networks made applying for patronage an appealing tactic for black church people. Second, these maps of the changing electoral support for the Readjusters and the VBSC promote greater understanding of political diversity among black Baptists and problematize premature or facile conclusions about black religious political engagement. For example, the maps suggest that Readjuster electoral success did not coincide with VBSC networks. Instead, these maps show that through their letters and convention journals, black Baptists intimated their "spatial imaginary"—their shared image of the landscape of their community.[102] In their copious listings of names and locations on petitions, in letters, and in the annual journals of the associations and conventions, black religious folks reinscribed the landscape with new boundaries and new geographies of belonging.

Map 5.1 illustrates this process of marking the landscape with community boundaries built on convention, petition, and letter networks, laid over the imprint of Mahone's canvass. While at first blush it appears that Mahone's canvass yielded a more comprehensive list—including both Baptist and Methodist churches—in a broad area including the Southside and Valley regions, the overlapping and reinforcing networks of the Baptist regional and state associations and conventions no doubt created a more robust epistemology of community for the Baptists. The convergences of the annual meetings of the associations and the exchanges of delegates and minutes allowed for more cross-pollination of ideas. This is especially true given that the conventions' geographic reach did not change during these years. Delegates from the same counties and many of the same churches attended these meetings. These regular meetings reinforced the sense of shared community ideas. Further, the fact that the regional associations tended to meet in August—at the start of canvassing season—makes speculating about these gatherings increasing black voter participation irresistible. A closer look at the minutes of the associations reveals that it was these connections that allowed black people to cultivate political community across geographic, regional, and political boundaries that fostered a politics of engagement.

In addition to the repetition of meetings reinforcing the network, the journals the associations printed and circulated were key tools for establishing

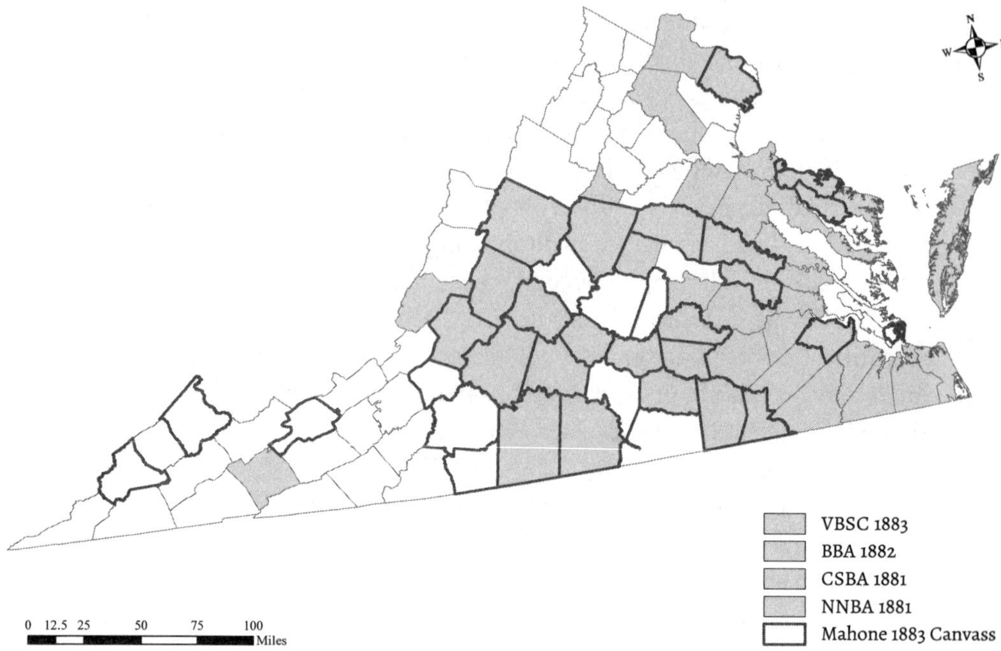

MAP 5.1 Comparative map of conventions and Mahone canvass, c. 1883. An interactive version can be found in the Fulcrum edition.

epistemology of community because of their content and because of their uses. The petitions for patronage from black Virginians from different counties rested on the cross-county alliances revealed in their data logs of churches, pastors, post-office addresses, and other information. From the start of the conventions, the recording secretary and later the statistical secretary kept a record of all the churches that sent delegates. These delegates usually came bearing a letter from the church clerk. Initially, these letters were read aloud, and if the records of the RZUA Church are any indication, the letters provided information about the status of the church's growth in membership, baptisms, purchases of property, and—for the successful church—cancellations of church debt. As time went on, the secretaries started printing a form in the convention journals to give churches a template for what information to provide and so the information could be easily cataloged in the journal. These journals were important identification tools for community members, because any delegates with their name printed in the journal could take their copy to another association's meeting and be seated—or recognized as a nonvoting participant. The different associations regularly printed hundreds of copies of the minutes for distribution to the churches, to delegates, and to other associations as a record of their own actions. In this way, they were able to share the developments within their bounds and learn about developments in other associations in the state and beyond. The use to which they put this data about who belonged to their community also allowed them to honor their evangelical mission of spreading the gospel to places, counties, and churches not yet included in their association. This focus was particularly evident in the VBSC's minutes, in which the statistician, who recorded the growing numbers of Baptists by race and geography from year to year, regularly followed the developments in other counties. In so doing, he showed not only where Baptist presence was strong but also where there was room for growth. Without examining the convention minutes from other states, I cannot say for certain that the distinct understanding and self-representation as "black Virginia Baptists" was unique, but it certainly was salient in the concern for the growth of the denomination among black people in the state. Their sense of community belonging was marked by racial and denominational terms and rooted in the spatial territory of the counties over which they laid their own convention and associational community boundaries.

Between 1879 and 1883, black Baptist churches from across the state—but especially in the Central, Tidewater, and Southside regions—sent information or delegates to the state and regional meetings in May and August of those years. By contrast, William Mahone's canvass yielded a snapshot of information about the existence of leaders of a few hundred Baptist and Methodist churches but little else. While knowing who these people were and how to reach them was an important part of political canvassing and turning out voters—some scholars have suggested he used this information and his later canvass to pay poll taxes to ensure black votes—the data points alone were weak compared to the dense network and interactions that the convention meetings represented. One simply cannot substitute canvass data for interaction and exchange and the cultivation of ideas and community that those networks represent. A sampling of the key issues in the conventions during those years attest to the ways community was built around shared ideas, experiences, and expectations about accountability, which did not always mean falling in lockstep, but instead meant supporting autonomy for churches and ministers.

In 1879, the Norfolk Union Baptist Church met August 14–17 at the Union Baptist Church in Northampton County, Virginia. One of the two major issues in the association at this time was the adoption of a resolution to reject participation in excursions and parades on Sundays, because those activities were viewed as unbecoming for the men and women of the community. A second resolution abolished the association playing a role in mediating conflicts between churches on the grounds that Baptist churches are independent, with no oversight agencies. This move might have removed a layer of accountability and exchange, but the sinews of connection remained very much intact by the presence of delegates from other regional associations, including Rev. Richard Wells from the VBSC. Wells was recognized and invited to have a nonvoting seat in the meeting. When one of the ministers who was scheduled to preach did not show up, Wells was recruited to preach in his stead.[103] This instance underscores how the associations sustained exchanges even though they rejected formal oversight bodies.

The Colored Shiloh Baptist Association met August 10–14, 1881, at the Zion Baptist Church in Portsmouth, Virginia. Among the regular business of the gathering, the attendees discussed several times the death of Elder E. G. Corprew, who had been a key figure in the convention for many years, and they strategized around the ways to memorialize the life of such a stalwart leader—whether by tombstone or worshipful meeting at his graveside.[104] They also offered up prayers for the U.S. president, James Garfield, who had been shot in an assassination attempt. In their resolution, they stated that they "earnestly sympathize with him in his condition and also with his family in their distress and anxieties"—circumstances that a people who had witnessed attempts to use violence to disrupt the everyday functions of their lives and their organizations in the immediate postemancipation period could understand. They sent a copy of the resolution to the secretary of state, James G. Blaine.[105]

In 1882, the Bethany Baptist Association met at Cool Spring Baptist Church, where they engaged in the work of establishing relationships between their churches. They posited that there should be districts, so that there could be meetings more frequently than once per year. They outlined the rules, duties, and responsibilities of ministers, deacons, and church members.[106] This relatively new association was doing the work of establishing the guidelines and boundaries for their work together. Laying a firm foundation was an important endeavor in the midst of the more complicated racial, political landscape in which they were operating.

While the canvass and VBSC maps show the ways black church associations fostered an epistemology of community that proved useful for political engagement, the changing maps of electoral results during the Readjuster era, along with the fairly stable VBSC map, invite reflection on how the

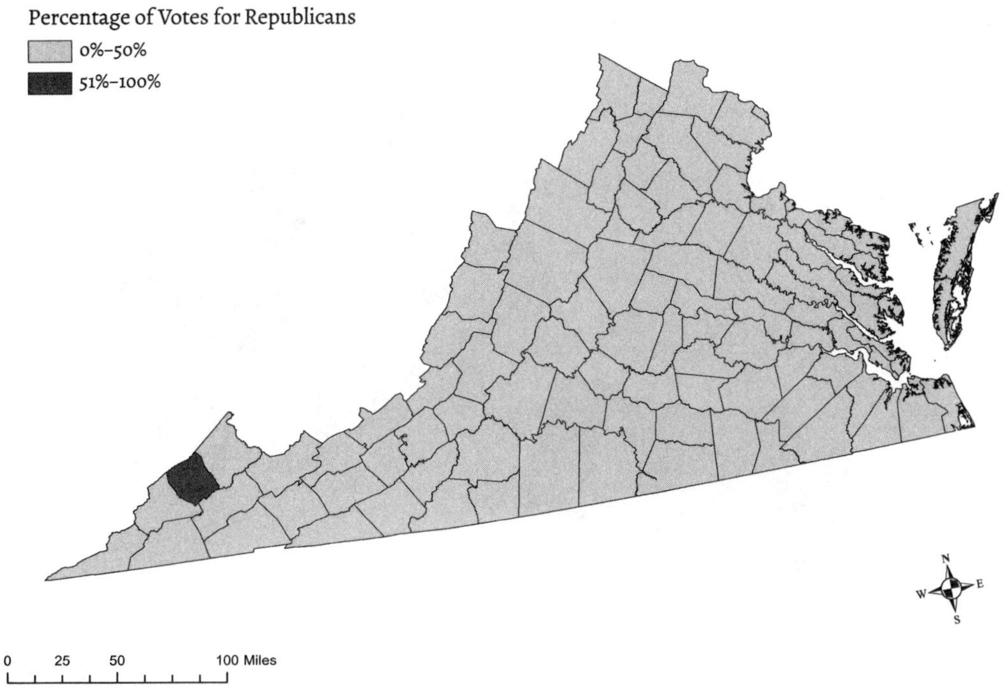

MAP 5.2 Map of 1877 gubernatorial election results. The Virginia Baptist State Convention of 1877 (outlined in white) did not encompass many of the very few counties that went strongly for Republicans in the 1877 gubernatorial election. Republicans and Readjusters had their work cut out for them in turning more of the state toward their goals. An interactive version of this map can be found in the Fulcrum edition. Sources: ICPSR; United States Historical Election Returns, 1824–1968 [computer file]; Minutes of the Virginia Baptist State Convention, 1879.

conventions might have influenced the political landscape. While the networks activated through patronage requests have uncanny resemblances to the cross-county networks encompassed in the associations, these networks do not predict political allegiances. Instead, an examination of the maps of the election results from 1877 to 1885, with the outline of the VBSC's network laid on top, raises intriguing questions about the relationship between religious associations and political outcomes even as it supports interpretation of the political efficacy of the religious networks in regard to patronage.

In 1877, the Virginia Baptist State Convention had the greatest representation from counties in the Southside, Tidewater, Northern, and Valley regions, but there was not a lot of support for the Republican Party in those areas or anywhere else. This was the period when the Republican Party lost

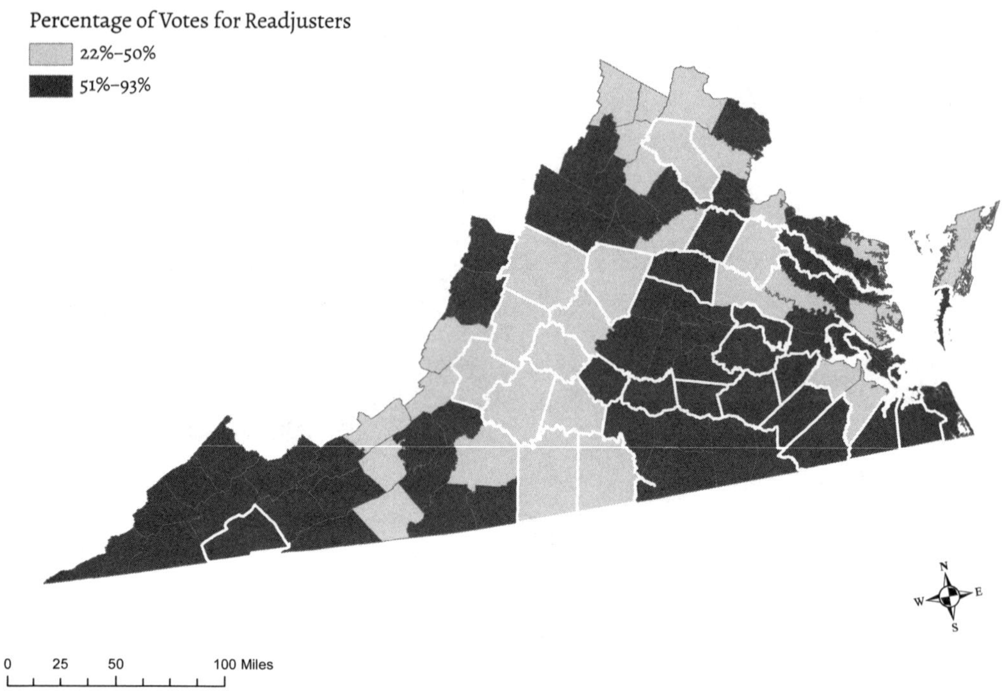

MAP 5.3 Map of 1881 gubernatorial election results. An interactive version of this map can be found in the Fulcrum edition. Sources: ICPSR; United States Historical Election Returns, 1824–1968 [computer file]; church data gathered from convention minutes.

its center of organization and subsequently its bases of support. Only two of the four counties that had strong support for the Republicans (Albemarle and Culpeper Counties in the northern part of the state) had churches that were part of the VBSC.

By 1881, when Readjuster gubernatorial candidate William C. Cameron won election to the post, support for the Readjusters varied among the counties that had churches represented at the VBSC. Levels of support seemed to vary according to region. The heaviest support was in the Tidewater, Central, and Southside regions, and in the western part of the state. In the Valley, Readjuster support was lowest. The Readjusters drew heavy support in the Southside counties of Mecklenburg, Brunswick, Greensville, and Lunenburg, but these counties were not represented at the VBSC that year. By contrast, several counties in the western part of the state supported the Readjusters and some churches from the region sent representation to the VBSC meeting. Of the thirty-two counties represented at the VBSC in 1881, just over half supported the Readjusters. This pattern suggests that there was not much correlation between the reach of the state convention and Readjuster support. Instead, the regional associations correlated with the highest levels of support that the Readjusters received. These differences illustrate that black Baptists were not monolithic in their political allegiances even as their networks reinforced participation.

As the 1885 gubernatorial election approached, the Readjuster coalition was falling apart and black religious politics started to reflect more of the racial critique of political processes. Some of the associations took an explicit stance against political involvement of ministers. Meanwhile, black antifusionist sentiments that had emerged early in the Readjuster movement gained greater support as terrorist violence in Danville suppressed black voter turnout and as the Readjusters doubled down on policies aimed at restricting black political freedom.

The minutes of the Bluestone Colored Baptist Association and the Bethany Baptist Association during this time suggest that there was a heavy political contest in the region and the ministers decided to stay out of it. Both associations passed resolutions that ministers would stay out of politics. At the 1885 BBA meeting held September 23–25 in Petersburg at the Gilfield Baptist Church, attendee M. Walker asked if it was right for ministers of the gospel to participate actively in political matters. The resolution passed in response to the query posited that because it was "currently reported that colored ministers of Virginia are easily and readily 'brought up' in political matters, therefore, Resolved, that we disapprove of ministers of the gospel taking an active part in politics, such often thereby causing dissensions in the church."[107]

However, the map suggests something that is also evident in the political record of the newspapers and in the minutes of the conventions. Perhaps it was the growing sense of racial identification and political efficacy that the association gatherings fostered that led to diminished support for the Readjusters. The discussions in the associations reinforced, reiterated, and expressed members' desire to have black teachers for black schools and training for black leaders to run black organizations that served the black community. The Readjuster Party had just come around to supporting the political goals that African American people put forward. In March 1881, black Petersburg residents who opposed the Readjusters called for an end to the poll tax, an end to the whipping post, and the maintenance of free schools—all policies that the Readjusters had come to embrace. Among the signers of the statement published in the newspaper was C. W. Tinsley and one hundred others, who were straight-out Republicans and who opposed fusionist alliances with Democrats.[108] The discussions about black political participation

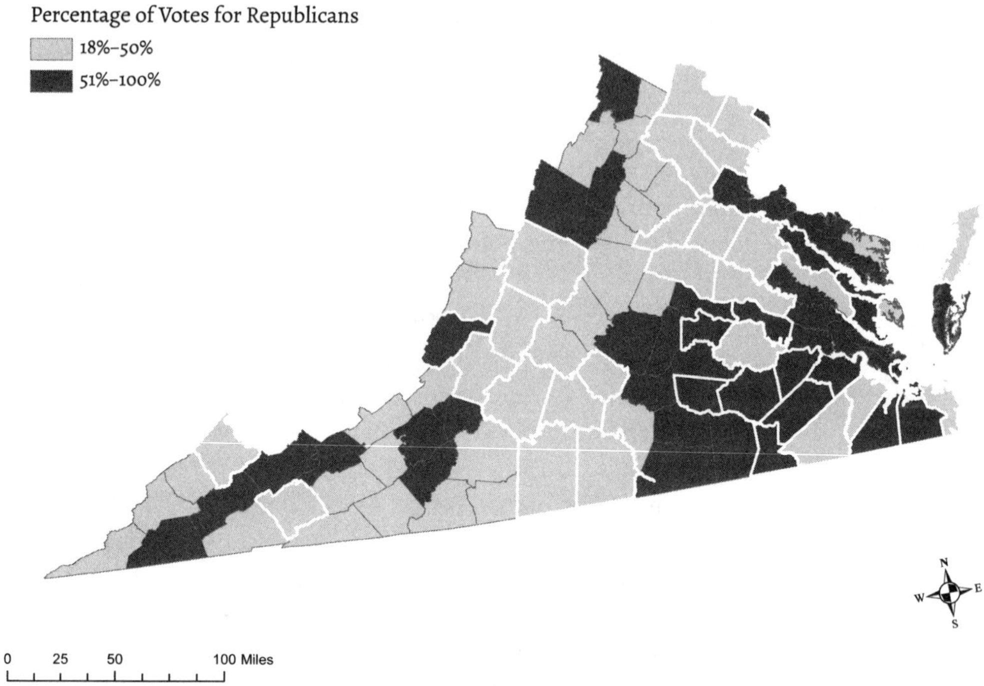

MAP 5.4 Map of 1885 gubernatorial election results. By 1885, when the Readjusters lost control of the legislature, most of the VBSC counties remained lukewarm supporters of the Republican-Readjuster ticket. An interactive version of this map can be found in the Fulcrum edition. Sources: ICPSR; United States Historical Election Returns, 1824–1968 [computer file]; Minutes of the Virginia Baptist State Convention, 1885.

that developed over the decade of the 1880s presented black people's political status as being subordinated on the basis of race, and it was. Their experiences running organizations, administering and teaching schools, funding and growing missionary and other endeavors, all confirmed the necessary acumen or skill to participate in politics at every level, but the Readjuster leadership tried to relegate them to state-level officeholding, effectively barring them from holding federal office.

By 1885, when the Readjusters lost the governor's post, the VBSC continued to have strong representation in the Tidewater and Valley regions of the state, with Southside excluded. Churches from Mecklenburg, Brunswick, and Lunenburg Counties never sent delegates to the the VBSC meeting during these years. However, Rev. Henry Williams, who was the statistician for both the BBA and the VBSC, attended all the meetings. In this way, Williams served as a connector between the associations so that they were not isolated. At the same time, the tendency for churches to send delegates to the regional but not the state association meetings reinforced the regional sensibilities reflected in the voting patterns. The Southside counties continued to demonstrate strong support for the Readjusters, while support weakened in most other parts of the state. The maps not only suggest the levels of support that the Readjusters gained from black voters throughout the state, but also the maps affirm the spatial imaginary of black Virginians, who saw themselves as members of individual churches and of regional and statewide communities.

At the same time that the Baptist regional and state meetings reinforced a statewide sense of black Baptist identity, the internal discussions about putting boundaries on the conventions reinforced the sense of the geography of belonging by setting literal geographic boundaries—refusing to admit North Carolina churches, for example—and doctrinal boundaries—rejecting the "Howellism" of the RZUA Church and any practices deemed to be not "baptistic."[109] These declarations illustrate that black religious identity was not monolithic. Along with these differences of geography and epistemology, the churches differed in their practices of interracial cooperation. Black Baptist Virginians like the Black Episcopalians regularly negotiated with fellow white believers in their denominations, though the Baptists generally did this from the positions of leadership in their own churches and organizations, while the Episcopalians did this as members of white churches or separate black churches but still united within the diocese. By contrast, the RZUA and AME churches were much more independent and had less formal mechanisms for interracial cooperation than their Baptist and Episcopalian counterparts. Consequently, while there was neither a monolithic black religious identity nor a monolithic interracial experience, the traditions of interracial cooperation that did exist fed into black Readjusterism and subsequent debates about black political allegiances along color lines.

Geographies of Belonging and Epistemologies of Community Converge in Black Religious Politics

In the Readjuster era, the black church conventions evinced the final evolution of a black religious politics that built on the networks of the black conventions and the overlapping use of political networks. It was best reflected in black people's efforts to secure black teachers for black schools and children and the election campaign of John Mercer Langston. In 1881, the

Education Committee of the VBSC enjoined its members not to send their children to any schools that did not employ black teachers. By 1882, this boycott turned into an active mobilization for black teachers, as Rev. Anthony Binga announced at the annual meeting. The discussion about increasing black representation in black schools replaced earlier injunctions against sending children to pedobaptist Sunday schools, which had previously consumed the convention attendees' attention.[110] These announcements acknowledged the struggle for black education and the political pressure that black people were putting on the cities of Petersburg and Richmond to hire black teachers.[111]

In this moment, black religious politics emerged in the form that captured the political power of black religious networks and their potential import for the political landscape. This organizing was met with the political violence that sought to undermine not just the Readjuster alliance but also the black religious political power-brokering that was crystallizing. The Danville massacre that preceded the 1883 election effectively stymied black participation in that election, and many Readjusters failed to secure offices. But the sense of the political efficacy of black networks and the desire for increased participation in politics and autonomous black leadership was not squelched. The VBSC began executing plans to establish an independent school at Lynchburg, an institution that would bring to light the vision of black teachers and administrators for black children. By the time John Mercer Langston began organizing to run for office in 1887 at the request of black voters in Prince Edward County, the notion that black people were prepared and ready to hold any office to which they aspired had thoroughly suffused convention discussions about education and the Lynchburg seminary. Many of the VBSC members were poised to break from the patronage of their white benefactors in the American Baptist Home Mission Society and likewise that of their political allies, the Readjusters. In Langston's campaign, the strength of black religious community's networks and knowledge of the same were visible.

In 1888, John Mercer Langston sought the office of U.S. Congressman for Virginia's majority-black Fourth Congressional District. Langston reported that he was asked to run by black voters in Farmville, Prince Edward County, at a meeting in September 1887.[112] He was strongly supported by black voters in Petersburg, as evidenced by the testimonies in the contested election hearings. He organized an effective campaign and poll-watching outfit, but he ultimately lost. Up the ballot, Benjamin Harrison and Levi Morton lost Virginia by 537 votes but beat incumbent U.S. president Grover Cleveland.[113] When the Democratic contender E. C. Venable was announced as the winner of the congressional election, Langston contested the results. He hired a team of lawyers, including former Readjuster governor William Cameron, to present his case to the Congressional Committee on Contested Elections. The committee completed its investigation and report in June 1889, but the congressional hearing was held up until September 1889. The Democrats used the filibuster tactic of refusing to show up for a vote so that a quorum could not be reached and Langston could not take office. Eventually the Republicans called all their members back to Washington in order to achieve a quorum. Having the majority afforded them the opportunity to do this.[114] For sixteen days Langston waited while Congress held hearings; finally, they voted to seat him on September 23, 1889.[115] While the story most often told is one of political gamesmanship, I put forward an alternative interpretation. This moment evidenced the strength of black political mobilization by black churches and the supporting discourses around race pride that were emerging in many locations—church conventions not the least of these.

Langston's 1888 election bid for Congress illustrated how knowledge of church-based networks could be used for political ends, but not in the ways we might expect. The connectedness of the church people and the broad-based support that churches and their leaders reflected informed the political project but were not deployed as simple political tools of the sort that would try to use a visit to a church as a means to secure black votes. The ways church networks operated was more nuanced than this. First, Langston's organizing network was robust, and a church member was a central part of the apparatus. Langston's poll-watching outfit was very well organized in the First and Sixth Wards of Petersburg, where many of the Gilfield Baptist Church members lived. One of Langston's main organizers in Petersburg was Gilfield church member J. A. C. Stevens. Stevens had been president of the Baptist schools in Petersburg for the previous five years and had held a number of roles in the Knights of Pythias and elected office as justice of the peace.[116] Over the course of nine days, Stevens testified before the congressional committee on Langston's behalf about the work he did to support the campaign. Stevens served as a poll watcher and was at the polls from sunup to sundown. While there, he recorded the names of all the voters who turned out for Langston. He read these names into the record as part of his testimony.[117]

He knew voters' selections as a consequence of the efforts to stymie black voter participation. The Democratically aligned election officials tried to hinder black voting by separating the voters into two separate lines—one for black voters and one for white voters. This caused a much slower voting process for the more numerous black voters, such that just under half of them did not get to vote before the polls closed.[118] It also produced an environment where the poll watchers were able to keep an eye on the process: Langston supporters called out that they had cast their vote, and the poll watcher recorded their names and counted their votes.[119] Through Stevens's report, Langston was able to obtain at the very least an accurate count of the number of black men who voted and a close if not exact count of the number of votes he received. This is the evidence that poll watcher J. A. C. Stevens provided.[120]

Second, Langston's broad-based network included black women who were stalwart figures not just in churches but also in politics. Langston's report of a critique made by a Mahone supporter who testified before the congressional committee actually shows Langston's political skill. Perhaps that is why Langston summarized these claims at some length in his autobiography.[121] The informant claimed that the young people did not know their history and so were willing to support Langston. Presumably the alternative would have been to honor the biracial coalition with the Readjusters. Some black folks knew their history all too well. They had risen out of the shackled limitations of slavery and political exclusion; their right was to hold office and to represent their own interests in the highest seats of government. Being prohibited from holding office on the basis of race was antidemocratic, and acknowledging this informed their pursuit of soul liberty. The conventions served as dramatic emphasis of this point. In his autobiography, Langston paraphrased the Mahone-supporting Republican who tried to characterize Langston's campaign as ill-informed and working outside the bounds of what was proper. Essentially this individual reprised the white supremacist arguments about black political incompetence evident in distorted depictions of black political participation as "Negro domination." He testified that Langston was able to stir up black voters by canvassing before the party had gotten started, by telling black people that they had the numerical advantage, and by galvanizing women, stirring them into religious fervor. However, parsing through this critique, we can see some of Langston's political genius, his independence, and his political networks. Efficacy is in the eye of the beholder. Langston used this testimony, which was offered to undermine his credibility, to actually underscore his effectiveness. Langston was organizing voters before Mahone had even begun to think about it. Langston worked with old and young people, and with men and women, while Mahone focused on ministers.

Though the informant tried to pathologize Langston's voter mobilization techniques by diminishing the women's participation as an expression of religious frenzy, Langston recognized the important supporting role that many black women played in political participation. Elsa Barkley Brown has argued that black women saw the vote as a communal property and importantly "voted" with their bodily presence in political hearings and conventions and in accompanying their men to the polls, often acting as a defensive phalanx armed to defend black male voters.[122] Langston affirmed that black women were also facilitators of black male participation. Far from frenzied support, daughters and wives provided cool-headed assistance to their male counterparts who were unable to read. They also played the role of enforcers of political choices. Langston writes that if a voter, "by reason of his ignorance or want of understanding, as to his duties on the premises, needed help, he was promptly aided by his more intelligent wife or daughter."[123]

Third, Langston drew his support from churches, but not in the ways that many seemed to expect. Though ministers were important figures in Langston's campaign, they were not the centerpieces. It is well known that black churches enforced Republican Party loyalty on ministers and members by ostracizing or expelling any who did not support the party.[124] In most cases, it was the congregation that wielded the power. One newspaper account obliquely supports this idea. The *Galveston Daily News* reported on the September 1888 Republican District Convention in which party leader William Mahone tried to limit Langston's delegates to thirty-one of the eighty-five positions. The black convention attendees rejected Mahone's move and separated into their own convention, where they unanimously nominated Langston.[125] While the black convention took place, Mahone held one in which he articulated his position that black people were not ready to hold national office.[126] The *Galveston Daily News* opined, "The Langston convention was by far the superior of the other and among its delegates were ten Negro preachers. The tone of their speeches was of strong defiance to Mahone, who was repudiated as a tyrant and condemned for his alleged recourse to the most fraudulent devices and systematic cheating. The general sentiment was that the negroes were redeeming themselves from political serfdom."[127] Though the *Daily News* made special note of the ten ministers who were very vocal Langston supporters, they did not identify the ministers by name.

It was not just significant that the ministers supported Langston, one contemporary observed. The ministers were Republicans because their members were.[128] The ministers represented the people's inclinations more than the political power of an individual leader. Like the eleven Howard University students who sought a patronage appointment for their professor, the ministers represented the will of the people, a population more numerous than the ten individuals at the convention. Given the growing strength of the conventions by this point, it is not too much to consider that those ten ministers represented a broader network of black ministers, churches, and church members in the Baptist associations—a network that encompassed the Fourth District and beyond. The mention of the ministers reflects again how onlookers might mistake the ministers as the central figures, when they were really couriers for the community's political will because they were generally referenced, but the many church members who were likely present and participants, individuals like J. A. C. Stevens and Richard Kennard, were not identified as church members. The fact that they were unnamed gave power to the position rather than to the communities they represented. Beyond editorial expediency, omitting the names of the ten ministers furthers a process of hiding the influence that hundreds of church members had and that made it possible for those ten ministers to be present. Identification of the ministers by name would signify the strength of the ministers in the political process. However, it is possible that Henry Williams Jr. or C. B. W. Gordon, pastors of two of Petersburg's largest churches, were among that number. Langston thanks Williams in his autobiography.[129] Though Gilfield church member and clerk Richard Kennard reported that he did not hear about the campaign in church, the overlap of religious community and political engagement is apparent.

LANGSTON'S SUPPORT FROM THE CHURCHES is not as apparent in the historical record. I located no headlines screaming that black churches gave Langston the election or that testimony from church operatives clinched the deal. In fact, at the death of Rev. Henry Williams Jr., one newspaper asserted that Williams did not engage in politics despite the fact that he briefly held political office early in his tenure as pastor of Gilfield Baptist Church and was a noted supporter of the controversial election bid of John Mercer Langston. Perhaps it was not the fact of his political service but the sentiment that there should be a separation between religion and politics that the article highlighted. Such a statement again evidenced how political church conventions were and how much they inculcated a political sensibility even if they did not explicitly engage in political discourse. However, in brief mentions of the involvement of church members and in the testimonies of individuals in the contested election hearing, the important networked supporting role that black churches played is evident. Langston's broad-based campaign is further evidence. He masterfully carried the premise of biracial political coalitions to its logical conclusion—that denying black people opportunities for political leadership based on race was inconsistent with the ideal of having free and fair elections in which any one qualified could run and in which voters could vote for whomever they pleased.[130] This political interpretation rested on decades of empirical evidence to support the claim and echoed the principle of soul liberty that black church people sought. Langston's aim to uphold these principles succeeded because of the ways church networks dug into and across communities. Mahone's subsequent canvassing of black churches in 1889 in order to test the waters for his own gubernatorial bid reinforces the sense of the organizing capacity of black churches.[131]

A generation after slavery ended, black churches were still mediating political engagement, but differently than they had immediately after emancipation. They shifted from being representations of black political acumen to being vehicles for participation and for self-determination. The way black people thought about their networks was influenced and enhanced by their very palpable sense of connection, fostered through church networks and annual meetings. Upon such a foundation, black people—one-third of Virginia's population and even more in some counties—could have confidence in advancing their own political aims and even, as James Tice Moore suggests, influencing white politicians like Mahone and the Readjusters to shift their policies.[132]

In this frame, the fact that the record book in which Mahone recorded the results of his 1889 canvass of black churches has, on the flip side, the results of a canvass of former Confederate soldiers appears more remarkable.[133] His strategy of building an interracial coalition of black people and former Confederates is striking. But I submit that the story of Mahone's black church canvasses in 1883 and again in 1889, as a response to the many instances of black cross-county political alliances that culminated in Langston's successful election, codifies the political significance of black church conventions and constitutes the final moment of the postemancipation evolution of black churches: the emergence of the church with the soul of a nation, built on the strength of its church networks.

Conclusion

Politically engaged black churches have a history, and Virginia's postemancipation story is just a small contribution to the narrative. Black Virginians' transition to freedom encompasses many facets of the experience that informed and influenced the development of black religious institutions. From land disputes and the place of women in congregations and conventions, to interracial cooperation, the establishment of educational institutions, and political participation, there was a dynamic exchange between the religious community and electoral politics. Pursuing soul liberty became the practice of political participation when it had once been a rhetorical and ideological battle against slavery and the dehumanization of black people. As Reconstruction unfurled, it placed demands on the nascent black church, causing a paradigm shift in the scope and practice of black church communities. Being the only stable black institution in the North and South, and intimately connecting white and black people, black churches shouldered a lot of the political transition to freedom. The church was a nexus between so many aspects of life—intraracial, interregional, interracial, and gender dynamics—it is a wonder it did not implode under the weight of all these competing forces. Instead, it evolved. Thus, this study has attempted to chronicle the evolution of black religious institutions, giving due attention to the social and political context, in order to capture the contingency of the moment and the results.

Churches and conventions rooted in the project of defining freedom and supporting black attempts to participate in American democracy became fragmented in their approaches once suffrage was obtained and the political terrain became more complicated. Friends and foes were no longer easily distinguished. Race, an important facet of religion, became an even more pronounced aspect of political negotiation and maneuvering. The attention to race and political alliances that the Readjuster movement and its demise drew made churches' political positioning all the more precarious.

The congressional candidacies of Joseph Evans in 1884 and John Mercer Langston in 1888 showed how much more complicated the intersection of religion and politics on the basis of race had become two decades into full-fledged freedom and political participation. Joseph Evans's unsuccessful run for the House of Representatives was the precursor to the successful if highly and hotly contested election of John Mercer Langston as U.S. congressman for Virginia's Fourth Congressional District. Opposed by Mahone in much the same way that Evans was, Langston used his considerable economic means to subvert Mahone's opposition, which had explicitly turned toward keeping black people out of federal positions.[1] Langston had enough money to purchase his own hall in Petersburg, where black people could regularly come to hear him speak. Thus, he could present his views without fear of being shouted down or otherwise kept from addressing the people, as would have been possible in other public political gatherings. And when Election Day came and Republicans and Democrats resorted to fraud to steal the election from him, Langston had enough means to hire a legal team to press his claims to the congressional seat. Langston became Virginia's first black congressman in 1890, and served only a few months before his term ended. There would not be another black congressman from the state for over one hundred years.[2]

Langston's triumph has been read as the result of racial politics; black people "drew the color line" and insisted on black officeholding even at the expense of what had been a fruitful interracial political coalition with Readjusters. What lingers within this turnabout, however, was the role of churches in securing Langston's victory. In reflecting on his victory, Langston thanked many ministers for their support, among them Rev. Henry Williams of Petersburg. On the one hand, some of these ministers went on to highlight their roles in successfully organizing people in 1888 when they shifted their support to Mahone during his 1889 gubernatorial campaign. On the other hand, some ministers vehemently opposed Langston's "drawing the color line."[3] Black churches were, as they had become during the Readjuster period, diverse in their political positioning and strategies.

In this moment, when the stakes of maintaining racial progress and recently secured advancements seemed high—and to some, those of pursuing further black political advancement seemed even higher—black churches became more than sites of inspiration and purveyors of messages of liberation; they became agents. Churches squeezed their broad missions of salvation, healing, and inspiration into the narrower goals of political significance and participation. They used the networks that drew them together as a religious community to influence the political machine and to make recognition of black humanity and democratic participation real.

Not only did these churches become complex prophetic agents as they facilitated political participation, but the ideas they supported were complicated and diverse. Perhaps the greatest evidence of the evolution of the practice of achieving soul liberty as prophetic activity is how black church conventions became mechanisms for political organizing. Initially operating under the model of the antebellum abolitionist church organization and the sense that unity in numbers was a strength, the conventions became the tools for pushing the political levers of change. Church leaders and members became constituents and agents for political party influence. Political operatives did not use them as the few letters in Mahone's collection might suggest. These black church agents had roots in bigger networks. They debated how involved in politics they should become, because the ethics of the political machine did not match the ethics of the church. Such considerations underscore how securing soul liberty included communal responsibility as a core value. Yet this value did not mean there was no conflict. Aided by the absence of a secret ballot for a while, churches enforced political positions on their constituents. The stakes were incredibly high, then, too. To be cut off from community meant a lack of cover in a variety of social and general life circumstances. Some democratic principles, such as support for a free and independent vote, did not translate well into the spiritual and communal norms of black churches, making Gilfield Baptist Church's chastisement of Henry Woodley for wantonly wielding his vote understandable (see chapter 3). But using the church to enforce political allegiances by running Democrat-supporting ministers out of their pulpits and members out of the pews did not reinforce biblical principles and undermined some of the very democratic ideals black people sought to achieve in the political arena.[4]

There was also the issue of race. Black people who were still struggling to define and secure recognition of their humanity were concerned about more than securing political office for black people or maintaining interracial alliances. Black people in the Episcopal Church met efforts by white bishops and clergy gathered at the 1884 Sewanee Conference to limit black access to leadership with resolve and fortitude.[5] Their struggle to have black people treated on equal footing in the church would continue for at least sixty more years. Meanwhile, the RZUA Church went its own way, separating from the Episcopal Church, and black Baptists split over whether to maintain their interracial alliance with white Baptists. Many members of the VBSC pursued a separatist path, convinced that the only way to secure black progress was through black independence, while a new organization of black Baptists—the Baptist General Association of Virginia—opted to remain affiliated. These approaches occurred along with white people's struggle to accept the reality of interracial religious polities. In this context, then, looking at religious institutions adds a much-needed dimension to understanding the "unfinished" elements of Reconstruction. By examining the extent to which these interracial negotiations within religious communities paralleled and even reinforced the interracial dynamics of politics, the causes of the breakdown in interracial coalitions appear more and clearly.[6]

With pressures placed on black religious institutions to navigate electoral politics and the cultural racial politics of emancipation, leadership was certainly an important element in the transition. But having men in leadership roles and as ministers did not mean that the power and meaning of those roles were not negotiated and refined according to the contingencies of the time. Pursuing soul liberty was limited in the realm of gender dynamics. Soul liberty when pursued in the electoral context had the unfortunate consequence of gendering ministerial leadership as male. This was due to the necessary negotiations between biblical and political norms and the pursuit of resources and political recognition. In addition to carving out ministry as a place for manhood to be expressed, establishing women's place was part of that construction as well, with women ultimately being placed in the ranks of teachers, fund-raisers, and community supporters. More remarkably, the occlusion of women's roles in political endeavors of the Readjuster movement demonstrates a limitation in Mahone's reliance on ministers to build alliances. He completely neglected black women, who proved to be key agents in facilitating and guiding black men's political participation. Meanwhile, the segmentation of women's roles within the denominations to finance and education (and not preaching or missionary work) reinforced their political exclusion even as it forced open new pathways for female leadership development in social organizations and in separate women's conventions.[7]

Through this project, I have endeavored to present a history of the postemancipation black churches of Virginia by following and chronicling the changes in mission, scope, and focus of the churches and conventions. This study did not presuppose political power and instead has depicted the contexts in which such political power could have and sometimes did arise. Churches and conventions certainly supported black suffrage, equal access to education, educational opportunities for women, and the notion that black teachers should teach black students. But their power to effect change largely resided in their communal nature and at once made them powerful and vulnerable institutions.

APPENDIX I

Black Politicians and Religious Affiliations, 1865–1890

TABLE 1 Black politicians and religious affiliations, 1865–1890

	Name	County	Occupation	Church Affiliation	Office Held
Politicians with Clear Religious Affiliation					
1	Cain, David W.	Petersburg	Storekeeper	Episcopalian	Virginia Black Convention, 1865
2	Carter, James W.	Petersburg	Contractor, carpenter		Petersburg City Council, School Board, Deputy Internal Revenue Collector, 1872–1874
3	Cook, Fields	Richmond	Barber, minister	Baptist	Grand Jury of U.S. Circuit Court, Richmond, 1867
4	Davis, Cephas L.	Mecklenburg	Minister, teacher	Baptist	Virginia Senate, 1879
5	Dawson, John M.	Williamsburg	Minister	Baptist	Williamsburg Common Council, 1874–1877
6	Dungee, Shed	Cumberland	Shoemaker, farmer, preacher		Virginia House of Delegates, 1879
7	Edwards, Ballard T.	Manchester, Chesterfield	Contractor, mason, teacher	Baptist	House of Delegates, 1869–1871; Virginia Black Convention, 1865; Overseer of the Poor, Justice of the Peace, Assistant Postmaster at Manchester
8	Munford, Edward	Petersburg	Storekeeper, laborer	Baptist	Petersburg City Council, 1872–1874
9	Powell, Guy	Brunswick	Preacher	Baptist	Virginia Senate, 1875–1878; Virginia House of Delegates, 1881–882
10	Shore, John K.	Petersburg	Barber	Baptist	Petersburg City Council, 1872–1874
11	Stevens, Christopher B.	Petersburg	Contractor	Baptist	Petersburg City Council, 1872–1874
12	Toler, Burwell	Hanover	Laborer, minister, carpenter	Baptist	Constitutional Convention, 1867–1868

13	Vandervall, Nelson	Richmond	Plasterer, storekeeper, minister	Baptist	Richmond City Council, 1873–1878, 1882
14	Williams, Jr., Henry	Petersburg	Minister	Baptist	Petersburg City Council, 1872–1874
Politicians with Possible Family Connections to Religious Associations					
15	Evans, Joseph P.	Petersburg	Minister, shoemaker		Virginia House of Delegates, 1871–1873
16	Hodges, Charles E.	Norfolk, Portsmouth	Minister	N/A	Virginia House of Delegates, 1869–1871
17	Hodges, William J.	Norfolk	Teacher, minister	N/A	Township supervisor, 1870; Superintendent of the Poor in Norfolk County
18	Holmes, James M. B.	Petersburg	Storekeeper	N/A	Petersburg City Council, 1872–1874
19	Morgan, Peter G.	Petersburg	Storekeeper, shoemaker	Episcopalian	Constitutional Convention, 1867–1868; Virginia House of Delegates, 1872–1874; Petersburg City Council
20	Moseley, William	Goochland	Farmer, boatman	N/A	Constitutional Convention, 1867–1868; Virginia Senate, 1869–1871
21	Stevens, J. A. C.	Petersburg	N/A	Baptist	Justice of the Peace
22	Stevens, William N.	Petersburg	Lawyer	Baptist	Virginia Senate, 1871–1878, 1881–1882
Politicians Whose Religious Affiliations Have Not Been Established					
23	Barrett, James D.	Fluvanna	Minister		Constitutional Convention, 1867–1868
24	Bayne, Thomas	Norfolk City	Minister	Wesleyan Methodist	Constitutional Convention, 1867–1868
25	Delaney, McDowell	Amelia	Minister	Baptist	Virginia House of Delegates, 1871–1873

(*continued*)

TABLE 1 (*continued*)

	Name	*County*	*Occupation*	*Church Affiliation*	*Office Held*
26	Dungee, Jesse W.	King William	Minister, shoemaker	N/A	Virginia House of Delegates, 1871–1873
27	Hodges, Willis A.	Norfolk, Princess Anne	Minister, farmer, editor	N/A	Constitutional Convention, 1867–1868
28	Moss, Francis (Frank)	Buckingham	Minister, farmer	N/A	Constitutional Convention, 1867–1868; Virginia Senate, 1869–1871; Virginia House of Delegates, 1874–1875
29	Patterson, William H.	Charles City	Minister	N/A	Virginia House of Delegates, 1871–1873
30	Peake, Thomas	Hampton, Elizabeth City	Minister	Baptist	Superintendent of the Poor
31	Perkins, Caesar	Buckingham	Minister	N/A	Virginia House of Delegates, 1869–1871, 1887–1888
32	Perkins, Fountain M.	Louisa	Minister	Baptist	Virginia House of Delegates, 1869–1871
33	Riddick, John	Cumberland	Minister, teacher, laborer	AME	Richmond City Council, 1872–1873
34	Willis	Dinwiddie	Minister, farmer	N/A	Virginia House of Delegates, 1869–1871

Sources: Jackson, *Negro Office-Holders*; Jackson, *Free Negro Labor*; Bratton, "Fields's Observations"; Lowe, *Republicans and Reconstruction*; Rachleff, *Black Labor in the South*; O'Brien, *Reconstruction in Richmond*; Dailey, *Before Jim Crow*; Moore, "Black Militancy in Readjuster Virginia"; Lowe, "Virginia's Reconstruction Convention"; Manuscript U.S. Census, 1870; Foner, *Freedom's Lawmakers*; Rabinowitz, *Race Relations*; *Dictionary of Virginia Biography*; Henderson, *Unredeemed City*; Taylor, *Negro in the Reconstruction of Virginia*, 1926.

APPENDIX II

Baptist Association Membership and Churches

Note: These tables offer a rough approximation of what portion of the black community was part of these Baptist associations during the 1880s. The total number of church members were reported by individual churches and recorded in the association minutes. The total black population is drawn from only those counties from which there were churches recorded in the association minutes. The percentage of the population that the Baptist association members made up in any given year is just an initial indicator of the churches' influence, as achieving membership status in a church had stricter requirements than being affiliated.

TABLE 2A Bethany Baptist Association (BBA)

	1882	*1885*	*1886*	*1887*	*1888*	*1889*
Number of Churches	66	75	73	77	78	80
Number of Church Members	17,252	18,696	20,026	19,873	20,561	22,471
Total Black Population in Related Counties (1880)	113,036	113,036	113,036	113,036	113,036	113,036
Percent of Black Population in Related Counties (1880)	15%	17%	18%	18%	18%	20%

Sources: "Minutes of the . . . Bethany Baptist Association . . . 1882, 1885–1889"; Historical Census Browser, University of Virginia, Geospatial and Statistical Data Center, accessed 30 April 2013, http://mapserver.lib.virginia.edu/index.html.

TABLE 2B Bluestone (Colored) Baptist Association (BCBA)

	1880	1884	1885	1886	1887	1888
Number of Churches	4	36	36	36	35	35
Number of Church Members	N/A	7,856	7,645	7,746	8,420	7,802
Total Black Population in Related Counties (1880)	39,188	49,102	49,102	49,102	49,102	49,102
Percent of Black Population in Related Counties (1880)	N/A	16%	16%	16%	17%	16%

Sources: U.S. Census 1880; "Minutes of the . . . Bluestone Baptist Association, 1880, 1884–1888"; Historical Census Browser, University of Virginia, Geospatial and Statistical Data Center, accessed 30 April 2013, http://mapserver.lib.virginia.edu/index.html.

TABLE 2C (Colored) Shiloh Baptist Association (CSBA)

	1881	1884	1885	1889
Number of Churches	94	101	96	75
Number of Church Members	32,640	37,824	32,180	N/A
Total Black Population in Related Counties (1880)	220,648	220,275	186,871	160,081
Percent of Black Population in Related Counties	15%	17%	17%	N/A

Sources: "Minutes of the . . . Shiloh Baptist Association, 1881, 1884, 1885, 1889"; Historical Census Browser, University of Virginia, Geospatial and Statistical Data Center, accessed 30 April 2013, http://mapserver.lib.virginia.edu/index.html.

TABLE 2D Virginia Baptist State Convention (VBSC)

	1880	*1881*	*1882*	*1883*	*1884*	*1885*	*1886*	*1887*	*1888*	*1889*
Number of Churches	78	76	73	82	102	101	90	88	87	91
Number of Church Members	44,437	40,741	42,177	47,912	51,991	54,416	38,314	36,304	39,641	45,532
Total Black Population in Related Counties (1880)	348,708	339,808	333,330	369,408	387,088	368,677	331,255	344,756	350,856	355,292
Percent of Black Population in Related Counties	13%	12%	13%	13%	13%	15%	12%	11%	12%	13%

Sources: "Minutes of the Virginia Baptist State Convention . . . 1880–1889"; Historical Census Browser, University of Virginia, Geospatial and Statistical Data Center, accessed 30 April 2013, http://mapserver.lib.virginia.edu/index.html.

Notes

Introduction

1. Petersburg Common Council Minutes, July 1, 1872 and November 1, 1872. Petersburg Council Record, Petersburg City Hall, Petersburg, VA.

2. Scholars of black religion concerned themselves with various aspects of the role of black churches in the lives of their constituents. Sociologists like W. E. B. Du Bois in the early 1900s and Benjamin E. Mays and Joseph Nicholson in the 1930s were extremely critical of the proliferation of black churches. Historian Carter G. Woodson was, however, judicious in his discussion of the political activism or lack of it among black ministers. Circumstances pushed some ministers into politics while others were able to stay completely out of the political realm, he explained. Context prevented oversimplified characterizations, though the concerns and critiques were legitimate. By the 1960s, however, critiques of black church activism grew more acerbic, with black religion being characterized as an "opiate" and the "otherworldly" aspects of spirituals being generalized to all of black religion. E. Franklin Frazier was the most influential proponent of the opiate idea, while Gary Marx was the more contentious. According to psychologist Jacqueline Mattis, the Frazier and Marx studies had the limitations of flattening the historical context and limiting the understanding of politics. Du Bois, *Negro Church*, 81, 85–86; Mays and Nicholson, *The Negro's Church*, 209–10, 12; Woodson, *History of the Negro Church*, 221–22; Frazier, *Negro Church in America*, 19–23; Marx, "Religion"; Mattis, "Religion and African American Political Life," 267. For more recent examinations of churches and politics, see Harris, *Something Within*; Savage, *Your Spirits Walk Beside Us*; Harper, *End of Days*. For discussion of complicating narratives of black religious history, see Young, "African Religions in the Early South."

3. For a more comprehensive discussion of these early generations of scholarship on black religion, see Savage, *Your Spirits Walk Beside Us*, chaps. 1–2.

4. Higginbotham, *Righteous Discontent*, 16. For discussion of this dialectic, see Lincoln and Mamiya, *Black Church in the African American Experience*, 222–23. Elsa Barkley Brown offers a thoughtful exposition of the transformation from political engagement to withdrawal in Richmond, Virginia. Brown, "Negotiating and Transforming the Black Public Sphere."

5. Frazier, *Negro Church in America*; Marx, "Religion"; Lincoln and Mamiya, *Black Church in the African American Experience*, 12–13, 23, 201; Wilmore, *Black Religion and Black Radicalism*, 268.

6. For more discussion of the relationship between black religious institutions and politics, see Paris, *Social Teaching of the Black Churches*.

7. For studies that incorporate ministers into the political context, see Du Bois, *Negro Church*; Woodson, *History of the Negro Church*; Montgomery, *Under Their Own Vine and Fig Tree*; Foner, *Reconstruction*; Hahn, *Nation under Our Feet*; Forsythe, "'But My Friends Are Poor'"; Frazier, *Negro Church in America*, chap. 3; Taylor, *Negro in the Reconstruction of Virginia*, 194.

8. See Appendix 1.

9. Hahn, *Roots of Southern Populism*, 6.

10. Scott, *Domination and the Arts of Resistance*; Kelley, "'We Are Not What We Seem'"; Kelley, *Race Rebels*; Hahn, *Nation under Our Feet*. One notable study of postemancipation political activities among black people is Berry, *My Face Is Black Is True*.

11. One example of the misdirection that black people continued to engage in after emancipation comes from Mary Allan-Olney, an Englishwoman living on a farm outside Lynchburg, Virginia, in the 1870s. Allan-Olney noted how difficult it was to interpret her black servants. When she asked them if they were ever beaten, they would smile and tell her no—responses that perplexed her and made her question if they were being honest. I discuss the transitions in labor, land, and education in the chapters that follow. Allan-Olney, *The New Virginians*, vol. 1. For discussions of the labor transition, see Hahn et al., *Freedom*. For discussions of the education transition, see Green, *Educational Reconstruction*; Williams, *Self-Taught*; James D. Anderson, *Education of Blacks in the South*; Woodson, *Miseducation of the Negro*.

12. Kolchin, *Sphinx on the American Land*, 94; Hildebrand, *Times Were Strange and Stirring*, xix–xxi.

13. For studies that depict freedpeople as dupes, see Morton, "Negro in Virginia Politics." For studies that depict freedpeople as naive, see Du Bois, *Black Reconstruction in America*; Taylor, *Negro in the Reconstruction of Virginia*.

14. Edmund Morgan demonstrates how central slavery was to the construction of American freedom. Reconstruction undid all that. Morgan, *American Slavery, American Freedom*.

15. James Tice Moore argues that the movement's roots lay in urban professionals rather than rural farmers. Moore, *Two Paths to the New South*, 45–46.

16. For the clearest and most concise account of the Readjuster movement, see Moore, *Two Paths to the New South*. For an updated and insightful analysis of the Readjuster movement's evolution, see Dailey, *Before Jim Crow*. For a studied approach to the intricacies of the debt legislation, see Pearson, *Readjuster Movement in Virginia*. On Readjuster policy, see Pearson, *Readjuster Movement in Virginia*, 127–28. On the Readjuster movement generally, see Morton, "Negro in Virginia Politics"; Taylor, *Negro in the Reconstruction of Virginia*; Wynes, *Race Relations in Virginia*, 6–15; Moger, *Virginia Bourbonism to Byrd*, 21–46; Pulley, *Old Virginia Restored*; Dailey, *Before Jim Crow*, 15–47; Hahn, *Nation under Our Feet*, 374–411.

17. For the Dunning School interpretation, see Morton, "Negro in Virginia Politics"; Pearson, *Readjuster Movement in Virginia*. For responses to the Dunning School interpretation, see Taylor, *Negro in the Reconstruction of Virginia*, 279; Du Bois, *Black Reconstruction in America*, 546; Hahn, *Nation under Our Feet*, 237–49.

18. For discussion of antebellum networks, see Errol A. Anderson, "Slave Religion, Slave Hiring"; Hahn, *Nation under Our Feet*, 33–43.

19. Lincoln and Mamiya, *Black Church in the African American Experience*, 206.

20. Kelley, *Race Rebels*, 36, 38–39; Lincoln and Mamiya, *Black Church in the African American Experience*, 99.

21. Floyd-Thomas, *Liberating Black Church History*, 45–46, 56. On black churches as a public sphere where ideas are exchanged, see Higginbotham, *Righteous Discontent*, chap. 1.

22. Sherwood, *Life of Charles B. W. Gordon*, 44–45.

23. For an extended discussion of the process of this CME church's formation, see Dvorak, *African-American Exodus*. For an institutional history of the Reformed ZUA Church, see General Education Board of the R.Z.U.A. Church, *History of the Reformed Zion Union Apostolic Churches of America*.

24. Collier-Thomas, *Jesus, Jobs and Justice*; Martha S. Jones, *All Bound Up Together*; Martha S. Jones, "'Make Us a Power'"; Braude, "Women's History Is American Religious History."

25. Orsi, "'He Keeps Me Going.'"

26. On the power of the purse held by women and church members generally, see Paul Harvey, *Redeeming the South*. On women's power of the vote within the church, see Elsa Barkley Brown, "Negotiating and Transforming the Public Sphere." On women in other spaces, see Higginbotham, *Righteous Discontent*; Butler, *Women in the Church of God in Christ*.

27. White, *Ar'n't I a Woman?*; Camp, *Closer to Freedom*; Jennifer L. Morgan, *Laboring Women*.

28. Elsa Barkley Brown, "'What Has Happened Here.'"

29. On positivist, masculinist, and objectivist epistemological underpinnings of GIS technology, see Pavlovskaya and St. Martin, "Feminism and Geographic Information Systems"; Crampton and Krygier, "Introduction to Critical Cartography"; Vincent Brown, "Mapping a Slave Revolt"; Yuan, McIntosh, and Delozier, "GIS as a Narrative Generation Platform"; Perry, *Vexy Thing*, chap. 6.

30. Brown and Kimball, "Mapping the Terrain of Black Richmond."

31. Pavlovskaya and St. Martin, "Feminism and Geographic Information Systems," 9.

32. For a discussion of the idea of historical consciousness and engagement, see Trachtenberg, "Unsung Heroes." For more discussion of how maps convey information and represent knowledge production, see Pavlovskaya and St. Martin, "Feminism and Geographic Information Systems."

33. Trachtenberg, "Unsung Heroes," 10.

34. On the development of the feminist subject, see Pavlovskaya and St. Martin, "Feminism and Geographic Information Systems," 6–7. For an example of how black people created their own communities and the debates about reflecting the communities as black people conceived them versus the way white city council members constructed them, see Brown and Kimball, "Mapping the Terrain of Black Richmond," 316.

35. I borrow this very eloquent way of relating a part to a whole in the realm of southern political development from Matthew Karp, who applied it to the much different political context of antebellum slave owners' foreign policy. Karp, "'This Vast Southern Empire."

Chapter One

1. Luther Porter Jackson, *Short History of the Gillfield Baptist Church*, 16.

2. Jeremiah R. V. Thomas to Maj. Gen. O. O. Howard, October 3, 1865, Records of the Office of the Assistant Commissioner of the State of Virginia, Bureau of Refugees, Freedmen and Abandoned Lands (BRFAL), Subordinate Field Offices, Letters and Orders Received, 1865–1869, Series 4180 [Freedmen and Southern Society Project (FSSP) A-7946].

I thank Leslie Rowland and the editorial staff for allowing me to use the Freedmen and Southern Society Project's files to get my bearings in the voluminous Freedmen's Bureau records. In accordance with the project's wishes, I include the project's file numbers in my citations, hereafter enclosed in brackets.

3. Charles E. Johnson to A. S. Flagg, Asst. Superintendent 2nd District, October 26, 1865, Records of the Office of the Assistant Commissioner of the State of Virginia, BRFAL, Subordinate Field Offices, Letters and Orders Received, 1865–1869, Series 4180 [FSSP A-7946].

4. Clarence E. Walker, *Rock in a Weary Land*, 84–85.

5. Charles E. Johnson to A. S. Flagg, October 26, 1865, Records of the Assistant Commissioner of the State of Virginia, BRFAL, Subordinate Field Offices, Letters and Orders Received, 1865–1869, Series 4180 [FSSP A-7946].

6. Emberton, *Beyond Redemption*, 77; Hahn et al., *Freedom*, 25; Penningroth, *Claims of Kinfolk*, chap. 2.

7. Mary Farmer-Kaiser, *Freedwomen and the Freedmen's Bureau*, 2.

8. On the intersections of race and religion, see Evans, *Burden of Black Religion*; Glaude, *African American Religion*, chap. 1.

9. Hahn, *Nation under Our Feet*, 48; Genovese, *Roll, Jordan, Roll*, 48, 284; Raboteau, *Slave Religion*, 331.

10. Camp, *Closer to Freedom*, 6–7. On enslaved women and movement, see Bell, "Self-Emancipating Women."

11. Eugene Genovese first articulated the notion that enslaved people identified with the people who owned them in Genovese, *Roll, Jordan, Roll*, 133–49.

12. Dvorak, *African-American Exodus*, 85 [quote], 118.

13. Sobel, *Trabelin' On*, 181–84; Raboteau, *Slave Religion*, 138.

14. Boles, *Masters and Slaves in the Household of the Lord*, 5.

15. *Unwritten History of Slavery*, 23–25, 81; Camp, *Closer to Freedom*, chap. 1; Creel, *"Peculiar People,"* 277.

16. Genovese, *Roll, Jordan, Roll*, 232, 35–36.

17. Camp, *Closer to Freedom*, 25–26.

18. Raboteau, *Slave Religion*, 232, 38–39.

19. Elizabeth, *Elizabeth, a Colored Minister of the Gospel*, 4–5; Perdue, Barden, and Phillips, *Weevils in the Wheat*, 55, 71, 99.

20. Perdue, Barden, and Phillips, *Weevils in the Wheat*, 55; Rachleff, *Black Labor in the South*, 8.

21. *Inventory of the Church Archives of Virginia*, iv–v.

22. *Unwritten History of Slavery*, 23, 150–51; Boles, *Masters and Slaves in the House of the Lord*, 10.

23. Bailey, *Down in the Valley*, 54. For an insightful discussion of the uses of the idea of religious freedom, see Wenger, *Religious Freedom.*

24. Julius Bailey suggests that it was both racism and denominational concern that prompted these separations. Bailey, *Down in the Valley*, 56.

25. Richard Allen, *Life, Experience, and Gospel Labours*, 16.

26. See, for example, Douglass, *Narrative of the Life of Frederick Douglass*, 77.

27. Blassingame, *Slave Testimony*, 411 [quote], 20, 35.

28. Harding, "Religion and Resistance," 114.

29. Luther Porter Jackson, *Short History of the Gillfield Baptist Church*, 5; Raboteau, *Slave Religion*, 142.

30. Luther Porter Jackson, *Short History of the Gillfield Baptist Church*, 11.

31. Luther Porter Jackson, *Short History of the Gillfield Baptist Church*, 17.

32. Bailey, *Down in the Valley*, 59.

33. Luther Porter Jackson, *Short History of the Gillfield Baptist Church*, 6.

34. On antebellum independent black churches, see Raboteau, *Slave Religion*, 138–42; Sobel, *Trabelin' On*; Bailey, *Down in the Valley*, chap. 3; Frey and Wood, *Come Shouting to Zion*; George, *Segregated Sabbaths*; Smith, *Climbing Jacob's Ladder*; Washington, *Frustrated Fellowship.*

35. First Baptist Church (Petersburg) had a similar pattern of leadership. It formed in the late eighteenth century and had black pastors until Nat Turner's rebellion, after which all of its pastors were white. Sherwood, *Life of Charles B. W. Gordon*, 52–53.

36. Sobel, *Trabelin' On*, 206.

37. On laws pertaining to independent black religious gatherings, see *Inventory of the Church Archives of Virginia*, v–vi.

38. Luther Porter Jackson, *Short History of the Gillfield Baptist Church*, 7.

39. Luther Porter Jackson, *Short History of the Gillfield Baptist Church*, 8.

40. Johnson, "A Tribute to the Rev. Henry Williams, D.D.," 41; Kennard, *Short History of the Gilfield Baptist Church*, 19.

41. Kennard, *Short History of the Gilfield Baptist Church*, 19; Luther Porter Jackson, *Short History of the Gillfield Baptist Church*, 18.

42. This point has been debated between the different early chroniclers of the church's history. Barnes, *Artisan Workers in the Upper South*, 133, 74.

43. Henderson, *Unredeemed City*, 85.

44. Martin, "Vindicated Faith."

45. Charles Irons and Beth Barton Schweiger push back against the notion that evangelical Christianity of the antebellum era was such a "handmaiden." Irons, *Origins of Proslavery Christianity*, 14; Schweiger, *Gospel Working Up*, 5.

46. Carole Emberton asserts that many freedpeople gathered in the cities, where there was strength and protection in numbers. Emberton, *Beyond Redemption*, chap. 3.

47. Shattuck, *Episcopalians and Race*, 8; Paul Harvey, *Through the Storm*, 69; Montgomery, *Under Their Own Vine and Fig Tree*, 42, 52.

48. Montgomery, *Under Their Own Vine and Fig Tree*, 59–73.

49. Harold T. Lewis points out that C. Eric Lincoln and Lawrence Mamiya, in their landmark sociological study of African American religion, omit discussion of black Episcopalians and other black people in predominantly white denominations. This is the trend in the study of black religious experience and deserves to be challenged. Lewis, *Yet with a Steady Beat*; Bailey, *Down in the Valley*, chap. 3.

50. Henderson, *Unredeemed City*, 85.

51. Perdue, Barden, and Phillips, *Weevils in the Wheat*, 39, 186; Levin, "William Mahone," 382.

52. Perdue, Barden, and Phillips, *Weevils in the Wheat*, 16, 32, 78, 129, 328.

53. "Accurate Early History of St. Stephens Church," 1, Carrie Bragg Campbell Papers, box 1, VSU.

54. "Accurate Early History of St. Stephens Church," 2, Campbell Papers, box 1, VSU.

55. Shattuck, *Episcopalians and Race*, 18.

56. See, for example, Dvorak, *African-American Exodus*; Bailey, *Down in the Valley*. A major corrective of this approach is Jualynne E. Dodson, *Engendering Church*.

57. Hahn, *Nation under Our Feet*, 48.

58. Gilmore, *Gender and Jim Crow*, 62–64.

59. For a discussion of narratives around black ministers, see Bailey, *Around the Family Altar*; Maffly-Kipp, *Setting Down the Sacred Past*, 3–4.

60. "Church History," 3, RZUA Papers, box 1, folder 2, VSU.

61. "Church History," 3, RZUA Papers, box 1, folder 2, VSU.

62. Allen notes that Howell's fundamentalism was also an impediment to his rise in the congregation. I follow what I believe is a narrative written by Rev. James Oliver Allen and published as part of RZUA Church history. General Education Board of the R.Z.U.A. Church, *History of the Reformed Zion Union Apostolic Churches*. Allen's sources for the early narrative of Howell's life are opaque, and I have not been able to locate Howell in the census.

63. "Church History," 1, RZUA Papers, box 1, folder 2, VSU.

64. "Church History," 1, RZUA Papers, box 1, folder 2, VSU.

65. "Church History," 1–2, RZUA Papers, box 1, folder 2, VSU.

66. "Church History," 3, RZUA Papers, box 1, folder 2, VSU.

67. "Church History," 4, RZUA Papers, box 1, folder 2, VSU.

68. "Church History," 5, RZUA Papers, box 1, folder 2, VSU.

69. "Church History," 15–16, RZUA Papers, box 1, folder 2, VSU; General Education Board of the R.Z.U.A. Church, *History of the Reformed Zion Union Apostolic Churches*, 8.

70. Mitchell, *Righteous Propagation*, 57; Summers, *Manliness and Its Discontents*, 4–5.

71. Corey D. B. Walker, *Noble Fight*, 147; Bailey, *Around the Family Altar*, 37.

72. Bailey, *Around the Family Altar*, 39; Martha S. Jones, *All Bound Up Together*, chaps. 3 and 5.

73. Bailey, *Around the Family Altar*, 39–40.

74. Farmer-Kaiser, *Freedwomen and the Freedmen's Bureau*, 2.

75. Eric Foner, *Reconstruction*, chap. 4.

76. Stewart Barnes to Gen. O. Brown, 11 May 1866, 12 May 1866, Records of the Assistant Commissioner of Virginia, BRFAL, Registered Letters Received, Dec.–May 1869, Series 3798 [FSSP A-7606]; Henderson, *Unredeemed City*, 67.

77. Henderson reported that the Freedmen's Bureau also paid money for the rebuilding of the church. Henderson, *Unredeemed City*. On First Baptist Church, Petersburg, see Sherwood, *Life of Charles B. W. Gordon*, 54.

78. Freedmen's Bureau agent J. W. Sharp reported on white attitudes toward black education. J. W. Sharp to Col. O. Brown, 21 July 1866, Records of the Office of the Assistant Commissioner of Virginia, Reports of Conditions of Bureau Affairs, January 1866–December 1868 [FSSP A-7453]. On violence against churches, see Ryan K. Smith, "Church Fire and Reconstruction."

79. Max Woodhull to Col. O. Brown, 16 April 1866, Records of the Office of the Assistant Commissioner of Virginia, Registered Letters Received, December 1865–May 1869 [FSSP A-7730].

80. Eric Foner, *Reconstruction*, 67–71; Hahn et al., *Freedom*, 201n2, 392–493.

81. Henderson, *Unredeemed City*, 45.

82. J. R. Stone to O. Brown, 27 January 1867, Petersburg Sub-Assistant Commissioner, Registered Letters Received, Vol. 1, A-B, 1866-67, Records of the Field Offices of the State of Virginia, BRFAL, microfilm 1913, roll 152.

83. Kerr-Ritchie, *Freedpeople in the Tobacco South*, 40.

84. Heinemann et al., *Old Dominion, New Commonwealth*, 243.

85. Monthly Report of Lands in the 2d District of Virginia for the Month of July 1866, Bvt. Maj. T. F. P. Crandon, Supt. 2d District VA; Monthly Report of Lands in the 2d Subdistrict VA for the Month of December, 1867, Land Reports, Records of the Field Offices for the State of Virginia, BRFAL, 1865–1872, microfilm 1913, roll 152.

86. Monthly Report of Lands in the 2d Subdistrict VA for the Month of March, 1867, Records of the Field Offices of the State of Virginia, BRFAL, 1865–1872, Land Reports, microfilm 1913, roll 156.

87. J. W. Sharp, Asst. Supt., to Col. O. O. Brown, 21 July 1866, Assistant Commissioner of Virginia, Narrative Reports of Conditions of Bureau Affairs, Jan. 1866–Dec. 1868, Series 3802 [FSSP A-7453].

88. J. W. Sharp, Asst. Supt., to Col. O. O. Brown, 21 July 1866. Assistant Commissioner of Virginia, Narrative Reports of Conditions of Bureau Affairs, Jan. 1866–Dec. 1868, Series 3802 [FSSP A-7453].

89. Henderson notes how unsuited to the work of aiding freedpeople many bureau agents were. Assistant Commissioner Orlando Brown was forced to choose among military officers to staff bureau offices, a selection criterion not attuned to the needs of the people or the position but to the financial administrative needs of the government. Henderson, *Unredeemed City*, 56–57.

90. Anonymous to Freedmen's Bureau, 29 March 1866; Emily Rodney to Gen. O. Brown, 2 April 1866; [J. P.?] Tukey to Bvt. Major W. S. How, AQM & Supt., 9 April 1866, Records of the Office of the Assistant Commissioner of Virginia, BRFAL, Registered Letters Received, December 1865–May 1869 [FSSP A-7707].

91. Kate Masur argues that there was more exchange between the freedpeople and the Freedmen's Bureau agents. Masur, *Example for All the Land*, chap. 2.

92. M. C. Fulton to Brig. Genl. Davis Tilson, 17 Apr. 1866, Unregistered Letters Received, ser. 632, GA Asst. Commissioner, BRFAL [FSSP A-5379]; Berlin and Rowland,

Families and Freedom, 185–87; Lynda J. Morgan, *Emancipation in Virginia's Tobacco Belt*, 192–93.

Chapter Two

1. Bratton, "Fields's Observations."

2. Bratton, "Fields's Observations," 92.

3. This law preventing enslaved people from being taught en masse came into effect after Turner's rebellion. Bratton, "Fields's Observations," 93n18.

4. For a discussion of the roots of the AME and AMEZ denominations as antiracist organizations, see Nash, *Forging Freedom*, 109, 18–19; George, *Segregated Sabbaths*. For a discussion of the independent black Baptist conventions' abolitionist and antiracist roots, see Martin, "Vindicated Faith," 14; Joseph Harris Jackson, *Story of Christian Activism*, 25; Washington, *Frustrated Fellowship*, x, 28. Gayraud Wilmore claims that these independent churches were part of the resistance to the institution of slavery. He writes that while the independent church formation can be interpreted as an expression of enslaved people's desire to have independent worship, "it was in fact a form of rebellion against the most accessible and vulnerable expression of white oppression and institutional racism in the nation: the American churches." Wilmore, *Black Religion and Black Radicalism*, 103.

5. Eric Foner, *Freedom's Lawmakers*; Hucles, "Many Voices, Similar Concerns," 553–54; Bratton, "Fields's Observations."

6. Wallace Shelton, who was a member of the Union Anti-Slavery Baptist Association in Ohio, reported visiting Elder William Troy in Richmond and Henry Williams in Petersburg. "Letter from the . . . ," *Scioto Gazette* (Chillicothe, OH), September 18, 1866. Washington points out that many of the leaders in the CABMC were from Virginia. Washington, *Frustrated Fellowship*, 61.

7. I surmise that this was the start date, since the Norfolk Union Baptist Association (NUBA) held its fifth annual meeting in 1868, the first year for which I have found minutes. "Minutes of the Fifth Annual Meeting of the Norfolk, Virginia, Union Baptist Association."

8. Washington, *Frustrated Fellowship*, 78–79.

9. Edwards, *Gendered Strife and Confusion*. These arguments were revived at the end of the nineteenth century with the advent of Jim Crow laws and practices. Hahn, *Nation under Our Feet*, 431–40.

10. "Minutes of the CSBA, 1865."

11. "Minutes of the CSBA, 1866."

12. "Minutes of the CSBA, 1866," 1.

13. "Minutes of the CSBA, 1865," 5–6.

14. Harper, *End of Days*. On narrative theology see also: Maffly-Kipp, *Setting Down the Sacred Past*.

15. "Minutes of the CSBA, 1865," 6.

16. This name varied. The organization started out as the Colored Shiloh Baptist Association in 1865, but in 1871 became the Shiloh Colored Baptist Association. In 1875, the organization dropped "colored" from its name entirely and became the Shiloh

Baptist Association. For consistency, I refer to it as the Colored Shiloh Baptist Association (CSBA).

17. "Minutes of the CSBA, 1865," 6.

18. "Minutes of the CSBA, 1866," 5.

19. "Minutes of the CSBA, 1866," 6.

20. "Minutes of the CSBA, 1866," 6.

21. "Minutes of the CSBA, 1867," 5–6.

22. Byrd, "Black Republicans, Black Republic," 2, 4; Martha S. Jones, *All Bound Up Together*, chap. 4; Eric Foner, *Reconstruction*.

23. Washington, *Frustrated Fellowship*, 14, 20–21.

24. "Report of the CABMC, 1869," 9.

25. Richard Lowe notes what he considers to be the comparatively mild nature of Virginia's Black Codes. Lowe, *Republicans and Reconstruction*, 46–48. On the return of the government, see 32–35.

26. Reconstruction Act of Thirty-Ninth Congress, "An act to provide for the more efficient government of the rebel states," passed March 2, 1867, in McPherson, *Political History of the United States of America*, 191–92; Du Bois, *Black Reconstruction*, 537.

27. Lowe, *Republicans and Reconstruction*, 70.

28. "Minutes of the CSBA, 1867," 6.

29. Scholars who assert the training ground thesis include Woodson, *History of the Negro Church*; Du Bois, *Black Reconstruction*; Frazier, *Negro Church in America*; Wilmore, *Black Religion and Black Radicalism*; Lincoln and Mamiya, *Black Church in the African American Experience*; Eric Foner, *Reconstruction*; Taylor, *Negro in the Reconstruction of Virginia*; Forsythe, "African American Churches"; Dodson, *Engendering Church*; Barr, *Black Texans*.

30. Corey D. B. Walker, *Noble Fight*, 131–32, 53.

31. Maffly-Kipp, *Setting Down the Sacred Past*, 10.

32. Maffly-Kipp, *Setting Down the Sacred Past*, 8–9.

33. "Report of the CABMC, 1871," 11.

34. "Report of the CABMC, 1871," 7. Roger Williams founded the first Baptist church in 1636 in Rhode Island. By the 1790s, there were Baptist churches in all the states. Du Bois, *Souls of Black Folk*, 18. Washington also begins the story of black Baptists with the early history of the denomination. Washington, *Frustrated Fellowship*, 4.

35. Harold Lewis's study of black Episcopalians hinges on the argument that black people relied on the foundational ecclesiology of the church to argue for their equality. Lewis, *Yet with a Steady Beat*.

36. "Journal of the Proceedings of the CSBA, 1867," 7; "Journal of the Proceedings of the CSBA, 1881," 4; "Minutes of the BBA, 1885," 8.

37. Washington, *Frustrated Fellowship*, 124–27.

38. On Cook's proposals, see "Minutes of the VBSC, 1871," 21; "Minutes of the VBSC, 1873," 13, 15; "Minutes of the VBSC, 1879," 19. For other associations with viva voce voting, see "Minutes of the BCBA, 1871," 3–4; "Minutes of the BCBA, 1884," 3. On the Funders, see Moore, *Two Paths to the New South*, 12–13, 25.

39. Washington notes that freedom was a key concept in the formation of independent churches, and so this made the churches political institutions in and of themselves.

The first independent churches had roots in American Revolutionary ideas, Washington argues. He did not, however, flesh out *how* the formation of the independent churches was political. Washington, *Frustrated Fellowship*, xi, 23.

40. Clarence Walker provides an in-depth discussion of the kind of competition that went on between the various denominations over participation in mission work among the freedpeople. Note that religious institutions were the first to conduct the "rehearsal for reconstruction," and that the Freedmen's Bureau relied on their established infrastructure of education for the freedpeople. Walker, *Rock in a Weary Land*. See also Engs, *Freedom's First Generation*, chap. 2.

41. "Minutes of the CABMC, 1869," 8.

42. "Minutes of the CABMC, 1869," 9.

43. Washington claims that the black Baptist associations began much like the white Baptist associations; the only difference was that the black Baptist associations were all antislavery. Washington, *Frustrated Fellowship*, 28–30.

44. Within the CABMC, there was debate about whether churches and ministers should be involved in politics, and Corresponding Secretary Rufus L. Perry argued that they should. Washington, *Frustrated Fellowship*, 115–22.

45. Much of the literature on gender and reconstruction highlights how perception of masculinity and femininity shaped white attitudes toward black political participation. In particular, Laura Edwards highlights the critique of black gender equality as part of the argument against black political participation. Edwards, *Gendered Strife and Confusion*; Schwalm, *Hard Fight for We*; Dailey, *Before Jim Crow*.

46. "Minutes of the VBSC, 1869," 20.

47. Imhoff, "Manly Missions," 146–48.

48. On gender and mission work see Becker, "Black Church."

49. "Minutes of the VBSC, 1869," 9, 21.

50. "Minutes of the VBSC, 1875," 12; "Minutes of the VBSC, 1878," 13; "Minutes of the VBSC, 1880," 13; "Minutes of the VBSC, 1883," 13.

51. Maggie Lena Walker was a singular woman and salient figure in Richmond and women's benevolent and financial work. She became president of a bank and served as the chief financial officer of First African Baptist Church, Richmond, in the late nineteenth and early twentieth centuries. Elsa Barkley Brown, "Constructing a Life and a Community."

52. "Minutes of the VBSC, 1868"; "Minutes of the VBSC, 1869"; "Minutes of the VBSC, 1870."

53. Higginbotham, *Righteous Discontent*, 161, 69; Collier-Thomas, *Jesus, Jobs and Justice*, 35–41; Montgomery, *Under Their Own Vine and Fig Tree*, 95.

54. On black women's financial circumstances and participation in benevolent associations, see Elsa Barkley Brown, "Constructing a Life and a Community," 29; Hunter, *To 'Joy My Freedom*, chap. 3; Rachleff, *Black Labor in the South*, 17, 20–21. On black women in the convention, see "Minutes of the VBSC, 1870," 11; "Minutes of the BCBA, 1873," 9; "Report of the CABMC, 1877," 33. On the general economic situation, see Hartzell, "Exploration of Freedom in Black Petersburg."

55. "Minutes of the VBSC, 1870," 12–13.

56. Montgomery, *Under Their Own Vine and Fig Tree*, 95.

57. For example: Henry Williams, sermon, 4–5, box 1, folder 18, and note, folder 21, box 1, Rev. Henry Williams Papers, VSU.

58. Gilmore, *Gender and Jim Crow*, xxi, Ch. 6.

59. "Minutes of the BCBA, 1873." James 1:25: "Religion that God our Father accepts as pure and faultless is this: to look after orphans and widows in their distress and to keep oneself from being polluted by the world."

60. "Report of the CABMC, 1877," 4, 22, 25; "Minutes of the CABMC, 1879," 36; "Minutes of the CSBA, 1881," 14.

61. Paul Harvey, *Through the Storm*, 153; Woodson, *History of the Negro Church*, chap. 8.

62. See Appendix I. The list of black politicians was compiled from the following sources: Dailey, *Before Jim Crow*; Eric Foner, *Freedom's Lawmakers*; Luther Porter Jackson, *Negro Office-Holders in Virginia*; Moore, *Two Paths to the New South*. I then cross-referenced the list with lists of members from the conventions, Gilfield Baptist Church, Rev. Henry Williams Papers, and Rev. Giles Buckner Cooke Papers. Though Eric Foner's *Freedom's Lawmakers* summarizes the religious affiliation of the 237 Reconstruction era politicians who were ministers, the study does not provide the names of ministers. Thus, my search has revealed more religiously affiliated politicians than just looking for ordained ministers or men who listed their occupations as ministers in the records would have. In addition to these fourteen, eight other politicians may have had family members who were convention participants.

63. The other religiously affiliated politicians were David W. Cain, James W. Carter, Shed Dungee, Ballard T. Edwards, Christopher B. Stevens, Edward Munford, and John K. Shore.

64. Foner, *Freedom's Lawmakers*, xiv, 252.

65. An autobiography attributed to Fields Cook was donated to the Library of Congress in 1902, but its provenance is unknown. The author never provides his full name, only his first name and that of his wife, Mary. By cross-referencing his birth date, age, general location, and family information, Mary J. Bratton, who provides the head note and analysis of his narrative, surmises that Fields Cook is the author of this narrative. Bratton, "Fields's Observations," 76–78.

66. Bratton, "Fields's Observations," 78.

67. Bratton, "Fields's Observations," 78.

68. Bratton, "Fields's Observations," 78–79.

69. Bratton, "Fields's Observations," 80.

70. Scully, *Religion and the Making of Nat Turner's Virginia*; Heyrman, *Southern Cross*, 223–24.

71. Bratton, "Fields's Observations," 80, 81.

72. Bratton, "Fields's Observations," 81.

73. Hahn, *Nation under Our Feet*, 111–15.

74. On commemorative practice and space, see Clark, *Defining Moments*; Kachun, *Festivals of Freedom*; Blight, *Race and Reunion*; Brown and Kimball, "Mapping the Terrain of Black Richmond."

75. "Meeting in Richmond, VA," *Christian Recorder*, April 29, 1865.

76. Brown and Kimball, "Mapping the Terrain of Black Richmond," 312.

77. "The Colored People's National Monument, to the Memory of Abraham Lincoln," *Christian Recorder*, July 15, 1865.

78. Rev. H. H. Garnett was the president of the association. Other notable members of the association included Rev. Leonard A. Grimes of Boston; Frederick Douglass of Rochester, NY; Rt. Rev. A. W. Wayman of Baltimore, MD; and Robert Smalls of Charleston SC (vice presidents); Rt. Rev. Daniel A. Payne, Rt. Rev. J. P. Campbell, Hon. Charles Sumner, Hon. Gerrit Smith, and Major M. R. Delany (life directors); Dr. James McCune Smith of New York City and Robert Robinson of Alexandria, VA (directors).

79. "The Colored People's National Monument, to the Memory of Abraham Lincoln," *Christian Recorder*, July 15, 1865.

80. Elsa Barkley Brown, "Negotiating and Transforming the Public Sphere," 113–14.

81. The Petersburg *Daily Express* reported that the five delegates were Fields Cook, Richard Wells, Wm. Williamson, Walter J. Snead, and T. Morris Chester.

82. "Latest News! The Richmond Colored Delegation," *Daily Express* (Petersburg, VA), June 19, 1865; "The Richmond Freedmen," New York *Tribune*, June 17, 1865; Rachleff, *Black Labor in the South*, 13–14.

83. "The Colored Mass Meeting," *Daily Express* (Petersburg, VA), June 9, 1865.

84. Foner and Walker, *Proceedings of the Black National and State Conventions*, 264.

85. Foner and Walker, *Proceedings of the Black National and State Conventions*, 264.

86. Foner and Walker, *Proceedings of the Black National and State Conventions*, 261, 67.

87. Foner and Walker, *Proceedings of the Black National and State Conventions*, 267.

88. Chesson, *Richmond after the War*, 88–91, 105–6.

89. Lowe, *Republicans and Reconstruction*, 41–47.

90. "An act to provide for the more efficient government of the rebel states," passed March 2, 1867, in McPherson, *Political History of the United States*, 191–92.

91. Rachleff, *Black Labor in the South*, 41; Taylor, *Negro in the Reconstruction of Virginia*, 211.

92. Taylor, *Negro in the Reconstruction of Virginia*, 211; McPherson, *Political Manual for 1866 and 1867*.

93. Taylor, *Negro in the Reconstruction of Virginia*, 218.

94. Taylor, *Negro in the Reconstruction of Virginia*, 219.

95. Taylor, *Negro in the Reconstruction of Virginia*, 220.

96. An article in the *Daily National Intelligencer* reported that Fields Cook and Dr. Sharp were the Republican candidates for the constitutional convention, and it listed several other conservative candidates. Neither Cook nor Sharp nor any of the conservatives were elected. Instead, the delegates from Richmond were Joseph Cox and Lewis Lindsey (black people) and James Hunnicutt, James Morrissey, and John Underwood (white people), all Republicans. "Nominations for Delegates to the Conventions—the Moderate Republicans—Eligibility of Candidates—General Wise," *Daily National Intelligencer* (Washington, DC), October 17, 1867; Rachleff, *Black Labor in the South*, 46.

97. Taylor, *Negro in the Reconstruction of Virginia*, 222.

98. Taylor, *Negro in the Reconstruction of Virginia*; Lowe, "Virginia's Reconstruction Convention," 342.

99. Henderson, *Unredeemed City*, 172.

100. Eric Foner, *Reconstruction*, 316–33.

101. For close examinations of the constitutional convention delegates and issues, see Lowe, "Virginia's Reconstruction Convention"; Hume, "Membership of the Virginia Constitutional Convention." For an alternative reading of the convention's salient issues, see Rosen, *Terror in the Heart of Freedom*.

102. Lowe, "Virginia's Reconstruction Convention," 353.

103. Samuel, *Debates and Proceedings of the Constitutional Convention of the State of Virginia*, 60–81; Rachleff, *Black Labor in the South*, 46–47.

104. Samuel, *Debates and Proceedings of the Constitutional Convention of the State of Virginia*, 150.

105. Taylor almost reduces the value of the black vote when he notes that black people did not play a significant role in shaping discourse about legislation but mostly just cast votes. Taylor, *Negro in the Reconstruction of Virginia*, 228.

106. Taylor, *Negro in the Reconstruction of Virginia*, 238–41.

Chapter Three

1. Record Book, 1868–1871, Gilfield Baptist Church Records, 1827–1939.

2. Hahn, *Nation under Our Feet*; Eric Foner, *Reconstruction*; Engs, *Freedom's First Generation*, 142–54; Kolchin, *First Freedom*; Rachleff, *Black Labor in the South*.

3. Higginbotham, *Righteous Discontent*, 47, 48; Roberson, *Fighting the Good Fight*, 196–99; Dvorak, *An African-American Exodus*, 127; Savage, *Your Spirits Walk Beside Us*, 36; Litwack, *Been in the Storm So Long*, 510; Montgomery, *Under Their Own Vine and Fig Tree*, 156–67; Paul Harvey, *Through the Storm*, 75; Woodson, *History of the Negro Church*, 221; Mays and Nicholson, *The Negro's Church*, 38; Frazier, *Negro Church in America*, chap. 3; Wheeler, *Uplifting the Race*, xv; Eric Foner, *Reconstruction*, 92–93.

4. Higginbotham, *Righteous Discontent*. For an approach that shows ministers' diverse interests, see Roberson, *Fighting the Good Fight*.

5. On ministers and congregations, see Savage, *Your Spirits Walk Beside Us*. For examples of works that highlight the factors that contribute to ministers' leadership, see Paul Harvey, *Through the Storm*; Paul Harvey, *Redeeming the South*; Eric Foner, *Reconstruction*; Woodson, *History of the Negro Church*, chap. 8.

6. Bestebreurtje, "Beyond the Plantation," 346–47; Robinson, *Race, Religion and the Pulpit*.

7. Raboteau, *Slave Religion*, 138, 42; Sobel, *Trabelin' On*, 206–7.

8. Irons, "North Carolina's Black Baptists," 31.

9. Sobel, *Trabelin' On*.

10. Gaines, *Uplifting the Race*; Gatewood, *Aristocrats of Color*.

11. See chapter 1.

12. Thompson, *Making of the English Working Class*, 42.

13. Heyrman, *Southern Cross*, prologue.

14. On Gilfield's requirement that members report each other, see Kennard, *Short History of the Gilfield Baptist Church*, 16. On the surveillance function of church meetings, see Harvey, *Redeeming the South*, 82–86; Sobel, *Trabelin' On*, 230.

15. Gilfield Record Book, 1868–1871.

16. 1860. U.S. Census. Petersburg, Virginia, population schedule, digital image, Ancestry.com (http://www.ancestry.com: accessed August 2, 2010); 1870 U.S. Census, Petersburg, Virginia, population schedule, digital image, Ancestry.com (http://www.ancestry.com: accessed August 2, 2010); 1880 U.S. Census, Petersburg, Virginia, population schedule, digital image, Ancestry.com (http://www.ancestry.com: accessed May 19, 2012)

17. Hartzell, "The Exploration of Freedom," 137. Margo Conk describes the difficulty in distinguishing between skilled and unskilled labor, a distinction that did not emerge until the early twentieth century among census takers. Even then, the specifications for what made an occupation skilled or unskilled was not scientific but rather based on social status (and hence race, ethnicity, class, and gender). Conk, "Occupational Classification in the United States Census."

18. Giggie, *After Redemption*, 36–38.

19. Gilfield Record Book, July 20, 1868.

20. Gilfield Record Book, June 2, 1868.

21. On the modernizing efforts of the postemancipation period, see Harvey, *Redeeming the South*, 77–106.

22. Gilfield Record Book, June 2, 1868, April 18, 1870; Penningroth, "Faith and Property."

23. Martha S. Jones, *Birthright Citizens*.

24. Penningroth, "Faith and Property," 2.

25. Barr, *Black Texans*, 42.

26. Kidada Williams, *They Left Great Marks on Me*; Rosen, *Terror in the Heart of Freedom*.

27. Elsa Barkley Brown, "To Catch the Vision of Freedom."

28. Gilfield Record Book, June 15, 1868. Note that by the Reconstruction Act of 1867, black men could vote, and they did vote for constitutional convention candidates in October 1867. On the election, see Henderson, *Unredeemed City*, 172.

29. Gilfield Record Book, June 16, 1868.

30. In August 1865, black people held a freedmen's convention in which suffrage was the main issue discussed. On October 18–20, 1867, black men voted for their delegates to the constitutional convention, showing that there had been ample discussion about their ability to exercise voting authority. Du Bois, *Black Reconstruction in America*, 537, 41.

31. During the 1867 constitutional convention, 90 percent of Virginia's black registered voters voted. Hahn, *Nation under Our Feet*, 194, 206.

32. On the difference between belonging and individual freedom, see Elsa Barkley Brown, "To Catch the Vision of Freedom."

33. Harvey, *Redeeming the South*, 169–70; Raboteau, *Slave Religion*, 136; Sobel, *Trabelin' On*, 206.

34. Gilfield Record Book, August 3, 1868. This incident may also be interpreted as a tension between what Paul Harvey calls "modernizers" of the late nineteenth century progressivism prevalent in the urban areas, and the Baptist democracy prevalent in the rural areas. It should be noted that these developments played out much earlier in Gilfield than Harvey's study suggests they should have. Harvey, *Redeeming the South*, 78.

35. Gilfield Record Book, September 7, 1868. The specific verses in 1 Corinthians 14:33–34 (KJV) enjoin women to "keep silence in the churches for it is not permitted unto them to speak but they are commanded to be under obedience as also saith the law. And if they will learn anything, let them ask their husbands at home for it is a shame for women to speak in church." And in 1 Timothy 2:11–15 (KJV): "Let the woman learn in silence with all subjection. But I suffer not a woman to teach, nor to usurp authority over the man, but to be in silence. For Adam was first formed, then Eve. And Adam was not deceived, but the woman being deceived was in the transgression. Notwithstanding she shall be saved in childbearing, if they continue in faith and charity and holiness with sobriety."

36. Butler, *Women in the Church of God in Christ*, chap. 1.

37. Martha S. Jones, *All Bound Up Together*, chap. 4.

38. Martha S. Jones, *All Bound Up Together*, 156–57.

39. One Gilfield member dated the start of the Sunday school as April 21, 1865. This date is seven months before Williams assumed the pastorate. Even if Williams did not start the school, the sense was that Williams started the work immediately. Annie Williams, "Gillfield Church on Sabbath Schools," 27.

40. By 1872, the AME Church saw Sunday school as being for children: "Bishop Campbell—Mr. Editor," *Christian Recorder*, November 16, 1872; Petersburg's Sunday School Union Meetings included adults: "Union Meeting of Sabbath Schools," *Petersburg Index-Appeal*, March 9, 1880. On adults in Sunday School, see Boylan, *Sunday School*; McMillen, *To Raise Up the South*.

41. Johnson, *Glimpse of the Happenings*, 37.

42. Johnson, *Glimpse of the Happenings*, 10.

43. "Death of Rev. Henry Williams," *Petersburg Progress*, February 19, 1900, reprinted in Johnson, *Sketch of the Life of Rev. Henry Williams, D.D.*, 9.

44. Johnson, *Glimpse of the Happenings*, 35.

45. Johnson, *Glimpse of the Happenings*, 35.

46. Johnson, *Glimpse of the Happenings*, 32.

47. Johnson, *Glimpse of the Happenings*, 24.

48. Johnson was elected on March 5, 1900. Luther Porter Jackson, *Short History of the Gillfield Baptist Church*, 20.

49. Sherwood, *Life of Charles B. W. Gordon*, 47.

50. Harvey captures this sense of inspiration that black men derived from their ministers in his account of William Heard, who felt inspired to "become a MAN" by Rev. William White, who Heard believed always forthrightly advocated for religion and the Republican Party. Paul Harvey, *Redeeming the South*, 56.

51. Woodson, *History of the Negro Church*, 247–65; LaVerne Byrd Smith, *Comprehensive History of First Baptist Church, South Richmond*, 2: 86–88.

52. Gilfield Record Book, July 20, 1868. Paul Harvey offers an alternative interpretation. See Harvey, *Redeeming the South*, 174.

53. Gilfield Record Book, October 3, 1868.

54. Paul Harvey, *Redeeming the South*, 167–70.

55. Gilfield Record Book, June 16, 1868.

56. Luther Porter Jackson, *Short History of the Gillfield Baptist Church*, 8; Paul Harvey, *Redeeming the South*, 82; LaVerne Byrd Smith, *Comprehensive History of First Baptist Church, South Richmond*, 1: 90–91.

57. Sobel, *Trabelin' On*, 230.

58. Elsa Barkley Brown, "Negotiating and Transforming the Public Sphere," 110.

59. Gilfield Record Book, 1861–1862.

60. Gilfield Record Book, January 19, 1862.

61. Hunter, *Bound in Wedlock*, 15.

62. Gilfield Record Book, March 7, 1861.

63. Hunter, *Bound in Wedlock*, chap. 6.

64. Perdue, Barden, and Phillips, *Weevils in the Wheat*, 95–96.

65. Proenza-Coles, "The Right to One's Relatives," 199–200.

66. Noralee Frankel contends that in addition to freedpeople defining marriage in their own ways, they also did not consider children born out of wedlock to be illegitimate. The Gilfield Record Book on which this chapter is based contradicts this claim. Frankel, *Freedom's Women*, xi–xii. On marriage and the courts, see Penningroth, "African American Divorce."

67. Sixteen out of approximately 138 cases pertained to childbearing out of wedlock during the 1861–62 period. This is a marked contrast to the higher number of cases (28) pertaining to marriage, husbands and wives not living together, and adultery. Gilfield Record Book, 1861–1862.

68. Gilfield Record Book, June 16, July 7, July 20, 1868.

69. Gilfield Record Book, 1868–1871.

70. Gilfield Record Book, October 4, November 15, December 20, 1869.

71. Gilfield Record Book, January 17, 1870.

72. Gilfield Record Book, May 16, 1870.

73. Gilfield Record Book, July 19, 1869.

74. Quoted in Washington, *Frustrated Fellowship*, 109.

75. Gilfield Record Book, June 20, 1870.

76. Gilfield Record Book, July 4, 1870.

77. Gilfield Record Book, July 4, 1870.

78. Hunter, *Bound in Wedlock*, chap. 6.

79. Elsa Barkley Brown, "Negotiating and Transforming the Public Sphere," 302–9.

80. Perrone, "Back into the Days of Slavery."

81. Elsa Barkley Brown, "Negotiating and Transforming the Public Sphere," 136–43.

82. Paul Harvey, *Redeeming the South*, 171.

83. Williams held offices in the following conventions: CSBA 1867–68, 1870; VBSC 1868, 1870, 1880–1884; CABMC, 1869; BBA 1882, 1886–87, 1889.

84. Wring, "Elder Rule and Southern Baptist Church Polity," 198–200.

85. A. E. Harvey, "Elders."

86. Johnson, "Tribute to the Rev. Henry Williams, D.D.," 44.

87. Harvey notes how important the stability of church community was in the postemancipation period. Paul Harvey, *Redeeming the South*; Frazier, *Negro Church in America*; Raboteau, *Slave Religion*.

88. Paul Harvey, *Redeeming the South*; Becker, "Black Church."

89. Matthew 18:15–17 (KJV): "Moreover if thy brother shall trespass against thee, go and tell him his fault between thee and him alone: if he shall hear thee, thou hast gained thy brother. But if he will not hear thee, then take with thee one or two more, that in the mouth of two or three witnesses every word may be established. And if he shall neglect to hear them, tell it unto the church: but if he neglect to hear the church, let him be unto thee as an heathen man and a publican."

90. It is notable that witnesses are not just permitted but required in cases involving rape or resulting in capital punishment. Deuteronomy 22. I thank Dr. Faith B. Harris of Virginia Union University for bringing this scripture to my attention.

91. John K. Shore, Richard Kennard, and James Carter were elected as representatives of Ward 6. They ran as Radicals and were elected, along with William Burgess, to represent the ward. Commissioner Return of Election, May 28, 1870, Petersburg Election Returns, 1870–1893, Library of Virginia.

92. Petersburg Common Council Minutes, 1865–1873, November 1, 1870, and April 24, 1871, Petersburg City Hall.

93. Edwards, *Gendered Strife and Confusion*, 49–52.

94. For discussions of how ministers separated religion and politics, see Martin, *For God and Race*, chap. 3. For a discussion of the origins of overlapping ministerial-political leadership, see Eric Foner, *Reconstruction*, 92–93.

Chapter Four

1. "JACPEVA, 1879," 84; Bond and Gundersen, "Episcopal Church in Virginia," 285; Bragg, *History of the Afro-American Group of the Episcopal Church*, 133–34; Neal, "Martha 'Pattie' Hicks Buford (1836–1901)."

2. The minutes of the 1878 ZUA meeting were lost. In 1880, Rev. Robb White attended the ZUA Annual Conference and inquired about the disposition of the minutes, which prompted the ZUA Church to include a resolution articulating its desire to remain separate from the Episcopal Church. "Minutes of the ZUA, 1880," 7.

3. For an extensive listing of schools, see Lester F. Russell, *Black Baptist Secondary Schools in Virginia*.

4. On cooperation, see J. Douglas Smith, *Managing White Supremacy*; Green, *Educational Reconstruction*; Hildebrand, *Times Were Strange and Stirring*.

5. "Minutes of the ZUA, 1880," 7.

6. Woodson, *History of the Negro Church*; Heather Andrea Williams, *Self-Taught*; James D. Anderson, *Education of Blacks in the South*.

7. Dailey, *Before Jim Crow*, 68–71.

8. Anderson, *Education of Blacks in the South*, 27–28; Butchart and Rolleri, "Secondary Education and Emancipation," 169.

9. Paul Harvey, *Redeeming the South*, 181–82.

10. Harvey claimed that the American Baptist Theological Seminary was the only school for educating black ministers. Paul Harvey, *Redeeming the South*, 169.

11. Raboteau describes how enslaved preachers were empowered by the spirit and not the formal structure of the church. This laid the foundation for postemancipation debates about trained ministers. Raboteau, *Slave Religion*, chap. 5. Paul Harvey, *Redeeming the South*, 60.

12. Bailey, *Down in the Valley*, 80.

13. Clarence E. Walker, *Rock in a Weary Land*; Powers, *Black Charlestonians*.

14. Clarence E. Walker, *Rock in a Weary Land*, 21–22; Raboteau, *Slave Religion*, 68–69.

15. Harvey offers the example of the Alabama Colored Baptist State Convention, which adopted this rule. Paul Harvey, *Redeeming the South*, 180; Allan-Olney, *The New Virginians*, 180.

16. "Church History," 25, RZUA Papers, box 1, folder 1.

17. "Church History," 30–31, 32–33, RZUA Papers, box 1, folder 1.

18. "Church History," RZUA Papers, box 1, folder 1.

19. This was the case in Virginia in 1865–78, but in New Orleans in 1890. Bennett, *Religion and the Rise of Jim Crow*, 136–61.

20. Norman, *James Solomon Russell*, chap. 1; Best, *Black Religious Leadership*, 29; Bond and Gundersen, "Episcopal Church in Virginia," 285; Ryan K. Smith, "Church Fire and Reconstruction," 37. For examples of this kind of work, see "Miss Pendleton's Work in Lexington," *Our Diocesan Work*, February 1881; "Mrs. Brent's Work among the Colored People," *Our Diocesan Work*, August 1881; Norman, "Pattie Buford's Missionary Work," *Brunswick Times Gazette*, January 18–February 8, 2012.

21. "JACPEVA, 1878," 161.

22. "JACPEVA, 1879," 22; Benton, *Church Cyclopaedia*, 805.

23. "JACPEVA, 1879," 223.

24. Bond and Gundersen, "Episcopal Church in Virginia," 285.

25. Bond and Gundersen, "Episcopal Church in Virginia," 285.

26. "JACPEVA, 1879," 37.

27. "JACPEVA, 1879," 38.

28. "Minutes of the ZUA, 1883."

29. "JACPEVA, 1879," 37.

30. Butchart, *Schooling the Freed People*.

31. "Minutes of the VBSC, 1880," 11.

32. "Minutes of the VBSC, 1880," 11.

33. "Minutes of the VBSC, 1880," 14.

34. Paul Harvey, *Redeeming the South*, 69; Higginbotham, *Righteous Discontent*.

35. It is important to note that there were black people who stayed in the southern Catholic and Methodist Episcopal churches after emancipation and well into the twentieth century. Bennett, *Religion and the Rise of Jim Crow*.

36. Shattuck, *Episcopalians and Race*, 12. For a discussion of black church membership declines in South Carolina and other places, see Shattuck, *Episcopalians and Race*, 8. Even with such small numbers of black communicants, there were some parishes that continued to perform services—baptisms, weddings, and funerals—for

black people. See "Parish Reports, JACPEVA, 1880"; Bond and Gundersen, "Episcopal Church in Virginia," 283.

37. Hayden, "After the War," 403.

38. Lewis, *Yet with a Steady Beat,* 48.

39. Bragg, *Colored Harvest,* 10.

40. Bragg, *Colored Harvest,* 10.

41. Toppin and Lee, "Early Account," 18, Toppin Papers, VSU. Campbell, "An Accurate History," Campbell Papers, VSU.

42. For a discussion of white southerners' desire to control the transition to freedom for black and white people, see Butchart, "Courage in the Classroom," 8–9.

43. For a discussion of the freedpeople-led education efforts of black southerners, see James D. Anderson, *Education of Blacks*; Heather Andrea Williams, *Self-Taught.* For a discussion of the involvement of southerners in the educational project, see Butchart, *Schooling the Freed People.*

44. James Solomon Russell, *Adventure in Faith.*

45. Graebner, "Episcopal Church and Race."

46. "Address on Freedmen," Giles B. Cooke Papers, Part A, Section 6, folder 2, VHS.

47. "Address on Freedmen," Giles B. Cooke Papers, Part A, Section 6, folder 2, VHS.

48. Bond and Gundersen, "Episcopal Church in Virginia," 285, 286.

49. Chandra Manning suggests that Confederate and Union soldiers' attitudes toward black people changed during the Civil War due to their encounters with enslaved and free black people. Manning, *What This Cruel War Was Over*; Taylor, *Negro in the Reconstruction of Virginia,* 151–52.

50. "JACPEVA, 1879," 37.

51. "JACPEVA, 1878," 102–3.

52. For a discussion about the unification, see "Church History," 32–33, RZUA Papers, box 1, folder 1. For the final resolution, see "Minutes of the ZUA, 1880," 7.

53. "JACPEVA, 1880," 60.

54. "JACPEVA, 1879," 88–89.

55. "JACPEVA, 1879," 89.

56. "JACPEVA, 1879," 83–84.

57. "JACPEVA, 1879," 83.

58. For a description of the ministry of education, see "JACPEVA, 1879," 221. For a discussion of the vital nature of preparatory school, see "JACPEVA, 1880," 49.

59. Shattuck, *Episcopalians and Race,* 11; Hayden, "After the War," 420.

60. "JACPEVA, 1879," 84.

61. Bond and Gundersen, "Episcopal Church in Virginia," 285.

62. Shattuck, *Episcopalians and Race,* 11.

63. The bishop echoes this idea that the situation represents a "crisis" for the diocese. "JACPEVA, 1879," 38, 39.

64. Lewis, *Yet with a Steady Beat,* 55.

65. "JACPEVA, 1880," 226.

66. See, for example, Lewis, *Yet with a Steady Beat,* 54.

67. Bederman, *"The Women had Charge of the Work Long Enough,"* 435.

68. Cullen, "I's a Man Now," 90. See also Horton, "Freedom's Yoke."

69. On the plantation household and gender dynamics, see Fox-Genovese, *Within the Plantation Household*; Glymph, *Out of the House of Bondage*; McCurry, *Masters of Small Worlds*.

70. Summers, *Manliness and Its Discontents*; Bederman, *Manliness and Civilization*.

71. Leslie Brown, *Upbuilding Black Durham*, 18–19, chap. 1.

72. Gilmore, *Gender and Jim Crow*, 18, chap. 2. See also Gasman, "Swept under the Rug."

73. Daniel B. Thorp describes an alternative, where the students were educated in shifts. Girls attended in the morning, and boys attended in the afternoon. This suggests that there were more diverse approaches to education and gender organization than Gilmore suggested. Thorp, "Beginnings of African American Education," 327.

74. Higginbotham, *Righteous Discontent*; Corey, *History of the Richmond Theological Seminary*.

75. Horst, *Education for Manhood*, Ch. 8.

76. Jacqueline Jones, *Soldiers of Light and Love*, chap. 2.

77. Elsa Barkley Brown, "Negotiating and Transforming the Public Sphere."

78. Higginbotham, *Righteous Discontent*, 21.

79. Cooper, *Voice from the South*, 76.

80. Cooper, *Voice from the South*, 44.

81. Cooper, *Voice from the South*, 76–78.

82. Cooper, *Voice from the South*, 50.

83. See also Wright, "Self-Determination."

84. Lester F. Russell, *Black Baptist Secondary Schools in Virginia*, 49.

85. "Minutes of the VBSC, 1880," 35–36.

86. "Minutes of the VBSC, 1880," 35–36.

87. "Minutes of the VBSC, 1880," 35.

88. Higginbotham, *Righteous Discontent*, 50, 58–60.

89. "Minutes of the VBSC, 1882," 19.

90. "Minutes of the BBA, 1882," 9. On educating black women see Shaw, "We Are Not Educating Individuals but Manufacturing Levers."

91. James Solomon Russell, *Adventure in Faith*, 20–21.

92. "Extracts from an Address Delivered by the Principal," *Southern Missioner*, November 1, 1892.

93. "Fourth Annual Report of the Principal," *Southern Missioner*, November 4–6, 1892.

94. See *Southern Missioner*, August 1892, March 1893, April 1893.

95. "The Bishop Payne Divinity School," *Southern Missioner*, October 4, 1893.

96. "Briefs," *Southern Missioner*, February 9, 1895, 4.

97. Cooper, *Voice from the South*, 45.

98. Butler, *Women in the Church of God in Christ*, chap. 2; Higginbotham, *Righteous Discontent*; Martha S. Jones, *All Bound Up Together*.

99. Butler, *Women in the Church of God in Christ*, 37–40.

100. Interestingly, Higginbotham effaces the existence and extent of contention within the black Baptist tradition by focusing on the extent to which black women supported the efforts at establishing schools, when they had also developed a gender consciousness that helped them to find ways to assert themselves in the church. Barbara

Savage presents an interesting image of Nannie Burroughs, the woman convention leader, who actually challenged men to stand up and take an active role in leading the church community. This gives just an inkling of the existence of tensions Higginbotham omits. Higginbotham, *Righteous Discontent*; Savage, *Your Spirits Walk Beside Us*; Martha S. Jones, *All Bound Up Together*, 151–71; Butler, *Women in the Church of God in Christ*.

101. Higginbotham, *Righteous Discontent*, 25.

Chapter Five

1. On segregation practices after Reconstruction ended, see Rabinowitz, "From Exclusion to Segregation"; J. Douglas Smith, *Managing White Supremacy*. On the later developments of race relations, see Hayter, *Dream Is Lost*; Harold, *New Negro Politics in the Jim Crow South*.

2. The archivist estimates the date of the endorsement to be 1882. Endorsement of Captain Gish by Freemen of Southwest Virginia, Mahone Papers, RBMSCL, Duke University.

3. While the petitioners identify these counties as being in the southwestern part of the state, they are now understood to be part of the Valley region.

4. First quote: Frazier, *Negro Church in America*, 14; second quote: Washington, *Frustrated Fellowship*, 135. See also Higginbotham, *Righteous Discontent*.

5. Moore, *Two Paths to the New South*, 70.

6. Moore, *Two Paths to the New South*, 70, 87, 91.

7. G. S. S. Wall et al., "Letter from the People to Jno. M. Langston on the President's Policy." *Christian Recorder*, June 21, 1877.

8. "Surrendered at Discretion," *Lynchburg Virginian*, March 18, 1881.

9. Eric Foner, *Reconstruction*, 577, 83–85.

10. Until 1913, U.S. Senators were elected by state legislatures rather than by popular vote. The 16th Amendment changed that. Dailey, *Before Jim Crow*, 50, 189n10.

11. *Journal of the Senate Commonwealth of Virginia*, 58.

12. "The Baltimore *Sun*'s Washington Correspondent, Who Is Usually Very Correct in His Statements, Says," *Lynchburg Virginian*, March 18, 1881.

13. Moore, *Two Paths to the New South*, 71; "Acts and Joint Resolutions Passed by the General Assembly of the State of Virginia during the Session of 1879–80"; "General Wickham, If Nominated by the Republicans for Senator in Virginia, Will Make the Race, Assured That the Bourbon Debt-Payers Will Come to Bis [*sic*] Support before They Will Go to That of Billy Mahone, the Conservative Readjuster," *Daily Inter Ocean*, December 10, 1879.

14. Johnston, "Participation of Negroes in the Government of Virginia," 259–62; Taylor, *Negro in the Reconstruction of Virginia*, 283.

15. Moore, *Two Paths to the New South*, 79.

16. "The Virginia Readjusters: The Character and Spirit of Their Convention," *Frank Leslie's Illustrated Newspaper*, June 25, 1881.

17. Pulley, *Old Virginia Restored*, 75; Forsythe, "African American Churches," 214. The Readjusters controlled the state legislature with a majority of twelve. According to this same source, black people throughout the state voted with the Readjusters.

E. B. C., "The Virginia Election—Cameron Elected with a Readjuster Legislature," *Petersburg Index-Appeal*, November 10, 1881. Election Returns, November 1881, in Petersburg Election Returns, 1870–1893, State Records Center, LVA, Richmond, VA.

18. See, for example, Rufus Bullock to Mahone, November 9, 1881; James Richardson to Mahone, 11 November 1881; C. J. Tower to Mahone, November 11, 1881, box 36, MP, RBMSCL, Duke University.

19. "The Virginia Campaign: What the Issue Is and What the Fight Will Be: Mahone's Plans, Purposes and Detailed Programme," *Washington Post*, June 15, 1881; "The New South," *Frank Leslie's Illustrated Newspaper*, Saturday, December 3, 1881.

20. The author claims that the election of 1881 was more about passion than reason, especially for black people. "The Canvass in Virginia: Speeches by Daniel and Cameron—the Uncertain Element," *Washington Post*, August 18, 1881.

21. E. B. C., in "The Virginia Election," reports that Republicans did not succeed in getting black people to vote with the Readjusters.

22. "Minutes of the VBSC, 1882"; "Minutes of the BBA, 1882."

23. Richard Wells was distinctive, because just as some churches participated in the movement, some ministers opposed emigration. "Minutes of the VBSC, 1879," 24. On responses to emigration, see Hahn, *Nation under Our Feet*, 343; Tarter, *Parte Virginia* (1880)."

24. "Minutes of the VBSC, 1879," 24.

25. "Minutes of the VBSC, 1880," 11. For more on vigilance over black representation in the media, see "Minutes of the VBSC, 1881," 20.

26. "Minutes of the VBSC, 1881," 34-35.

27. "Minutes of the VBSC, 1881," 17; "Minutes of the VBSC, 1882," 19.

28. "Minutes of the VBSC, 1878," 20.

29. "Minutes of the VBSC, 1881," 17. See also "Minutes of the VBSC, 1882," 19. They advocated hiring black teachers and principals in schools.

30. "Minutes of the VBSC, 1880," 14; "Minutes of the VBSC, 1881," 16.

31. "Minutes of the VBSC, 1880," 19, 24, 33; "Minutes of the VBSC, 1881," 16.

32. "Minutes of the VBSC, 1880," 19.

33. "Minutes of the VBSC, 1880," 24.

34. "Minutes of the VBSC, 1882," 21.

35. Minutes of the VBSC, 1882," 3.

36. See, for example, "Minutes of the ZUA Church, 1880," 2.

37. This is based on the 1880 census returns. See Appendix II. In 1882, 39 percent of black people in Greensville were Baptist. In 1881, black Baptists were 29 percent of the black population in Albemarle and 34 percent of the black population in Charles City. In 1881, black VBSC members made up 43 percent of the black population in Prince George (2,238 people), 34 percent in Prince Edward (2,200), 27 percent in Powhatan (2,200), and 28 percent in Portsmouth (5,082). In 1883, black VBSC members made up 35 percent of the black population in Nansemond (3,359), 32 percent in Portsmouth (5,854), and 38 percent in Prince Edward (2,481). In 1881, the Readjuster candidate for governor, William Cameron, won the following counties with at least 59 percent of the vote: Powhatan (65 percent black), Prince Edward (68 percent black), and Prince George (68 percent black).

38. One can see from the maps of cities and counties represented in the various conventions the broad geographic bases these conventions represented and the parallels to the broad networks represented in the Gish and Gregory letters. This is just the aerial view, which could be further refined by looking at the names and addresses of annual members, delegates, and other attendees. Such information could allow for a detailed mapping of political and social networks, a valuable approach that is beyond the means of the present project.

39. The VBSC (statewide organization) was the only association under study here to meet in May. The other more regional associations met in August or, in the case of the Bethany Baptist Association, September.

40. "Minutes of the CSBA, 1881"; "Minutes of the VBSC, 1869"; "Minutes of the BBA, 1885."

41. "Minutes of the BBA, 1882," 8.

42. For a discussion of the formation of black consciousness and black nationalism, see Washington, *Frustrated Fellowship*, 52–53; Higginbotham, *Righteous Discontent*, 6.

43. Moore, *Two Paths to the New South*, 78n32.

44. Bragg, *Hero of Jerusalem*, 12.

45. Bragg, *Hero of Jerusalem*, 10–12.

46. Moore, *Two Paths to the New South*, 93–94.

47. Dailey, *Before Jim Crow*, 65.

48. Dailey, *Before Jim Crow*, 13.

49. Dailey, *Before Jim Crow*, 70–75.

50. Dailey, *Before Jim Crow*, chap. 2.

51. On the use of patronage for political loyalty, see Bensel, *American Ballot Box in the Mid-Nineteenth Century*.

52. J. Douglas Smith, *Managing White Supremacy*, 21. For a contrasting view of the development of patronage, see McDonald, Introduction.

53. This perception of the use of patronage as the machine's basic substance seems to be more often subscribed to by Dunning school historians like Charles C. Pearson, who argues that patronage undid the solid South. Pearson, *Readjuster Movement in Virginia*, 177. On the matter of the centrality of Mahone to this narrative, Alrutheus Taylor most strongly argues for Mahone's centrality in using patronage to build the Readjuster coalition. He writes: "The Negro was treated racially but justly along with others. The Readjusters did not claim to be interested in race, but in a square deal for the poor. In this way the party attracted sufficient whites and Negroes to dominate the State for a decade through an efficient political machine controlled by William Mahone doing more successfully through Federal patronage what the Conservatives had been doing through fraud and intimidation. Negroes shared the spoils." Taylor, *Negro in the Reconstruction of Virginia*, 283. Charles Wynes also places Mahone at the center of the political universe when he writes, "From 1879–1883 his hopes were again raised and his future brightened as the Readjusters, under the leadership of Mahone, accorded him the greatest measure of justice and liberal reform that had yet been his lot." Wynes, *Race Relations in Virginia*, 5. Steven Hahn deemphasizes the use of patronage in building political alliances, emphasizing instead that black people built coalitions according to what they thought was politically expedient for

themselves. He depicts the Readjuster biracial coalition as weak. In fact, he argues that Mahone's distribution of patronage to black people was the undoing of the biracial coalition because white people did not like it. Hahn, *Nation under Our Feet,* 376–78, 400–402.

54. For other examples of what appear to be unsolicited group referrals or endorsements, see Referral of Robert E. Payne (Colored) of Charlottesville, Albemarle County, VA, May 21, 1881, box 187, MP, RBMSCL. Payne received the endorsement of five county committeemen and fourteen other men of the county, including two ministers, Rev. M. T. Lewis and Rev. James Johnson.

55. Petition in support of Professor James M. Gregory [April 1881–82], box 187, MP, RBMSCL.

56. Jones describes how this was true in the antebellum African Methodist Episcopal churches of Baltimore. Martha S. Jones, *Birthright Citizens,* 77. See also William H. Johnson, *History of the Bethany Baptist Sunday School Convention,* 84.

57. For a discussion of community formation under enslavement, see Penningroth, *Claims of Kinfolk,* chapter 3.

58. See, for example, Johnson, *History of the Bethany Baptist Sunday School Convention,* 5–6, 11.

59. On patronalism, see Downs, *Declarations of Dependence.* "Virginia, List of Appointments from 1867–1881," box 187, MP, RBMSCL. One example of the thinking about connections: "White Teachers in Colored Schools," scrapbook, Clippings on Race Relations, Politics, Slavery and Negro Education, 1897–1930, George Freeman Bragg Papers, Moorland Spingarn Research Center.

60. Cheek, "John Mercer Langston," 101.

61. Simmons, *Men of Mark,* 638.

62. Petition in support of Professor James M. Gregory [April 1881–2], MP, box 187.

63. Bragg, *Hero of Jerusalem,* 13.

64. Moore, *Two Paths to the New South,* 104.

65. Moore, *Two Paths to the New South,* 105.

66. Dailey, *Before Jim Crow,* 70–75; "Minutes of the VBSC, 1881," 16; "Minutes of the VBSC, 1882," 21.

67. Moore, *Two Paths to the New South,* 105.

68. According to Allen W. Moger, Mahone sought only to control the votes of the church members. Mahone was not the only one who used these networks to buy votes; so did the Democrats. Steven Hahn claims that once Mahone discovered these networks, he used them to mobilize voters by paying their poll taxes. Thus, he simply applied an organizational structure to these already existing networks. Moger, *Virginia Bourbonism to Byrd,* 379–81.

69. Ethington and Toyosawa, "Inscribing the Past," 75–77.

70. Circular letter, Wm. Mahone, Chairman, Petersburg, VA, to County Chairman, March 24, 1883, MP, box 189, folder: Subject Files: Politics, Canvassing Black Churches and Ministers, 1883.

71. Forsythe, "African American Churches," 215–16.

72. Dailey, *Before Jim Crow,* 74–75; Moore, *Two Paths to the New South,* 103.

73. Forsythe, "'But My Friends Are Poor,'" 414.

74. Circular letter, J. P. Schermerhorn, Richmond, VA, to Gen. Wm. Mahone, Mar. 24, 1883, MP, box 189, folder: Subject Files: Politics, Canvassing Black Churches and Ministers, 1883. See also M. Watson, Jennings Ordinary, VA, to Gen. Wm. Mahone, April 7, 1883.

75. O. L. Hardy to Hon. Wm. Mahone, Washington, DC, n.d., MP, box 189, folder: Subject Files: Politics, Canvassing Black Churches and Ministers, 1883.

76. W. E. Craig, Staunton, VA, to Gen. Wm. Mahone, April 9, 1883, MP, box 189, Canvassing Folder.

77. Henry G. Wale, Louisa C.H. to Gen. Wm. Mahone, April 5, 1883, MP, box 189, folder: Subject Files: Politics, Canvassing Black Churches and Ministers, 1883.

78. Geo W. C. Clements to Gen. Wm. Mahone, ND, MP, box 189, folder: Subject Files: Politics, Canvassing Black Churches and Ministers, 1883.

79. Tankensby, J. A., Liberty, VA, to Gen. Wm. Mahone, April 12, 1883, MP, box 189.

80. "Colored Ministers & Churches, Hanover Co.," Mahone Papers, box 189, folder: Politics, Canvassing.

81. Moore, *Two Paths to the New South*, 149.

82. Circular letter, V. Jainer, Greensville, March 24, 1883, MP, box 189, folder: Subject Files: Politics, Canvassing Black Churches and Ministers, 1883.

83. Colored Churches and Preachers in Appomattox, MP, box 189, folder: Subject Files: Politics, Canvassing Black Churches and Ministers, 1883. See also Portsmouth report from John R. White and Nottoway County Report from M. Watson.

84. J. A. Tankensby, Liberty, VA, to Gen. Wm. Mahone, April 12, 1883; Alfred L. Kelley, Lynchburg to Gen. Wm. Mahone, March 27, 1883, MP, box 189.

85. Circular letter, John R. White, Portsmouth, VA, to Gen. Wm. Mahone, March 24, 1883, MP, box 189, folder: Politics, Canvassing.

86. G. W. Kilgore, Wise Court House, VA, to Hon. Wm. Mahone, April 8, 1883. See also Jas. Hibbitts report regarding Buchanan County; Robert Wylie re: Bland County, March 29, 1883, MP, box 189, folder: Subject Files: Politics, Canvassing.

87. John A. Gibson to Gen. Wm. Mahone, Job Hawxhurst response to circular, 1883, MP, box 189, Folder: Subject Files: Politics, Canvassing.

88. Staunton River/Riceville, MP, box 189.

89. The poll tax had been ended by the 1881–82 legislature. Tax assessments did remain an issue, but this would have been more of an individual issue than a mass issue. For a discussion of the Republican Coalition Club's aims to address tax assessment in 1882, see Johnston, "Participation of Negroes," 263–67.

90. Forsythe, "'But My Friends Are Poor,'" 423; Hahn, *Nation under Our Feet*, 233.

91. Forsythe, "'But My Friends Are Poor,'" 414.

92. Forsythe, "'But My Friends Are Poor,'" 423, 25.

93. Forsythe, "'But My Friends Are Poor,'" 419.

94. "Minutes of the VBSC, 1883."

95. Virginia also had churches that tended to be larger than those in other states. "Minutes of the VBSC, 1883," 29.

96. "Minutes of the VBSC, 1883," 42.

97. "Minutes of the VBSC, 1883," 34, 36–38.

98. "Minutes of the BCBA, 1884."

99. See Appendix II.

100. "Minutes of the BBA, 1882."

101. See Appendix II.

102. Ethington and Toyosawa define a spatial imaginary as a "mental image of any spatial environment, held by participants in a symbolic discourse." Ethington and Toyosawa, "Inscribing the Past," 75.

103. "Minutes of the VBSC, 1879," 5.

104. "Minutes of the CSBA, 1881."

105. "Minutes of the CSBA, 1881," 18.

106. "Minutes of the BBA, 1882."

107. "Minutes of the BBA, 1885," 13.

108. "The Other Side: Address to the People of Virginia by the Anti-Mahone Members of the Petersburg Colored Convention," *Lynchburg Virginian*, March 18, 1881.

109. "Minutes of the BCBA, 1873," 9–10; "Minutes of the BBA, 1888," 13.

110. "Minutes of the VBSC, 1881"; "Minutes of the VBSC, 1882." On pedobaptists, see "Minutes of the CSBA, 1868." The discussion about pedobaptists did not completely go away in every convention, as the Bethany Baptist Association was still discussing the issue at the 1888 association meeting. "Minutes of the BBA, 1888."

111. Dailey, *Before Jim Crow*, 68–71.

112. On the Farmville meeting, see Langston, *From the Virginia Plantation to the National Capitol*, 438–39, 40.

113. Cheek, "Negro Runs for Congress."

114. Langston, *From the Virginia Plantation to the National Capitol*, 497.

115. "'Few Die and None Resign,'" *New York Age*, September 20, 1890.

116. "Contested Election Case of John M. Langston vs. E. C. Venable from the Fourth Congressional District of Virginia," 118.

117. "Contested Election Case of John M. Langston vs. E. C. Venable from the Fourth Congressional District of Virginia," 122, 27.

118. Dinnella-Borrego, "From the Ashes of the Old Dominion," near note 60.

119. Langston, *From the Virginia Plantation to the National Capitol*, 476–77.

120. "Contested Election Case of John M. Langston V. E. C. Venable."

121. Langston, *From the Virginia Plantation to the National Capitol*, 471.

122. Elsa Barkley Brown, "To Catch the Vision of Freedom," 81–82.

123. Langston, *From the Virginia Plantation to the National Capitol*, 478.

124. Giggie, "'Disband Him from the Church'"; Elsa Barkley Brown, "To Catch the Vision of Freedom"; Cheek, "Negro Runs for Congress."

125. "New York All Right: The Democrats Have a Clean Grab on the Electoral Vote," *Galveston Daily News*, September 21, 1888; "The Split in Virginia," *New York Age*, September 29, 1888.

126. "The Split in Virginia," *New York Age*, September 29, 1888.

127. "New York All Right: The Democrats Have a Clean Grab on the Electoral Vote," *Galveston Daily News*, September 21, 1888.

128. Cheek, "Negro Runs for Congress."

129. Langston, *From the Virginia Plantation to the National Capitol*.

130. Langston, *From the Virginia Plantation to the National Capitol*, 449–50.

131. Forsythe, "African American Churches," 212.

132. Moore, "Black Militancy in Readjuster Virginia, 1879–1883," 183.

133. Preachers White & Colored [canvass book], MP, box 190, Folder: Canvassing Black Ministers, 1889.

Conclusion

1. Langston, *From the Virginia Plantation to the National Capitol*, 444–45.

2. Cheek, "A Negro Runs for Congress." Robert Cortez "Bobby" Scott was elected in 1992.

3. For a highly critical view of black people who supported John Mercer Langston, see Johnston, "Participation of Negroes in the Government of Virginia." For a more neutral account, see Forsythe, "African American Churches," 216.

4. Third Baptist Church in Petersburg ran its minister out of town when he dared to support a Democratic candidate. For discussions of this behavior in other locales, see Elsa Barkley Brown, "Negotiating and Transforming the Public Sphere"; Giggie, "'Disband Him from the Church'"; Ford, "Black Spiritual Defiance and the Politics of Slavery."

5. Bragg, *History of the Afro-American Group*; Shattuck, *Episcopalians and Race*, chap. 2.

6. W. Scott Poole and Edward Blum introduce this idea of studying religion as a means of depicting some aspects of Reconstruction. Poole and Blum, *Vale of Tears*, 1–14.

7. Higginbotham, *Righteous Discontent*; Gilmore, *Gender and Jim Crow*. On the use of financial security and respectability, see Dabel and Jenrich, "Co-opting Respectability."

Bibliography

Primary Sources

Manuscript Collections

Archives of the Episcopal Church, Austin, TX
  Saint Paul Normal and Industrial School Records
Bishop Payne Library, Protestant Episcopal Theological School of Virginia, Alexandria, VA
  Bishop Payne Divinity School Records, 1885–1953
  Protestant Episcopal Theological Seminary of Virginia, Board of Trustees Minutes
Duke University Rare Book, Manuscript & Special Collections Library, Durham, NC
  William Mahone Papers, 1853–1895
Freedmen & Southern Society Project, University of Maryland, College Park, MD
Johnston Memorial Library, Virginia State University, Petersburg, VA
  Carrie Bragg Campbell Papers
  Colson-Hill Family Papers
  Dr. Edgar Toppin Papers
  Henry Williams Papers
  Major William Henry Johnson Papers
  Reformed Zion Union Apostolic Church Papers, 1876–1974
Library of Congress, Washington, DC
  Contested Election Case of John M. Langston vs. E. C. Venable, from the Fourth Congressional District of Virginia, US. 51st Congress, 1889–1891, House, Washington, Government Printing Office, 1889
Library of Virginia, Richmond, VA
  Church Records, Sixth Mount Zion Church 130th Anniversary Committee
  Military Rule Election Records
  Petersburg Election Returns, 1870–1893
  Petersburg Poll Books, 1882–1894
Moorland Spingarn Research Center, Washington, DC
  George Freeman Bragg Papers
  John Mercer Langston Collection
Petersburg City Hall, Petersburg, VA
  Petersburg Council Record, 1865–1873
Saint Paul's College, Lawrenceville, VA
  Miscellaneous Letters
  Saint Paul Bulletin
Virginia Historical Society, Richmond, VA
  Giles Buckner Cooke Papers, 1864–1937
  William Kennedy Papers

Church and Convention Minutes

Gilfield Baptist Church Records, 1827–1939, Accession #10041. Albert and Shirley Small Special Collections Library, University of Virginia, Charlottesville, Va.

"Journal of the . . . Annual Council of the Protestant Episcopal Church in Virginia Held . . . 1879–1888."

"Journal of the Proceedings of the Colored Shiloh Baptist Association of Virginia, Held in the Town of Manchester, at Its Third Annual Session, on the 7th, 8th, 9th, and 10th of August 1867."

"Minutes of the . . . Annual Meeting of the Bethany Baptist Association (Colored) Held . . . 1882, 1885, 1886–1889."

"Minutes of the . . . Annual Meeting of the Zion Union Apostolic Church in America Held . . . 1876, 1880, 1883–1884, 1886–1887."

"Minutes of the . . . Annual Session of the Bluestone Colored Baptist Association, Held . . . 1871, 1873, 1884, 1885."

"Minutes of the . . . Annual Session of the Colored Shiloh Baptist Association of Virginia Held . . . 1865–1866, 1870, 1878, 1880, 1881, 1884."

"Minutes of the . . . Annual Session of the Virginia Baptist State Convention, Held . . . 1868–1871, 1873, 1875, 1878–1883."

"Minutes of the Fifth Annual Meeting of the Norfolk, Virginia Union Baptist Association Held in the Meeting-House of the First Baptist Church, Catharine St., Norfolk, VA, Oct. 16th, 17th, 19th and 20th, 1868."

"Minutes of the First Anniversary of the Virginia Baptist State Convention Held in Norfolk, Virginia May 13th to 15th, A.D. 1868."

"Report of the . . . Annual Meeting of the Consolidated American Baptist Missionary Convention . . . , 1869, 1871, 1877."

Government Records

"Acts and Joint Resolutions Passed by the General Assembly of the State of Virginia during the Session of 1879–80." Richmond: R. F. Walker, Superintendent Public Printing, 1880.

City of Petersburg Register of Free Negroes, 1850–1858.

City of Petersburg Register of Free Negroes, 1859–1864.

"Contested Election Case of John M. Langston Vs. E. C. Venable from the Fourth Congressional District of Virginia." Edited by U.S. 51st Congress, 1889–1891. House. Washington: Government Printing Office, 1889.

Dinwiddie County Register of Free Negroes, 1850–1864.

Journal of the Senate Commonwealth of Virginia: Begun and Held at the Capitol in the City of Richmond on Wednesday, December 3, 1879, Being the One Hundred and Fourth Year of the Commonwealth. R. E. Frayser, Superintendent Public Printing, 1879–1880.

Records of the Field Offices for the State of Virginia, Bureau of Refugees, Freedmen and Abandoned Lands, 1865–1872 (M1913).

Samuel, W. H. *The Debates and Proceedings of the Constitutional Convention of the State of Virginia. Assembled at the City of Richmond, Tuesday, December 3, 1867; Being a Full and Complete Report of the Debates and Proceedings of the Convention, Together with the Reconstruction Acts of Congress and Those Supplementary Thereto, the Order of the Commander of the First Military District Assembling the Convention, and the New Constitution*. Richmond, VA, 1868.

Virginia. Petersburg. 1860 U.S. census, population schedule. Digital images. *Ancestry.com* http://www.ancestry.com: 2010.

Virginia. Petersburg. 1870 U.S. census, population schedule. Digital images. *Ancestry.com*. http://www.ancestry.com: 2010.

Virginia. Petersburg. 1880 U.S. census, population schedule. Digital images. *Ancestry.com*. http://www.ancestry.com: 2012.

Printed Sources

Allan-Olney, Mary. *The New Virginians*. 2 vols. Edinburgh: William Blackwood and Sons, 1880. Google e-book.

Allen, Richard. *The Life, Experience, and Gospel Labours of the Rt. Rev. Richard Allen to Which Is Annexed the Rise and Progress of the African Methodist Episcopal Church in the United States of America Containing a Narrative of the Yellow Fever in the Year of Our Lord 1793: With an Address to the People of Colour in the United States*. Philadelphia: Martin and Boden, 1833. https://docsouth.unc.edu/neh/allen/allen.html.

Benton, A. A. *The Church Cyclopaedia: A Dictionary of Church Doctrine, History, Organization and Ritual*. New York: James Pott, 1883.

Berlin, Ira, and Leslie S. Rowland, eds. *Families and Freedom: A Documentary History of African-American Kinship in the Civil War Era*. New York: New Press, 1996.

Blassingame, John W., ed. *Slave Testimony: Two Centuries of Letters, Speeches, Interviews and Autobiographies*. Baton Rouge: Louisiana State University Press, 1977.

Bragg, George F. *The Colored Harvest in the Old Virginia Diocese*. 1901.

———. *The Hero of Jerusalem; in Honor of the One Hundredth Anniversary of the Birth of General William Mahone of Virginia*. Baltimore, MD: Church Advocate Press, 1926.

———. *History of the Afro-American Group of the Episcopal Church*. Baltimore, MD: Church Advocate Press, 1922.

Bratton, Mary J. "Fields's Observations: The Slave Narrative of a Nineteenth-Century Virginian." *Virginia Magazine of History and Biography* 88, no. 1 (January 1980): 75–93.

Bureau of the Census. "Historical Statistics of the United States, 1789–1945: Statistics of the United States Colonial Times to 1970: Part 1." Washington, DC: Government Printing Office, 1975.

———. *Ninth Census: Volume I: The Statistics of the Population of the United States*. Washington, DC: Government Printing Office, 1872.

———. *Religious Bodies: 1906. Part II. Separate Denominations: History, Descriptions and Statistics*. Washington, DC: Government Printing Office, 1910.

Cooper, Anna Julia. *A Voice from the South*. New York: Oxford University Press, 1988. First published 1892 by Aldine Printing House (Xenia, OH).

Corey, Charles H. *A History of the Richmond Theological Seminary with Reminiscences of Thirty Years' Work among the Colored People of the South.* Richmond, VA: J. W. Randolph, 1895.

Douglass, Frederick. *Narrative of the Life of Frederick Douglass, an American Slave, Written by Himself.* 2nd ed. Edited by David W. Blight. Boston: Bedford/St. Martin's, 2003.

Du Bois, W. E. B. *The Negro Church: Report of a Social Study Made under the Direction of Atlanta University; Together with the Proceedings of the Eighth Conference for the Study of Negro Problems, Held at Atlanta University, May 26th, 1903.* Walnut Creek, CA: Altamira Press, 2003.

———. *The Souls of Black Folk.* New York: Dover, 1994.

Hahn, Steven, Steven F. Miller, Susan E. O'Donovan, John C. Rodrigue, and Leslie S. Rowland, eds. *Freedom: A Documentary History of Emancipation, 1861–1867.* Series 3, vol. 1, *Land and Labor, 1865.* Chapel Hill: University of North Carolina Press, 2008.

Inter-university Consortium for Political and Social Research. United States Historical Election Returns, 1824–1968 [Computer File]. ICPSR00001-v3. Ann Arbor, MI: Inter-university Consortium for Political and Social Research [distributor], 1999-04-26. Doi:10.3886/ICSPR00001.v3

Johnson, William H. *A Glimpse of the Happenings of the Gillfield Baptist Sabbath School.* Petersburg, VA: s.n., 1928.

———. *A History of the Bethany Baptist Sunday School Convention, Southside, Virginia, Organized 1888.* Petersburg, VA: Owen Printing, 1926.

———. *A Sketch of the Life of Rev. Henry Williams, D.D., Late Pastor of the Gilfield Baptist Church.* Petersburg, VA: Fenn & Owen Printers and Binders, 1901.

———. "A Tribute to the Rev. Henry Williams, D.D." In *A Sketch of the Life of Rev. Henry Williams, D.D.*, 41–45. Petersburg, VA: Fenn & Owen Printers and Binders, 1901.

Kennard, Richard. *A Short History of the Gilfield Baptist Church of Petersburg, Virginia.* Petersburg, VA: Presses of Frank A. Owen, 1903.

Langston, John Mercer. *From the Virginia Plantation to the National Capitol or the First and Only Negro Representative in Congress from the Old Dominion.* New York: Arno Press and the New York Times, 1969.

McPherson, Edward. *The Political History of the United States of America during the Period of Reconstruction.* New York: Negro Universities Press, 1969. First published 1871 by Philp and Solomons (Washington, DC).

———, ed. *A Political Manual for 1866 and 1867, or Executive, Legislative, Judicial, Politico-Military, and General Facts from April 15, 1865 to April 1, 1867.* Washington, DC, 1867.

Perdue, Charles L., Jr., Thomas Barden, and Robert K. Phillips, eds. *Weevils in the Wheat: Interviews with Virginia Ex-Slaves.* Charlottesville: University Press of Virginia, 1976.

Russell, James Solomon. *Adventure in Faith: An Autobiographic Story of St. Paul Normal and Industrial School, Lawrenceville, Virginia.* New York: Morehouse, 1936.

———. "Extracts from an Address Delivered by the Principal of St. Paul's School before the Young People's Association of St. Mathews Church, Philadelphia, Friday Evening, Oct. 21." *Southern Missioner*, November 1892.

———. "Fourth Annual Report of the Principal." *Southern Missioner*, November 4–6, 1892.

Sherwood, Rev. William Henry. *Life of Charles B. W. Gordon, Pastor of the First Baptist Church, Petersburg, Virginia, and History of the Church*. Petersburg, VA: John B. Ege, 1885.

Simmons, William J. *Men of Mark: Eminent, Progressive and Rising*. Cleveland: George M. Rewell, 1887.

Smith, LaVerne Byrd. *A Comprehensive History of First Baptist Church, South Richmond, 1821–1993*. Vol. 1, *First Baptist, South Richmond, Today and the First Fifty Years, 1821–1871*. Richmond: First Baptist Church South Richmond, 1994.

———. *A Comprehensive History of First Baptist Church, South Richmond, 1821–1993*. Vol. 2, *The 133-Year Journey after the Civil War, 1865–1998*. Richmond: First Baptist Church, South Richmond, 1999.

Statistical Abstract of the United States. New York: Johnson Reprint, 1885.

Unwritten History of Slavery: Autobiographical Accounts of Negro Ex-Slaves. Washington, DC: Microcards Editions, 1968. First published 1945 as *Unwritten History of Slavery* by Social Science Institute, Fisk University (Nashville).

Secondary Sources

Anderson, Errol A. "Slave Religion, Slave Hiring and the Incipient Proletarianization of Enslaved Black Labor: Developing Du Bois' Thesis on Black Participation in the Civil War as a Revolution." *Journal of African American Studies* 19, no. 2 (June 2015): 192–213.

Anderson, James D. *The Education of Blacks in the South, 1860–1935*. Chapel Hill: The University of North Carolina Press, 1988.

Bailey, Julius H. *Around the Family Altar: Domesticity in the African Methodist Episcopal Church, 1865–1900*. Gainesville: University Press of Florida, 2005.

———. *Down in the Valley: An Introduction to African American Religious History*. Minneapolis: Fortress Press, 2016.

Barnes, L. Diane. *Artisan Workers in the Upper South, Petersburg, Virginia, 1820–1865*. Baton Rouge: Louisiana State University Press, 2008.

Barr, Alwyn. *Black Texans: A History of African Americans in Texas, 1528–1995*. 2nd ed. Norman: University of Oklahoma Press, 1996.

Becker, William H. "The Black Church: Manhood and Mission." In *African-American Religion: Interpretive Essays in History and Culture*, edited by Timothy E. Fulop and Albert J. Raboteau, 177–99. New York: Routledge, 1997.

Bederman, Gail. *Manliness and Civilization: A Cultural History of Gender and Race in the United States, 1880–1917*. Chicago: University of Chicago Press, 1995.

———. "The Women Have Had Charge of the Church Work Long Enough": The Men and Religion Forward Movement of 1911–1912 and the Masculinization of Middle Class Protestantism." *American Quarterly*. 41, no. 3 (September 1989): 432–65.

Bell, Karen. "Self-Emancipating Women, Civil War and the Union Army in Louisiana and Low-Country Georgia, 1861–1865." *Journal of African American History* 101, no. 2 (Winter–Spring 2016): 1–22.

Bennett, James B. *Religion and the Rise of Jim Crow in New Orleans*. Princeton, NJ: Princeton University Press, 2005.

Bensel, Richard Franklin. *The American Ballot Box in the Mid-Nineteenth Century*. Cambridge: Cambridge University Press, 2004.

Berry, Mary Frances. *My Face Is Black Is True: Callie House and the Struggle for Ex-Slave Reparations*. New York: Alfred A. Knopf, 2006.

Best, Felton O., ed. *Black Religious Leadership from the Slave Community to the Million Man March: Flames of Fire*. Black Studies 3. Lewiston, NY: Edwin Mellen Press, 1998.

Bestebreurtje, Lindsey. "Beyond the Plantation: Freedmen, Social Experimentation, and African American Community Development in Freedman's Village, 1863–1900." *Virginia Magazine of History and Biography* 126, no. 3 (2018): 334–65.

Blight, David. *Race and Reunion: The Civil War in American Memory*. Cambridge, MA: Belknap Press of Harvard University Press, 2001.

Boles, John B., ed. *Masters and Slaves in the Household of the Lord: Race and Religion in the American South, 1740–1870*. Lexington: University Press of Kentucky, 1988.

Bond, Edward L., and Joan R. Gundersen. "The Episcopal Church in Virginia, 1607–2007." *Virginia Magazine of History and Biography* 115, no. 2 (2007): 163–344.

Boylan, Anne M. *Sunday School: The Formation of an American Institution, 1790–1880*. New Haven, CT: Yale University Press, 1988.

Braude, Ann. "Women's History Is American Religious History." In *Religion and American Culture: A Reader*, edited by David G. Hackett, 159–78. New York: Routledge, 2003.

Brown, Elsa Barkley. "Constructing a Life and a Community: A Partial Story of Maggie Lena Walker." *OAH Magazine of History* 7, no. 4 (Summer 1993): 28–31.

———. "Negotiating and Transforming the Public Sphere: African American Political Life in the Transition from Slavery to Freedom." In *The Black Public Sphere: A Public Culture Book*, edited by the Black Public Sphere Collective. Chicago: University of Chicago Press, 1995.

———. "To Catch the Vision of Freedom: Reconstructing Southern Black Women's Political History, 1865–1880." In *African American Women and the Vote, 1837–1965*, edited by Ann D. Gordon, 66–99. Amherst: University of Massachusetts, 1997.

———. "'What Has Happened Here': The Politics of Difference in Women's History and Feminist Politics." *Feminist Studies* 18, no. 2 (summer 1992): 295–312.

Brown, Elsa Barkley, and Gregg D. Kimball. "Mapping the Terrain of Black Richmond." *Journal of Urban History* 21, no. 3 (March 1995): 296–346.

Brown, Leslie. *Upbuilding Black Durham: Gender, Class and Black Community Development in the Jim Crow South*. Chapel Hill: University of North Carolina Press, 2008.

Brown, Vincent. "Mapping a Slave Revolt: Visualizing Spatial History through the Archives of Slavery." *Social Text* 33, no. 4 (December 2015): 134–41.

Butchart, Ronald E. "Courage in the Classroom: When Teachers Faced Violence and Worse for Their Activism and Advocacy on Behalf of Black Freedom." *Georgia Social Studies Journal* 3, no. 1 (Winter 2013): 7–15.

———. *Schooling the Freed People: Teaching, Learning, and the Struggle for Black Freedom, 1861–1876*. Chapel Hill: University of North Carolina Press, 2010.

Butchart, Ronald E., and Amy F. Rolleri. "Secondary Education and Emancipation: Secondary Schools for Freed Slaves in the American South, 1862–1875." *Paedogogica Historica* 40, no. 1–2 (April 2004): 157–81.

Butler, Anthea. *Women in the Church of God in Christ: Making a Sanctified World.* Chapel Hill: University of North Carolina Press, 2007.

Byrd, Brandon R. "Black Republicans, Black Republic: African-Americans, Haiti, and the Promise of Reconstruction." *Slavery and Abolition* 36, no. 4 (2014): 1–23.

Camp, Stephanie M. H. *Closer to Freedom: Enslaved Women and Everyday Resistance in the Plantation South.* Chapel Hill: University of North Carolina Press, 2004.

Cheek, William F. "John Mercer Langston: Black Protest Leader and Abolitionist." *Civil War History* 16, no. 2 (June 1970): 101–20.

———. "A Negro Runs for Congress: John Mercer Langston and the Virginia Campaign of 1888." *Journal of Negro History* 52, no. 1 (January 1967): 14–34.

Chesson, Michale B. *Richmond after the War, 1865–1890.* Richmond: Virginia State Library, 1981.

Clark, Kathleen Ann. *Defining Moments: African American Commemoration and Political Culture in the South, 1863–1913.* Chapel Hill: University of North Carolina Press, 2005.

Collier-Thomas, Bettye. *Jesus, Jobs and Justice: African American Women and Religion.* New York: Alfred A. Knopf, 2010.

Conk, Margo Anderson. "Occupational Classification in the United States Census: 1870–1940." *Journal of Interdisciplinary History* 9, no. 1 (Summer 1978): 111–30.

Crampton, Jeremy W., and John Krygier. "An Introduction to Critical Cartography." *ACME: An International e-Journal for Critical Cartographies* 4, no. 1 (2006): 11–33.

Creel, Margaret Washington. *"A Peculiar People": Slave Religion and Community-Culture among the Gullahs.* New York: New York University Press, 1988.

Cullen, Jim. "I's A Man Now": Gender and African American Men. In *Divided Houses: Gender and the Civil War*, edited by Catherine Clinton and Nina Silber, 76–91. New York and Oxford: Oxford University Press, 1992.

Dabel, Jane E., and Marissa Jenrich. "Co-opting Respectability: African American Women and Economic Redress in New York City, 1860–1910." *Journal of Urban History* 43, no. 2 (March 2017): 312–31.

Dailey, Jane. *Before Jim Crow: The Politics of Race in Postemancipation Virginia.* Chapel Hill: University of North Carolina Press, 2000.

Dictionary of Virginia Biography. Richmond: Library of Virginia, 1998–2006.

Dinnella-Borrego, Luis-Alejandro. "From the Ashes of the Old Dominion: Accommodation, Immediacy, and Progressive Pragmatism in John Mercer Langston's Virginia." *Virginia Magazine of History and Biography* 117, no. 3 (June 2009): 215–49.

Dodson, Jualynne E. *Engendering Church: Women, Power, and the AME Church.* Lanham, MD: Rowman & Littlefield, 2002.

Downs, Gregory P. *Declarations of Dependence: The Long Reconstruction of Popular Politics in the South, 1861–1908.* Chapel Hill: University of North Carolina Press, 2011.

Du Bois, W. E. B. *Black Reconstruction in America, 1860–1880.* New York: Free Press, 1935, 1962.

Dvorak, Katharine L. *An African-American Exodus: The Segregation of the Southern Churches.* Brooklyn, NY: Carlson, 1991.

Edwards, Laura F. *Gendered Strife and Confusion: The Political Culture of Reconstruction.* Urbana: University of Illinois Press, 1997.

Elizabeth. *Elizabeth, a Colored Minister of the Gospel, Born in Slavery.* Philadelphia: Tract Association of Friends, 1889. Accessed 5 February 2011. http://docsouth.unc.edu/neh/eliza2/eliza2.html.

Emberton, Carole. *Beyond Redemption: Race, Violence, and the American South after the Civil War.* Chicago: University of Chicago Press, 2013.

Engs, Robert F. *Freedom's First Generation: Black Hampton, Virginia, 1861–1890.* Philadelphia: University of Pennsylvania Press, 1979. Reprinted with a new introduction. New York: Fordham University Press, 2004.

Ethington, Philip J., and Nobuko Toyosawa. "Inscribing the Past: Depth as Narrative in Historical Spacetime." In *Deep Maps and Spatial Narratives,* edited by David J. Bodenhamer, John Corrigan, and Trevor M. Harris, 72–101. Bloomington: Indiana University Press, 2015.

Evans, Curtis. *The Burden of Black Religion.* Oxford: Oxford University Press, 2008.

Farmer-Kaiser, Mary. *Freedwomen and the Freedmen's Bureau: Race, Gender, and Public Policy in the Age of Emancipation.* New York: Fordham University Press, 2010.

Floyd-Thomas, Juan M. *Liberating Black Church History: Making It Plain.* Nashville: Abingdon Press, 2014.

Foner, Eric. *Freedom's Lawmakers: A Directory of Black Officeholders during Reconstruction.* New York: Oxford University Press, 1993.

———. *Reconstruction: America's Unfinished Revolution, 1863–1877.* New York: Perennial Classics, 1988.

Foner, Philip S., and George E. Walker, eds. *Proceedings of the Black National and State Conventions.* Vol. 1. Philadelphia: Temple University Press, 1986.

Ford, Bridget. "Black Spiritual Defiance and the Politics of Slavery in Antebellum Louisville." *Journal of Southern History* 78, no.1 (February 2012): 69–106.

Forsythe, Harold S. "African American Churches, Fusion Politics in Virginia, and the Republican Gubernatorial Campaign in 1889." In *Afro-Virginian History and Culture,* edited by John Saillant, 211–26. New York: Garland, 1999.

———. "'But My Friends Are Poor': Ross Hamilton and Freedpeople's Politics in Mecklenburg County, Virginia, 1869–1901." *Virginia Magazine of History and Biography* 105, no. 4 (Autumn 1997): 409–38.

Fox-Genovese, Elizabeth. *Within the Plantation Household: Black and White Women of the Old South.* Chapel Hill: University of North Carolina Press, 1988.

Frankel, Noralee. *Freedom's Women: Black Women and Families in Civil War Era Mississippi.* Bloomington: Indiana University Press, 1999.

Frazier, E. Franklin. *The Negro Church in America.* New York: Schocken Books, 1963.

Frey, Sylvia and Betty Wood. *Come Shouting to Zion: African American Protestantism in the American South and British Caribbean.* Chapel Hill: University of North Carolina Press, 1998.

Gaines, Kevin. *Uplifting the Race: Black Leadership, Politics, and Culture in the Twentieth Century.* Chapel Hill: University of North Carolina Press, 1996.

Gasman, Marybeth. "Swept under the Rug? A Historiography of Gender and Black Colleges." *American Educational Research Journal.* 44, no. 4 (December 2007): 760–805.

Gatewood, Willard B. *Aristocrats of Color: The Black Elite, 1880–1920.* Fayetteville: University of Arkansas Press, 2000. First published 1990 by Indiana University Press (Bloomington).

General Education Board of the R.Z.U.A. Church. *History of the Reformed Zion Union Apostolic Churches of America.* Lawrenceville, VA: Brunswick, 1998.

Genovese, Eugene D. *Roll, Jordan, Roll: The World the Slaves Made.* New York: Pantheon Books, 1974.

George, Carol V. R. *Segregated Sabbaths: Richard Allen and the Emergence of the Independent Black Churches, 1760–1840.* New York: Oxford University Press, 1973.

Giggie, John. *After Redemption: Jim Crow and the Transformation of African American Religion in the Delta, 1875–1915.* Oxford: Oxford University Press, 2008.

———. "'Disband Him from the Church': African Americans and the Spiritual Politics of Disfranchisement in Post-Reconstruction Arkansas." *Arkansas Historical Quarterly* 60, no. 3 (Autumn 2001): 245–64.

Gilmore, Glenda. *Gender and Jim Crow: Women and the Politics of White Supremacy in North Carolina, 1896–1920.* Chapel Hill: University of North Carolina Press, 1996.

Glaude, Eddie S., Jr. *African American Religion: A Very Short Introduction.* Oxford: Oxford University Press, 2014.

Glymph, Thavolia. *Out of the House of Bondage: The Transformation of the Plantation Household.* Cambridge: Cambridge University Press, 2008.

Graebner, N. Brooks. "The Episcopal Church and Race in Nineteenth-Century North Carolina." *Anglican and Episcopal History* 78, no. 1 (March 2009): 85–93.

Green, Hilary. *Educational Reconstruction: African American Schools in the Urban South, 1865–1890.* New York: Fordham University Press, 2016.

Hahn, Steven. *A Nation under Our Feet: Black Political Struggles in the Rural South from Slavery to the Great Migration.* Cambridge, MA: Belknap Press of Harvard University Press, 2003.

———. *The Roots of Southern Populism: Yeoman Farmers and the Transformation of the Georgia Upcountry, 1850–1890.* New York: Oxford University Press, 1983.

Harding, Vincent. "Religion and Resistance among Antebellum Slaves, 1800–1860." In *African-American Religion: Interpretive Essays in History and Culture*, edited by Timothy E. Fulop and Albert J. Raboteau, 107–30. New York: Routledge, 1997.

Harold, Claudrena N. *New Negro Politics in the Jim Crow South.* Athens: University of Georgia Press, 2016.

Harper, Matthew. *The End of Days: African American Religion and Politics in the Age of Emancipation.* Chapel Hill: University of North Carolina Press, 2016.

Harris, Fredrick C. *Something Within: Religion in African-American Political Activism.* New York: Oxford University Press, 1999.

Hartzell, Lawrence L. "The Exploration of Freedom in Black Petersburg, Virginia, 1865–1902." In *The Edge of the South: Life in Nineteenth-Century Virginia,* edited by Edward L. Ayers and John C. Willis, 134–56. Charlottesville: University Press of Virginia, 1991.

Harvey, A. E. "Elders." *Journal of Theological Studies* 25, no. 2 (October 1974): 318–32.

Harvey, Paul. *Redeeming the South: Religious Cultures and Racial Identities among Southern Baptists, 1865–1925.* Chapel Hill: University of North Carolina Press, 1997.

———. *Through the Storm, through the Night: A History of African American Christianity.* Lanham, MD: Rowman & Littlefield, 2011.

Hayden, J. Carleton. "After the War: The Mission and Growth of the Episcopal Church among Blacks in the South, 1865–1877." *Historical Magazine of the Protestant Episcopal Church* 42, no. 4 (December 1973): 403–27.

Hayter, Julian. *The Dream Is Lost: Voting Rights and the Politics of Race in Richmond, Virginia.* Lexington: University Press of Kentucky, 2017.

Heinemann, Ronald L., John G. Kolp Jr., Anthony S. Parent, and William G. Shade. *Old Dominion, New Commonwealth: A History of Virginia, 1607–2007.* Charlottesville: University of Virginia Press, 2007.

Henderson, William D. *The Unredeemed City: Reconstruction in Petersburg, Virginia: 1865–1874.* Washington, DC: University Press of America, 1977.

Heyrman, Christine Leigh. *Southern Cross: The Beginnings of the Bible Belt.* Chapel Hill: University of North Carolina Press, 1997.

Higginbotham, Evelyn Brooks. *Righteous Discontent: The Women's Movement in the Black Baptist Church, 1880–1920.* Cambridge, MA: Harvard University Press, 1993.

Hildebrand, Reginald F. *The Times Were Strange and Stirring: Methodist Preachers and the Crisis of Emancipation.* Durham, NC: Duke University Press, 1995.

Horst, Samuel L. *Education for Manhood: The Education of Blacks in Virginia during the Civil War.* Lanham, MD: University Press of America, 1987.

Horton, James Oliver. "Freedom's Yoke: Gender Conventions among Antebellum Free Blacks." *Feminist Studies* 12, no. 1 (Spring 1986): 51–75.

Hucles, Michael. "Many Voices, Similar Concerns: Traditional Methods of African-American Political Activity in Norfolk, Virginia, 1865–1875." *Virginia Magazine of History and Biography* 100, no. 4 (October 1992): 543–66.

Hume, Richard L. "The Membership of the Virginia Constitutional Convention of 1867–1868: A Study of the Beginnings of Congressional Reconstruction in the Upper South." *Virginia Magazine of History and Biography* 86, no. 4 (October 1978): 461–84.

Hunter, Tera W. *Bound in Wedlock: Slave and Free Marriage in the Nineteenth Century.* Cambridge, MA: Belknap Press of Harvard University Press, 2017.

———. *To 'Joy My Freedom: Southern Black Women's Lives and Labors after the Civil War.* Cambridge, MA: Harvard University Press, 1997.

Imhoff, Sarah. "Manly Missions: Jews, Christians and American Religious Masculinity, 1900–1920." *American Jewish History* 97, no. 2 (April 2013): 139–58.

Inventory of the Church Archives of Virginia: Negro Baptist Churches in Richmond. Richmond, VA: Historical Records Survey of Virginia, 1940.

Irons, Charles F. "North Carolina's Black Baptists and the Predicament of Emancipation." In *Between Freedom and Fetters: African American Baptists since Emancipation*, edited by Edward R. Crowther and Keith Harper, 28–56. Macon, GA: Mercer University Press, 2015.

———. *The Origins of Proslavery Christianity: White and Black Evangelicals in Colonial and Antebellum Virginia*. Chapel Hill: University of North Carolina Press, 2008. Kindle.

Jackson, Joseph Harris. *A Story of Christian Activism: The History of the National Baptist Convention, U.S.A.* Nashville, TN: Townsend Press, 1980.

Jackson, Luther Porter. "Christianity for All: 1760–1790." *Journal of Negro History* 16, no. 2 (April 1931): 168–70.

———. *Free Negro Labor and Property Holding in Virginia, 1830–1860*. New York: D. Appleton-Century Company, Inc., 1942.

———. "Free Negroes of Petersburg, Virginia." *Journal of Negro History* 12, no. 3 (July 1927): 365–88.

———. *Negro Office-Holders in Virginia, 1865–1895*. Norfolk, VA: Guide Quality Press, 1945.

———. *A Short History of the Gillfield Baptist Church of Petersburg, Virginia.* Petersburg, VA: Virginia Printing, 1937.

Johnston, James Hugo. "The Participation of Negroes in the Government of Virginia from 1877 to 1888." *Journal of Negro History* 14, no. 3 (July 1929): 251–71.

Jones, Jacqueline. *Soldiers of Light and Love: Northern Teachers and Georgia Blacks, 1865–1873*. Chapel Hill: University of North Carolina Press, 1980.

Jones, Martha S. *All Bound Up Together: The Woman Question in African American Public Culture, 1830–1900*. Chapel Hill: University of North Carolina Press, 2007.

———. *Birthright Citizens: A History of Race and Rights in Antebellum America.* Cambridge: Cambridge University Press, 2018.

———. "'Make Us a Power': African American Methodists Debate the 'Woman Question,' 1870–1900." In *Women and Religion in the African Diaspora*, edited by R. Marie Griffith and Barbara Dianne Savage, 128–54. Baltimore: Johns Hopkins University Press, 2006.

Kachun, Mitch. *Festivals of Freedom: Memory and Meaning in African American Emancipation Celebrations, 1808–1915*. Amherst: University of Massachusetts Press, 2003.

Karp, Matthew. "'This Vast Southern Empire': The South and the Foreign Policy of Slavery, 1833–1861." PhD diss., University of Pennsylvania, 2011.

Kelley, Robin D. G. *Race Rebels: Culture, Politics, and the Black Working Class.* New York: Free Press, 1994.

———. "'We Are Not What We Seem': Rethinking Black Working-Class Opposition in the Jim Crow South." *Journal of American History* 80, no. 1 (June 1993): 75–112.

Kerr-Ritchie, Jeffrey R. *Freedpeople in the Tobacco South: Virginia, 1860–1900*. Chapel Hill: University of North Carolina Press, 1999.

Kolchin, Peter. *First Freedom: The Responses of Alabama's Blacks to Emancipation and Reconstruction.* Westport, CT: Greenwood Press, 1972. Reprinted with a new preface. Tuscaloosa: University of Alabama Press, 2008.

———. *A Sphinx on the American Land: The Nineteenth-Century South in Comparative Perspective.* Baton Rouge: Louisiana State University Press, 2003.

Levin, Kevin M. "William Mahone, the Lost Cause and Civil War History." *Virginia Magazine of History and Biography* 113, no. 4 (2005): 378–412.

Lewis, Harold T. *Yet with a Steady Beat: The African American Struggle for Recognition in the Episcopal Church.* Valley Forge, PA: Trinity Press International, 1996.

Lincoln, C. Eric, and Lawrence H. Mamiya. *The Black Church in the African American Experience.* Durham, NC: Duke University Press, 1990.

Litwack, Leon F. *Been in the Storm So Long: The Aftermath of Slavery.* New York: Random House, 1979.

Lofton, Kathryn E. "The Preacher Paradigm: Promotional Biographies and the Modern-Made Evangelists." *Religion and American Culture: A Journal of Interpretation* 16, no. 1 (Winter 2006): 95–123.

Lowe, Richard. *Republicans and Reconstruction in Virginia, 1856–1870.* Charlottesville: University Press of Virginia, 1991.

———. "Virginia's Reconstruction Convention: General Schofield Rates the Delegates." *Virginia Magazine of History and Biography* 80, no. 3 (July 1972): 341–60.

Lundy-Wagner, Valerie, and Marybeth Gasman. "When Gender Issues Are Not Just about Women: Reconsidering Male Students at Historically Black Colleges and Universities." *Teachers College Record* 113, no. 5 (May 2011): 934–68.

Maffly-Kipp, Laurie F. *Setting Down the Sacred Past: African-American Race Histories.* Cambridge, MA: Belknap Press of Harvard University Press, 2010.

Manning, Chandra. *What This Cruel War Was Over: Soldiers, Slavery, and the Civil War.* New York: Alfred A. Knopf, 2007.

Martin, Sandy Dwayne. *For God and Race: The Religious and Political Leadership of AMEZ Bishop James Walker Hood.* Columbia: University of South Carolina Press, 1999.

———. "Vindicated Faith, Not a Lost Cause: African American Baptist Identity and Vision in the Civil War and Postwar Eras, 1850–1900." In *Between Freedom and Fetters: African American Baptists since Emancipation*, edited by Edward R. Crowther and Keith Harper, 9–26. Macon, GA: Mercer University Press, 2015.

Marx, Gary. "Religion: Opiate or Inspiration of Civil Rights Militancy among Negroes?" *American Sociological Review* 32, no. 1 (February 1967): 64–72.

Masur, Kate. *An Example for All the Land: Emancipation and the Struggle over Equality in Washington, D.C.* Chapel Hill: University of North Carolina Press, 2010.

Mattis, Jacqueline S. "Religion and African American Political Life." *Political Psychology* 22, no. 2 (June 2001): 263–78.

Mays, Benjamin Elijah, and Joseph William Nicholson. *The Negro's Church.* New York: Russell & Russell, 1933, 1969.

McCurry, Stephanie. *Masters of Small Worlds: Yeoman Households, Gender Relations and the Political Culture of the Antebellum South Carolina Low Country.* New York: Oxford University Press, 1995.

McDonald, Terrence. Introduction to *Plunkett of Tamany Hall: A Series of Very Plain Talks on Practical Politics by William L. Riordon*. Edited by Terrence McDonald. Boston: Bedford Books, 1994.

McMillen, Sally G. *To Raise Up the South: Sunday Schools in Black and White Churches, 1865–1915*. Baton Rouge: Louisiana State University Press, 2001.

Mitchell, Michele. *Righteous Propagation: African Americans and the Politics of Racial Destiny after Reconstruction*. Chapel Hill: University of North Carolina Press, 2004.

Moger, Allen. *Virginia Bourbonism to Byrd, 1870–1925*. Charlottesville: University Press of Virginia, 1968.

Montgomery, William E. *Under Their Own Vine and Fig Tree: The African-American Church in the South, 1865–1900*. Baton Rouge: Louisiana State University Press, 1993.

Moore, James Tice. "Black Militancy in Readjuster Virginia, 1879–1883." *Journal of Southern History* 41, no. 2 (May 1975): 167–86.

———. *Two Paths to the New South: The Virginia Debt Controversy, 1870–1883*. Lexington: University Press of Kentucky, 1974.

Morgan, Edmund S. *American Slavery, American Freedom: The Ordeal of Colonial Virginia*. New York: W. W. Norton, 1975.

Morgan, Jennifer L. *Laboring Women: Reproduction and Gender in New World Slavery*. Philadelphia: University of Pennsylvania Press, 2004.

Morgan, Lynda J. *Emancipation in Virginia's Tobacco Belt, 1850–1870*. Athens: University of Georgia Press, 1992.

Morton, Richard L. "The Negro in Virginia Politics, 1865–1902." PhD diss., University of Virginia, 1918.

Nash, Gary B. *Forging Freedom: The Formation of Philadelphia's Black Community, 1720–1840*. Cambridge, MA: Harvard University Press, 1988.

Neal, Gay W. "Martha 'Pattie' Hicks Buford (1836–1901)." *Dictionary of Virginia Biography*. Library of Virginia (1998–), 2001. Accessed 2 May 2019. https://www.lva.virginia.gov/public/dvb/bio.asp?b=Buford_Pattie_Hicks.

Norman, Worth E., Jr. *James Solomon Russell: Former Slave, Pioneering Educator and Episcopal Evangelist*. Jefferson, NC: McFarland, 2012.

———. "Pattie Buford's Missionary Work (Five Part Series)." *Brunswick Times Gazette*, 18 January–8 February 2012.

O'Brien, John T. "Reconstruction in Richmond: White Restoration and Black Protest, April–June 1865." *The Virginia Magazine of History and Biography* 89, no. 3 (July 1981): 259–81.

Orsi, Robert A. "'He Keeps Me Going': Women's Devotion to Saint Jude Thaddeus and the Dialectics of Gender in American Catholicism, 1929–1965." In *Religion and American Culture: A Reader*, edited by David G. Hackett, 331–54. New York: Routledge, 2003.

Paris, Peter J. *The Social Teaching of the Black Churches*. Philadelphia: Fortress Press, 1985.

Pavlovskaya, Mariana, and Kevin St. Martin. "Feminism and Geographic Information Systems: From a Missing Object to a Mapping Subject." *Geography Compass* 1, no. 3 (2007): 583–606.

Pearson, Charles Chilton. *The Readjuster Movement in Virginia.* New Haven, CT: Yale University Press, 1917.

Penningroth, Dylan C. "African American Divorce in Virginia and Washington, D.C., 1865–1930." *Journal of Family History* 33, no. 1 (January 2008): 21–35.

———. *The Claims of Kinfolk: African American Property and Community in the Nineteenth Century South.* Chapel Hill: University of North Carolina Press, 2003.

———. "Faith and Property in African American History." Paper presented at The Future of the African American Past, sponsored by the American Historical Association and the National Museum of African American History, Washington, DC, May 19–21, 2016.

Perrone, Giuliana. "'Back into the Days of Slavery': Freedom, Citizenship, and the Black Family in the Reconstruction-Era Courtroom." *Law and History Review* 37, no. 1 (2019): 125–61.

Perry, Imani. *Vexy Thing: On Gender and Liberation.* Durham, NC: Duke University Press, 2018.

Poole, W. Scott and Edward J. Blum, "Introduction." In *Vale of Tears: New Essays on Religion and Reconstruction*. First edition, edited by Edward J. Blum and W. Scott Poole, 1–14. Macon, GA: Mercer University Press, 2005.

Proenza-Coles, Christina. "The Right to One's Relatives: The Conventions and Consequences of Denying Paternity for Mixed-Race Children in Colonial and Antebellum Virginia," In *Voices within the Veil: African Americans and the Experience of Democracy*, edited by William H. Alexander, Cassandra Newby-Alexander and Charles H. Ford, 187–206. United Kingdom: Cambridge Scholars Publishing, 2008.

Pulley, Raymond. *Old Virginia Restored: An Interpretation of the Progressive Impulse, 1870–1930.* Charlottesville: University Press of Virginia, 1968.

Rabinowitz, Howard N. "From Exclusion to Segregation: Southern Race Relations, 1865–1890." *Journal of American History* 63, no. 2 (September 1976): 325–50.

Raboteau, Albert J. *Slave Religion: The "Invisible Institution" in the Antebellum South.* Oxford: Oxford University Press, 1978.

Rachleff, Peter J. *Black Labor in the South: Richmond, Virginia, 1865–1890.* Philadelphia: Temple University Press, 1984.

Roberson, Houston Bryan. *Fighting the Good Fight: The Story of the Dexter Avenue King Memorial Baptist Church, 1865–1977.* New York: Routledge, 2005.

Robinson, Julia Marie. *Race, Religion and the Pulpit: Rev. Robert L. Bradby and the Making of Urban Detroit.* Detroit: Wayne State University Press, 2015.

Rosen, Hannah. *Terror in the Heart of Freedom: Citizenship, Sexual Violence, and the Meaning of Race in the Postemancipation South.* Chapel Hill: University of North Carolina Press, 2009.

Russell, Lester F. *Black Baptist Secondary Schools in Virginia, 1887–1987.* Metuchen, NJ: Scarecrow Press, 1981.

Savage, Barbara Dianne. *Your Spirits Walk Beside Us: The Politics of Black Religion.* Cambridge, MA: Belknap Press of Harvard University Press, 2008.

Schwalm, Leslie. *A Hard Fight for We: Women's Transition from Slavery to Freedom.* Urbana: University of Illinois Press, 1997.

Schweiger, Beth Barton. *The Gospel Working Up: Progress and the Pulpit in Nineteenth Century Virginia.* New York: Oxford University Press, 2000.

Scott, James C. *Domination and the Arts of Resistance: Hidden Transcripts.* New Haven, CT: Yale University Press, 1990.

Scully, Randolph Ferguson. *Religion and the Making of Nat Turner's Virginia: Baptist Community and Conflict, 1740–1840.* Charlottesville: University of Virginia Press, 2008.

Shattuck, Gardiner H., Jr. *Episcopalians and Race: Civil War to Civil Rights.* Lexington: University Press of Kentucky, 2000.

Shaw, Stephanie. "We Are Not Educating Individuals but Manufacturing Levers": Creating a Black Female Professional Class During Jim Crow." *OAH Magazine of History* 18, no. 2 (January 2004): 17–21.

Smith, Edward D. *Climbing Jacob's Ladder: The Rise of Black Churches in Eastern American Cities, 1740–1877.* Washington: Smithsonian Institution Press, 1988.

Smith, J. Douglas. *Managing White Supremacy: Race, Politics, and Citizenship in Jim Crow Virginia.* Chapel Hill: University of North Carolina Press, 2002.

Smith, Ryan K. "A Church Fire and Reconstruction: St. Stephen's Episcopal Church, Petersburg, Virginia." Master's thesis, College of William and Mary, 1998.

Sobel, Mechal. *Trabelin' On: The Slave Journey to an Afro-Baptist Faith.* Princeton, NJ: Princeton University Press, 1988.

Summers, Martin. *Manliness and Its Discontents: The Black Middle Class and the Transformation of Masculinity.* Chapel Hill: University of North Carolina Press, 2004.

Tarter, Brent. "*Ex Parte Virginia* (1880)." *Encyclopedia Virginia.* Virginia Foundation for the Humanities, 2018. https://www.encyclopediavirginia.org/Ex_Parte_Virginia_1880.

Taylor, Alrutheus Ambush. *The Negro in the Reconstruction of Virginia.* Washington, DC: Association for the Study of Negro Life and History, 1926.

Thompson, E. P. *The Making of the English Working Class.* New York: Pantheon Books, 1963.

Thorp, Daniel B. "The Beginnings of African American Education in Montgomery County." *Virginia Magazine of History and Biography* 121, no. 4 (2013).

Trachtenberg, Alan. "Unsung Heroes: History in the Making." In *A Stirring Song Sung Heroic: African Americans from Slavery to Freedom, 1619–1865,* 5–10. Haverford, PA: Hurford Center for the Arts and Humanities and the Lehigh University Art Galleries, 2013.

Walker, Clarence E. *A Rock in a Weary Land: The African Methodist Episcopal Church during the Civil War and Reconstruction.* Baton Rouge: Louisiana State University Press, 1982.

Walker, Corey D. B. *A Noble Fight: African American Freemasonry and the Struggle for Democracy in America.* Urbana: University of Illinois Press, 2008.

Washington, James Melvin. *Frustrated Fellowship: The Black Baptist Quest for Social Power.* Macon, Georgia: Mercer University Press, 1986.

Wenger, Tisa. *Religious Freedom: The Contested History of an American Ideal.* Chapel Hill: University of North Carolina Press, 2017.

Wheeler, Edward L. *Uplifting the Race: The Black Minister in the New South, 1865–1902.* Lanham, MD: University Press of America, 1986.

White, Deborah Gray. *Ar'n't I a Woman? Female Slaves in the Plantation South.* Rev. ed. New York: W. W. Norton, 1999.

Williams, Annie. "Gillfield Church on Sabbath Schools." In Kennard, *Short History of the Gilfield Baptist Church*, 27–28. Petersburg, VA: Presses of Frank A. Owen, 1903.

Williams, Heather Andrea. *Self-Taught: African American Education in Slavery and Freedom.* Chapel Hill: University of North Carolina Press, 2005.

Williams, Kidada. *They Left Great Marks on Me: African American Testimonies of Racial Violence from Emancipation to World War I.* New York: New York University Press, 2012.

Wilmore, Gayraud S. *Black Religion and Black Radicalism: An Interpretation of the Religious History of African Americans.* Maryknoll, NY: Orbis Books, 1998.

Woodson, Carter G. *The History of the Negro Church.* 3rd ed. Washington, DC: Associated, 1972.

———. *The Mis-education of the Negro.* Trenton, NJ: Africa World Press, 1964. First published in 1933.

Wright, Stephanie R. "Self-Determination, Politics and Gender on Georgia's Black College Campuses, 1875–1900." *The Georgia Historical Quarterly* 92, no. 1 (2008): 93–119.

Wring, Robert A. "Elder Rule and Southern Baptist Church Polity." *Journal for Baptist Theology and Ministry* 3, no. 1 (Spring 2005): 188–212. Accessed 12 March 2018. http://www.baptists.net/history/author/bob/.

Wynes, Charles. *Race Relations in Virginia, 1870–1902.* Charlottesville: University of Virginia Press, 1961.

Young, Jason. "African Religions in the Early South." *Journal of Southern Religion* 14 (2012).

Yuan, May, John McIntosh, and Grant Delozier. "GIS as a Narrative Generation Platform." In *Deep Mapping and Spatial Narratives*, edited by David J. Bodenhamer, John Corrigan, and Trevor M. Harris, 179–202. Bloomington: Indiana University Press, 2015.

Index

Note: Information in figures is indicated by page numbers in *italics*.

MIX
Paper from
responsible sources
FSC® C008955
FSC
www.fsc.org